Why We
Did It

Why We Did It

A Travelogue from the Republican Road to Hell

Tim Miller

HARPER

An Imprint of HarperCollinsPublishers

HarperCollins books may be purchased for educational, business, or sales promotional use. For information, please email the Special Markets Department at SPsales@harpercollins.com.

FIRST EDITION

Designed by Nancy Singer

Library of Congress Cataloging-in-Publication Data
Names: Miller, Tim, 1981– author.
Title: Why we did it : a travelogue from the Republican road to Hell / Tim Miller.
Description: First edition. | New York : HarperCollins Publishers, 2022. | Includes index.
Identifiers: LCCN 2022004536 (print) | LCCN 2022004537 (ebook) | ISBN 9780063161474 (hardcover) | ISBN 9780063161481 (ebook)
Subjects: LCSH: Republican Party (U.S. : 1854–) | Trump, Donald, 1946– | United States—Politics and government—2017–2021. | United States—Politics and government—2021–
Classification: LCC JK2356 .M57 2022 (print) | LCC JK2356 (ebook) | DDC 324.2734—dc23/eng/20220318
LC record available at https://lccn.loc.gov/2022004536
LC ebook record available at https://lccn.loc.gov/2022004537

22 23 24 25 26 LBC 7 6 5 4 3

For Toulouse
"I'm tryin' real hard to be the shepherd."

Any real change implies the breakup of the world as one has always known it, the loss of all that gave one an identity, the end of safety. And at such a moment, unable to see and not daring to imagine what the future will now bring forth, one clings to what one knew, or thought one knew; to what one possessed or dreamed that one possessed. Yet, it is only when a man is able, without bitterness or self-pity, to surrender a dream he has long cherished or a privilege he has long possessed that he is set free—he has set himself free—for higher dreams, for greater privileges.

—James Baldwin, "Faulkner and Desegregation"

Contents

Introduction

America never would have gotten into this mess if it weren't for me and my friends.

We were the "normal" Republicans. The pragmatic and practical. The "adults in the room" you hear so much about. Back in the early 2010s you might have found us networking with reporters at a bipartisan Bobby Van's happy hour. Or making you wait one more second for our attention while we typed out an urgent missive on our BlackBerry device. Or appearing as the token right-winger on some onanistic Beltway panel.

Our Facebook profile picture may have been a backstage shot with Paul Ryan in his half-zip pullover. On Twitter we delivered devilish barbs mocking the Democrats for their disarray, tongue often planted in cheek.

We worked at corporate affairs firms or in "Boehner World." We were Republican campaign apparatchiks and former Bush officials you see on the tube. We were opposition party operatives in exile, thriving in the meretricious capital, anxiously anticipating the moment when it was our turn to be the brash Josh Lymans conducting brisk walk-and-talks in the White House's hallowed halls.

We may have been partisans, but the puckish sort. The "good ones," unlike those *crazy, mouth-breathing ideologues*. Sure, we had conservative impulses. Fancied tax cuts and protecting babies and cutting red tape and what have you. We repped 'murica in a jejune back-to-back world war champs kinda way and could cite chapter and verse of Reagan's Liberty State Park homily declaring that our nation's golden door was the last best hope of man on earth.

You wouldn't have confused us with populist revolutionaries. We wore pleated khakis, for Pete's sake. (Well, I didn't, but generally speaking.) At the time, populist revolutionaries weren't even really a thing in D.C., besides the weird tricornered-hat cosplayers on the National Mall whose votes we cultivated but kept at several arms' distance from our day-to-day lives.

When the Trump Troubles began there wasn't a single one in our ranks who would have said they were in his corner. To a person we found him gauche, repellant, and beneath the dignity of the public service we bestowed with bumptious regard. We didn't take him seriously. We didn't watch *The Apprentice.* We didn't get off on the tears of immigrant children. And you wouldn't have caught us dead in one of those gaudy red baseball caps.

But, at first gradually and then suddenly, nearly all of us decided to go along. The same people who roasted Donald Trump as an incompetent menace in private served his rancid baloney in public when convenient. They continued to do so even after the mob he summoned stained the party and our ideals and the halls of the Capitol with their shit.

A few of us had tried to stand athwart the madness yelling stop before it was too late. Most tucked away their worries in a little box, easing their mind with a fanciful self-assurance that the Troubles would soon blow over. As they quietly acquiesced, others went whole hog, giddily swimming in his slop.

How did it all go to hell so fast? To what end did so many go along with something that had been anathema? And why didn't the insurrectionist denouement make them say "enough" to this carnage of our creation?

These were my people. I should know.

• • •

A week after the Capitol riot I was in my pandemic bed/office when the messages started to roll in. My husband was the first, sending a link to our core friend group's Lovelies text chain. The headline from the Associated Press: "Records: Trump Allies Behind Rally That Ignited Capitol Riot."

"Lots of Wren content," he wrote.

The physical response came before the reality of the news had really sunk in. My stomach turned, palms dampened, heart sank.

"Wren" was not just another in the endless parade of loathsome Trump cronies. She wasn't one of those former colleagues whom I had come to consider with a mix of disgust and aghastment as the years went by. Wren wasn't even "Wren," to me.

She was Caroline. My friend. My campaign confidante. My concert buddy. Or, at least, she had been.

Then came another text and more cringing. According to the *Wall Street Journal,* Wren was named as a "VIP Advisor" on an attachment to the permit for the January 6, 2021, rally that preceded the deadly insurrection at the Capitol and she had worked on it with none other than InfoWars founder Alex Jones. The SMS that alerted me to this is still burned into my retinas. It read, "Caroline Wren texting people that Alex Jones is actually nice is too much for me."

What in the actual fuck.

I reluctantly clicked. Despite being primed by that horrifying summary, the article itself managed to be more shocking than I anticipated.

"In text messages Ms. Wren sent to another organizer and reviewed by the Journal, Ms. Wren defended Mr. Jones. 'I promise he's actually WAY nicer than he comes off.. . . . I'm hoping you'll [sic] can become besties,' Ms. Wren wrote."

The best you can say about those few dozen gobsmacking words is that it might be technically true that Alex Jones is "way nicer than he comes off," given that he comes off as the acrid embodiment of everything that is wrong in our society. As for the possibility of becoming "besties" with him, well, even taking into account the most generous possible reading of that text, even recognizing that I had myself played footsie for professional purposes with similarly awful people, it is still hard to wrap one's mind around how a person could type that without becoming overwhelmed with revulsion at oneself. This is Alex Jones, after all. The human ass-pimple best known for defaming and harassing the mourning parents whose innocent little children had just been executed by a monster at Sandy Hook Elementary School. Just think of how warped and wicked you have to be to target, without any remorse, people coping with the most intense grief that can be imposed on a human being. Now my friend is in the newspaper, saying he isn't all that bad. That if people got to know him, they might be "besties."

How am I supposed to comprehend that?

Later that day a reporter texted posing that very query. "How {did} she fall prey to this deal? Just thirst?"

I paused to consider it. Nine years earlier we had worked together on the campaign of the most moderate Republican presidential candidate of the twenty-first century. In the ensuing decade, we had become genuine friends. Not the type of D.C. "friend" that is really just a work acquaintance whom you make small talk with at happy hours. An actual friend. We went to see Portugal. The Man together, about a half decade before they were on the radio. She'd hassle me over text until I got out of bed to meet her for a drink because she was only in town for the night. We browned out at a club in Miami and in some dive bar in Columbia and at the 9:30 Club and in her basement and well . . . lots of places. I was invited to her yearly "Wrenpalooza" birthday party. Our closeness persisted even when we weren't partying. She was the kind of friend with whom I would share private worries and fears that only a small group of people were privy to. I leaned on her when my husband and I were going through adoption troubles after our first attempt went south. And she on me when a relationship hit the skids.

How did we end up so far apart?

Here's how I responded to the reporter: "Thirst. Likes being in the mix. Thought it was a fun game and people were overreacting. Oops."

That was my theory, at least. But I didn't actually know if it was the truth.

By the time I had sent that text, Caroline and I were no longer "friends" in the active sense. In March 2016, I texted her, cheekily, "Stop with the Trump stuff. I will unfriend u." But what I thought was an empty threat at the time became our reality.

By 2021 we were still "friendsish," to use a technical term. But we weren't sharing secrets. I didn't know what was going on in her personal life. We weren't even able to talk about one of the most consequential matters facing both of us—our work, the president, the state of the country.

It had been almost two years since I had seen her, and the last time we had gotten together, I had purposefully avoided the tiny-handed elephant in the room. She had come to Oakland and hung out with my husband and daughter, whom she adores (obvs). Along with a mutual friend, the five of us went to dinner at a foodie restaurant by Lake Merritt. We talked about the latest childhood milestones and gossiped about old mutuals. For most of the dinner, there was no real discussion of "the news," unless you count sharing a little goss about who various political figures were hooking up with.

Toward the end of the night, our pleasant détente was broken when my husband couldn't resist and made a swipe. Both of their necks turned a shade of eggplant, and they parried. I don't remember the specifics of the quarrel. I tuned it out, focused on breathing deep breaths, and pretended to attend to some unnecessary toddler parenting until the exchange came mercifully to an end. It wasn't exactly the most courageous move. But I had had enough relationships go sour over Trump by that point and had decided that when it came to resentment of past pals, my heart was full up. That night I never even asked her about her foray into Trump world. Didn't learn that she was about to take a senior role as the finance director on his reelection campaign.

I just compartmentalized this part of our life. As the weeks went forward and she became increasingly intermingled with the Trump high command, I unfollowed her on Snapchat and muted her Instagram stories to protect my blood pressure from the spikes of seeing her in social settings with random MAGA maroons. A year later, she was across the bridge in San Francisco and invited me to join her for drinks with Donald Trump Jr. and his girlfriend, former Fox News talker Kim Guilfoyle. She was planning to take them to the Tonga Room, a classic tiki bar in the finance district, because, according to her, Kim would "love the scene."

For a moment, I considered it, if only for the story. I mean, how often do you get invited to an intimate happy hour with one of the most loathsome people on the planet and also Donald Trump Jr.? But I couldn't imagine how we could have survived even a single drink without risking a physical altercation, given how plain my disdain for them would be. I have the world's worst

poker face and a tendency toward blurting out my internal mono-
logue. It was possible I would have told Don to go fuck himself
the moment he came inside my field of vision. I did the prudent
thing and declined.

After that, we basically just ghosted each other.

All this is to say, I didn't *truly* know exactly how she "fell
prey to this whole deal," how a former pal had become a coup
conspirator . . . because we didn't talk about it. Was it really all just
a big game, like I had assumed? Did the person who I thought was
a like-minded Republican in Name Only (RINO) squish genuinely
want to overthrow our democracy to install Donald Trump as an
unelected quasi-autocrat?

To find out, I would have to reanimate the relationship we had
once had.

So, five months after the insurrection pregame party that she
had organized on the Mall, Caroline and I found ourselves sitting
by the bay windows in the Hotel Casa del Mar's Terrazza Lounge,
looking out at the Ferris wheel on the Santa Monica Pier, sun beating down through the glass. I was nervous, the palms of my feet
and hands dampening.

How exactly do you start a conversation that requires a complete rewiring of your friendship? That might end it for good? Part
of me wanted to just lean right in. To shout, *How are you still going
along with this shit?* But a fight about Donald Trump wouldn't illu-
minate anything; we've all had plenty of those.

In order to truly understand what happened, I needed to not
just listen to her rationalizations and explanations about January
6th. I needed to figure out where our parting had started. Whether
the common ground I thought we had shared ever really existed at
all. I needed to look at myself through her and try to understand
what it was I had done that made all those whom I had worked and

partied alongside feel so comfortable going along with something so horrible.

• • •

Why We Did It is a book about the people who submitted to every whim of a comically unfit and detestable man who crapped all over them and took over the party they had given their life to. It's about the army of consultants, politicians, and media figures who stood back and stood by as everything they ever fought for was degraded and devalued. The people who privately admitted they recognized all the risks but still climbed aboard for a ride on the SS *Trump Hellship* that they knew would assuredly sink.

I suspect that prospect will excite many of my fellow Trump detesters who come to this book craving a dollop of delicious schadenfreude and the satisfying comfort food that can only be baked by an apostate Republican validating all their liberal readers' prior biases. And, well, I cannot tell a lie: there will be some of that warm apple pie to come.

But my objective is not to execute one continuous Dr. Dunkenstein jam that lays waste to the craven former colleagues who submitted to their new idiocratic overlord. Nor to disembowel Trump's most deranged and debased allies: the racists and the conspiracists and the sociopaths who clung to his stink. There has been plenty of that already. And, if you are feeling a dearth of dunking in your life, well, my Twitter feed is a smartphone away.

Why We Did It aims to get at something deeper than that. To dig through the wreckage of the party I once loved and come to understand how so many of my friends allowed something that was so central to our identity to become so unambiguously monstrous. And why they had continued to do so once the monster became uncontrollable.

Grappling with that requires first understanding how our actions helped lead us to that dystopian escalator ride. How we got people familiar enough with unseriousness and cruelty that they would giddily glide down with him. I'm sure a student of history might be able to trace it back to the Southern Strategy or Lee Atwater or, hell, maybe even Mark Hanna (give him a Google).

But my soul required coming to terms with something that was more intimate than that. A question that I had grappled with throughout the entire Trump era.

Why in the fuck did the vast, vast, vast majority of seemingly normal, decent people whom I worked with go along with the most abnormal, indecent of men? And why hadn't I seen it coming? If we are to summon even a hint of value from our manifest failures throughout this whole sordid mess, to find any guideposts for bringing people into the light—those were the questions that needed answering. Answering them required plumbing the complicated motivations of real, living humans.

So, I decided to retrace their steps and mine.

The first half of this book examines the journey I took walking right up to the ledge. From the McCain/Palin prelude to playing footsie with Steve Bannon and the worst of the alt-right. It covers the red flags I saw and ignored. The ones I missed. The secrets I kept. The brutal slams I imposed on my imagined enemies. The friends I made along the way. That solipsistic reflection will, I hope, shed some light on how damn easy we made it for others to take the plunge right on over the cliff I managed to veer away from.

Some of the stories will be familiar—after all, they were news. However, you'll now have a chance to view them in a more reflective light from a person who was orchestrating them. Things like Mitt Romney's IBS-riddled dog being strapped to the car roof or the origins of Crooked Hillary.

There will be other stories and anecdotes that might have

otherwise been lost to history, but which I revive because they are emblematic of the various complexes that led us to this distressing moment. The first is how many of the players in the upper echelons of American political life treated their duties as a big game, where they awarded themselves the status of public service while minimizing the responsibilities of that service in favor of performance and skulduggery. How success in this era was so often completely removed from political beliefs. *Should it have come as a surprise that a game show host was so successful at co-opting a system as puerile as that?*

You'll also see how the Republican ruling class dismissed the plight of those we were manipulating, growing increasingly comfortable using tactics that inflamed them, turning them against their fellow man. How often we advanced arguments that none of us believed. How we made people feel aggrieved about issues we had no intent or ability to solve. How we spurred racial resentments and bigotry among voters while prickling at anyone who might accuse us of racism. And how these tactics became not just unchecked but supercharged by a right-wing media ecosystem that we were in bed with and that had its own nefarious incentives, sucking in clicks and views through rage hustling without any intention of delivering something that might bring value to ordinary people's lives. *Should it have come as a surprise that a charlatan who had spent decades duping the masses into joining his pyramid schemes and buying his shitty products would excel in such an environment? Someone who had a media platform of his own and a reptilian instinct for manipulation? Someone who didn't hesitate to say the quiet part aloud?*

This brings us to our second, more complex psychological journey. After our past sins were anthropomorphized into an Archie Bunkeresque president, what to make of those who saw his defects clearly and went along anyway?

What was it about them or the system that rewarded such behavior? Going full MAGA was never clearly prestigious or in service to their ideological priors. There was no certainty that the ends would justify the means. Many who threw in with Trump were ruined by him. Why strive for proximity to power when the costs are so great and you don't even know what you want to get out of that power when it falls in your lap? That's the puzzle.

Throughout this reflection, I attempt to put forth a more fully formed, you might say *actualized*, understanding of my own rationalizations—as a gay man who worked for homophobes, an oppo research magnate who giddily stirred up artificial animus, a clear-eyed Trump loather who still took a bite of the poisoned apple (we'll get to that).

It's through this process that I hope to inhabit the mindset of those who came to terms with Trump. Because—and this is important—many of the people who did so are not all that different from me. In our conversations they defended their choice using many of the same justifications I had in the past. These people are not all barbarians or megalomaniacs. They are flawed men and women with shadow wants and desires. It's just that in this case those desires allowed them to accept an unusual evil.

Some of their rationalizations were unique to the Republican Party; others were the more universal failings replicated throughout industries and societies and political ideologies across the sands of time. Some of them were in the ballpark of defensible; others will fill them rightly with shame. Some are still grappling with these choices, while others have given up and embraced their complicity.

The manner in which people made these allowances for themselves will be told through the vantage point of my colleagues on the Republican autopsy, a project that had proposed a more welcoming and uplifting trajectory for the GOP and featured a representative sample of the key men and women in the fallen former Republican establishment. The actions of these characters—and of an additional representative few who either volunteered to come to church or required an involuntary dunk in the font—will, I hope, paint a complete picture of why those in proximity to power did what they did and why it's going to be so hard to get any of them to reverse course.

One of Trump's most shameless enablers is a congressman from Texas named Dan Crenshaw. Crenshaw is seen by some as a rising star in the party. He is like many of the characters you will meet over the course of this book. Someone who knew better and told us he knew better but went along with the hateful, bigoted, blundering Trump anyway. He wrote this in his book on "leadership": "After every failure, after every hardship, we create a personal narrative to account for that moment. We tell ourselves a story."

On this count, Crenshaw is exactly right. He and his fellow accomplices committed one of the biggest failures of the modern era. They decided to abet a man that they all understood to be a danger. A man who remains a fundamental threat to the very fabric of our democracy even after his defeat.

What I will submit to you are the stories, the narratives, that those who are a party to this failure tell themselves to account for their actions. In all their hypocritical, oblivious, self-indulgent, resentful, and at times well-meaning glory.

I will warn you. This journey is a depressing one in toto. But our peripatetic path to the abyss won't be bereft of levity, as it is written in the spirit of my most sacred maxim.

In trying to understand what's happening in politics, when in doubt, remember it is always, always *Veep* . . . not *House of Cards*. As a result, there will be no shortage of Jonads and sphincters, and jolly green jizzfaces to lighten the load.

Enjoy . . . if you can.

Why We Did It

1

The Comforting Lie

Eleven straight questions about immigration reform. At least that's how I remember it. I haven't punished myself by going back to watch the video. Maybe it was only six straight questions. It felt like eleven to me.

It was May 2007. I was the Iowa spokesperson for John McCain's presidential campaign, and things weren't looking so hot. The comprehensive immigration reform bill known colloquially by the political class as "McCain-Kennedy" and by Republican voters as "amnesty for illegals" was about to be reintroduced in the U.S. Senate. This legislation was about as popular with potential Iowa Caucus attendees as getting a raging hemorrhoid flareup during the September soybean harvest.

Amnesty consumed the discussion on conservative talk radio, both the big national shows like Rush Limbaugh and local talk, most notably WHO Newsradio 1040—the central Iowa "blowtorch" that reached much of the state. Ronald Reagan had worked at the station as a sports announcer in 1933, a point of pride among the local Republican set. By 2007, WHO's lineup consisted of a morning drive-time show with newsreaders and light banter, agriculture reports, and conservative rabble-rousing. The station's most successful rouser, Jan Mickelson, aired from 9 to 11:30, which might not be a prime hour in some markets, but in Iowa made him the king of the combine. Mickelson garnered twice the audience of anyone else in the state, and his relentless expostulation of McCain and the other RINOs who maintained a soft line on immigration bled over to his fans.

The field staffers who worked alongside me in the McCain campaign were the canaries in our nativist coal mine. They spent the bulk of their day talking to Republican regulars and thus bore the brunt of their ire. As the PR flack, I hadn't had that type of personal exposure. I'd been dispatched to the far back corner of the Iowa headquarters because the boss wanted my desk as socially distant from the volunteer area as possible thanks to my not very "Iowa nice" high-wattage cursing when on the phone with reporters.

After a long day of working the phones or attending county Republican dinners, the field guys and gals would trudge back to my desk and plop down, completely deflated by the hostile reception they had been receiving over our candidate's support for "amnesty." They dreaded slogging through their call quotas, having to hear person after person hurl invective over the amnesty bill. One recalled being shaken by a woman who had suggested that we put all the "illegals" on train cars back to Mexico and said that it would be okay if some lives were lost.

So I knew it was bad, but I didn't fully comprehend how bad until I saw it up close and personal in Council Bluffs, or Counciltucky, as the campaign staff referred to it. (Urban Dictionary offers an alternate, more colorful nickname: the "dingy asshole of America.")

We were holding a breakfast event in a soulless conference room inside the dingy asshole's gleaming new Mid-America Center. For McCain, it was the penultimate stop of a two-day swing through the state, and most of his campaign high command was either at the headquarters in Arlington, Virginia, or awaiting the candidate's arrival at the last stop in Fort Dodge. This left me with the now quaint-seeming task of updating the bosses on the proceedings via BlackBerry PIN message.

I was lost in the conference room maze, nervous that I was going to be late, and suffering from hangover sweats, having had a few too many bourbon-and-Cokes at the local casino the night before. I arrived right as the candidate was about to go on, grabbed a stale croissant and a disgusting coffee, and squeezed into the back right corner just as he took the stage. Senator McCain kicked off his stump speech. "I want to do the hard things, not the easy things," he said, before hitting all the usual notes. Winning the war on terror. Tales of heroism. Cutting wasteful spending. You know the drill. I zoned out a bit and sent an occasional snarky PIN to my campaign colleagues rather than focus on the particulars.

Then he turned to the Q&A portion.

This is where Mr. Straight Talk Express would often shine. I can remember the moment at a different town hall where he brought me to the brink of tears pushing back against the Bush administration's "enhanced interrogation" regime, which I had mindlessly supported before joining the campaign. "One of the things that kept us going when I was in prison in North Vietnam was that we knew that if the situation were reversed, that we would not be doing to our captors what they were doing to us," he said. He went on to denounce waterboarding, declaring that "we are a better nation than that."

I changed my mind on the spot. He spoke to one of the core reasons I became a Republican in the first place, the belief that America was a special, essential nation. That we were different. That we had a noble and necessary role to play in the world that we had to live up to.

In my *West Wing*ified imagination, with answers like that, we would claw back into the race one Q&A at a time, winning over the hearts and minds of Iowans who, like me, yearned for a politician who wanted to inspire us to be better, one who would *tell it like it is*. That's what people wanted in a president. The truth! Not those blow-dried phonies who fed the crowd platitudes that flattered their biases. Right?

I looked up from my BlackBerry with anticipation, awaiting the first moment of McCain magic to send back to HQ, but my hopeful optimism didn't last long. One by one, the cranky questioners went at him with asperity. Amnesty. Illegals. Mexicans. The border. The wall. The NAFTA superhighway (this was a popular conspiracy theory at the time; I was always a little surprised Trump never revived it). Illegals. Amnesty. Amnesty. Amnesty. Amnesty. Amnesty. Amnesty. Amnesty.

McCain would parry with his interrogators, but the straight talk was not landing. He was up there taking body blows like one of the patsies they put up against Mike Tyson after he got out of jail. But McCain was a stubborn mule who could take a few hooks to the gut. He was not a man who wanted to tell crowds exactly what they wanted to hear. In fact, at times he seemed to relish being the contrarian. Even though I could sense his growing frustration, he managed to maintain a wry mien.

Finally, at long last, a reprieve seemed to be in the offing. The first question he got after the immigration gauntlet was from a darling little old lady in the first row. She wanted to know what his stance was on abortion. I let out a sigh of relief in the back, no longer wanting to live my Sorkinian fantasy, just hoping for a crowd-pleaser on an issue where my candidate was in step with the audience.

But John McCain hadn't trekked to Counciltucky to please the mob that pummeled him.

He looked that grandma right in the eye and said he wanted to give her some "straight talk" instead. (At this point, I nearly threw up the stale breakfast croissant. I have a weak constitution.) While I might be pro-life, McCain answered, I'm also for stem cell research—a controversial hot button with the pro-life set at the time.

The sweet old lady slumped her shoulders. The crowd groaned. I fired off a PIN to the boss and walked outside to sneak a Parliament Light before the roiling catastrophe came to a close, and our tormentors filed out past me.

Eight weeks later, I was off the campaign. The juggernaut that had been planned foundered, and the campaign had to downsize. That the front-runner had faltered so dramatically out of the gate presaged our populist future. Republican kingmakers' ability to force-feed anointed candidates upon their voters was weakening, and a few dozen staffers on McCain's nascent presidential campaign, me among them, were proto-casualties of an internecine war that the populists had not yet won.

A few months later, the campaign resurrected. But as part of the turn in his political fortunes, the Maverick would eventually give little bits of himself over to the base that distrusted him. It was the politician's survival instinct at work. While he held the line on the Iraq War troop surge, he pivoted to the right on immigration to meet the voters where they were. During a November interview with Mickelson, he wouldn't concede that even the most sympathetic immigrants—Dreamers brought to America by their undocumented parents when they were young children—should be given special treatment. When Mickelson asked about these "kids of illegals," McCain replied: "Well, I think that we are a compassionate nation and we don't punish innocent people, but I have to say to ya again there's so much mistrust out there, there's so much anger, there's so much passion, that we'd have to convince a majority of

Americans even on a program such as that, that the borders are secure."

To McCain, at the time, that pivot didn't seem like much of a sacrifice.

It wasn't as if he had changed his position on immigration. He had simply said that his preferred position could no longer be achieved until some imaginary future date where people believe the border is secure. He had transitioned from taking a confrontational stance with the audience to using the politician's "comforting lie." The comforting lie centers the mob's feelings, their *anger*, their *passion*, over the uncomfortable realities of governing. It was a small change but a meaningful one.

From McCain's perspective, telling the comforting lie was more honorable than the path that was taken by most of his contemporaries, and there's no doubt that was the case. He had engaged in a good-faith attempt to solve the immigration crisis in a bipartisan manner and hadn't wavered on his underlying commitment to reform. What was his reward for this? Rabid crowds shouting him down. Sinking poll numbers. Racist GOP gadfly Tom Tancredo sending him an order of nachos when they both happened to be shaking hands at the same restaurant in Manchester, New Hampshire.

Meanwhile, he looked around at the rest of the field and saw charlatans straight-out lying about their views on immigration to gain an advantage over him. None did this more blatantly than Willard Mitt Romney. McCain considered preposterous the notion that the moderate Massachusetts governor was some immigration hard-liner. Romney had flip-flopped on the other salient social issues of the moment—abortion, gay rights, guns—so it seemed certain that his border hawkishness was merely a confidence game, given that it was the one cultural issue where Romney didn't carry the same baggage as the other primary contenders.

During the campaign, the erudite Romney would awkwardly attempt to take on the populist mantle by lambasting McCain and his wingman Lindsey "Grahmnesty" over their moderate immigration positions. At a South Carolina cattle call on Senator Graham's home turf, Romney declared that their proposed "Z" visa (which would allow undocumented immigrants a legal work permit) should be called an "A" visa because "it's amnesty and that's what it stands for." He was rewarded with thundering applause, for the limpest of lines. Romney carried his affected border hawkishness for years as a sop to the distrustful base. This performative overcompensation would wind up catching up to him, when in 2012 he proposed a policy of "self-deportation" that was so preposterous even Donald Trump mocked it as "crazy." But back in 2008, it was working and Romney, for a moment, used it to take the front-runner mantle.

The transparent phoniness of Romney's immigration shtick grated on McCain—for good reason! And it contributed to him rationalizing his own change in tone.

It may have been strategically justified, but everyone else being a phony doesn't negate the fact that McCain himself made this nearly undetectable pivot of convenience from straight talk to comforting lie on immigration in order to sustain his comeback in that primary.

That minor sacrifice was a harbinger of the much more dangerous panders to come, from other politicians who didn't share his prudence, or Romney's for that matter.

Months after winning the nomination, McCain solidified his bona fides with the base by ignoring his instinct to run on a "unity ticket" with conservative Democrat Joe Lieberman. Instead he went with Alaska governor Sarah Palin, the Trumpian forerunner who was able to fire up the faithful with the punchy anti-Obama zingers that just didn't come naturally to the nominee.

This was, by all accounts, a bitter pill for the Maverick to swallow.

His desire for Lieberman was so strong that, years later, those in the McCain high command confessed to me that he spent more than a week sulking. He refused until the last moment to come to grips with the fact that he had to settle on a Plan B.

As McCain weighed his options, campaign manager Steve Schmidt and other strategists argued that they needed a "transformative, electrifying" jolt to the campaign, which Palin might bring.

The final decision came after a closely held confab at McCain's ranch in Arizona. There, Schmidt would be the one who made the closing argument for Palin, while another close aide pitched Tim Pawlenty, a milquetoast Minnesota governor. Schmidt, who eventually admitted he was "frightened" by the notion of Palin being a heartbeat from the presidency, did a career 180 and later founded the anti-Trump Lincoln Project, which aimed to slay her populist spawn. But that day in Sedona he was focused solely on blazing a path to the White House. So he turned a blind eye to his fears. He could see victory, and a future as a top aide to President McCain, from that ranch.

At the time, there was a bit more logic to the choice than it might seem in retrospect. In Alaska, Palin had positioned herself as an anticorruption outsider, not the troll queen she would become. Had Schmidt and McCain known that the brash, independent-minded Sarah from Alaska would not evolve into a Maverick Apprentice but instead into an uncontainable lib-owning, trash-talking, reality TV Frankenstein monster, perhaps they wouldn't have made this sacrifice. Maybe McCain would have told Schmidt and the other advisors to stuff it and stuck to his guns on Lieberman.

Who knows? What we do know is that Palin showed the base that it's more fun to support someone who will baby-bird their grievances and unfounded beliefs right back to them than to hold their nose for someone who they know is reluctantly succumbing to their desires. Palin's events drew a motley, feral crowd dotted with the types of "deplorables" who would later turn Trump's rallies into a late-era Lynyrd Skynyrd tour. Unlike his future contemporaries, McCain refused complete submission to that mob. He famously admonished the voter who called Obama an "Arab" and scolded the crowd who had booed the then president-elect during a graceful and unifying concession speech.

But for a Maverick to survive in the GOP he still needed to fall back on the comforting lies that got him the nomination. A few years later, in one of the most uncomfortable political ads in memory, McCain demanded that the Obama administration "Complete the Danged Fence," a nakedly halfhearted version of the Build. The. Wall. chant that was to come. He did it to help fend off J. D. Hayworth, a Tea Party weirdo with a talk radio background who was challenging him in a Senate primary.

Viewers of the ad were meant to believe that the candidate emphasized "danged" to show how much he supported the fence, but those with a keen McCain ear knew he said "danged" because he thought it was so freaking stupid that he had to do the ad in the first place. The "danged" was akin to the frustrated lament of an employee who has been assigned a stupid project by the boss and just has to finish the danged thing before he could meet his friends for a drink. In this case, it was the mob who was the boss. And McCain knew it.

He managed to maintain his integrity as well as, or better than, most. But the moral sacrifices that would be required to stay in the future GOP were preordained on that Sedona ranch. Anyone seeing clearly, unencumbered by ambition or blinders or grievance, should have recognized it.

I know I did.

A part of me realized that the party I had started volunteering for as an early pubescent teen was slipping away from me and the trajectory we were on was a dark one. The Republican voters I saw in Counciltucky weren't looking for straight talk or paeans to national purpose. What they really wanted was to stick it in the other's eye and be comforted by convenient lies. They just needed a leader shameless enough to give it to them.

In retrospect, departing the McCain campaign should have been the moment when I pulled the ripcord and began charting a different course for my life. But I allowed myself to get sucked back in, telling myself many of the same stories that eight years later led otherwise rational people to decide that they should go along with Donald Trump. Pretending I thought we should build a danged fence, if that's what it took to win.

2

Compartmentalizer-in-Chief

After McCain, I moved back to D.C. and began the first of a few transitional periods that would eventually lead me to this book. This was the first time since before I could drive that I was watching politics as an outsider, and frankly, I didn't like most of what I saw. I had taken a job at Berman and Company, a PR firm that specializes in creating astroturf groups that would advocate on behalf of corporate interests. Astroturfing is not exactly the Lord's work, and while some of our activities were skeevy, the firm's libertarian bent, relatively normal working hours, and super gay staff allowed me the space to do some self-examination outside the slog of a political campaign. Among the many clarifying realizations during this period was the one that has been the most important of my entire life: I came to grips with the fact that I had to come out of the closet.

I want to detail for straight folk how and why this moment of clarity happened when it did. This is an important exercise, because what I have discovered is that the brainteasers I was playing with my closeted self parallel what I saw in my future former GOP friends during the Trump era. I would see the relief on the faces of people who left his orbit and came clean, just as clearly as the pain on the faces of people like Mike Pence who wouldn't admit to themselves what is obvious to everyone else.

Before I got to Berman, I could never envision for myself a happy gay life. I knew I wanted kids. I knew I didn't want to risk losing my devout Catholic family or my straight bro besties. So it seemed like staying in the closet and faking it till I made it with women was the best of not-great options. After all, the equipment worked—sorry for the TMI, but this is an important consideration for some—so I could just suppress the wrong thoughts and ride it out.

I was never going to break away from this line of thinking until I allowed myself to see people who were both gay and leading open lives that I could envision for myself. For years, thanks to my compartmentalization superpower, I couldn't do so, despite the fact that Berman was not actually the first time I had been exposed to a diverse array of gay people. I graduated from the George Washington University, for God sakes—one of the gayest spaces in all of American life, no exaggeration. The now cancel-worthy malapropism that kids from other schools bestowed on my alma mater was "Gay Double Jew," due to the preponderance of both on campus. While I was there, I had one or two encounters (okay, fine, definitely two, but I'm trying to mentally expunge the second one), but, if anything, those drove me deeper into the closet. They made me more embarrassed. More self-conscious. More ashamed. More hostile to people who were open about their sexuality, because I couldn't have what they had, or at least that's what I told myself.

So I just stopped seeing anyone or anything that inconvenienced my chosen reality. This tunnel vision was so intense that if you asked 2005 me, I would have genuinely told you that the only people that I thought were living openly gay lives were hairdressers or the flamboyant types who hosted *Queer Eye for the Straight Guy* and that the only other gays in the world were the creepy closet cases who stared at me on the Metro. GW was the Baskin Robbins thirty-one flavors of homos and I managed to flatten that entire universe into queens and creeps. (PS: *I love queens! I hate that I thought this!*)

Some of the very same people who would become my dearest friends just three years later were sitting in my classes, going to parties, and doing all the shit I wished I was doing on that rare occasion when I let myself daydream. Instead I cleaved off my gayness from the rest of my identity in large part because I didn't feel like the "gay lifestyle" was compatible with how I saw myself and my future. Such is the power of the brain's ability to lock away things that aren't convenient.

I finally escaped this mental maze one Friday afternoon when, nervous as all get-out, I went down the hall to awkwardly ask Justin, the gay coworker whom I was the least close with, to meet up for a mysterious drink. Tagging him in this book as someone I didn't particularly care for at the time is going to seem like an unnecessarily rude neg. I get it. But it's a crucial detail if you are to understand the deluded closeted mind.

I had convinced myself that this *coworker* was not *really* a part of my life, so even after I told him my big gay secret, I would still have the option to change my mind and go back straight. If things went south, I figured that I could just excise him from my existence forever. No harm, no foul.

Now, I'm not sure that I had fully thought through the long-term implications of that strategic plan, as it is unclear whether this excision would have included me quitting the new job I was using to pay off the gambling debts that I had accrued at Iowa's Indian casinos or whether I was planning to simply avoid Justin in the office kitchen for an indeterminate amount of time.

Nevertheless, my hastily organized cryptic happy hour came to pass. We sat in the very unromantic and uncomfortable chairs that marked the sidewalk patios outside the K Street nightclubs near our downtown D.C. office. We drank a couple of overpriced cocktails that I hope I paid for. After an interminable few minutes of small talk and office gossip, my entire body experiencing extreme diaphoresis, I stutteringly spit out the words that I had never said aloud before. I'm gay.

Justin, whom I had been insulting in my head as being an utterly replaceable part of my life a few minutes earlier, was absolutely wonderful in response. He had his whole spiel down pat, seeing as I was the umpteenth person to come out of the closet to him. He gave me a book to read, *The Best Little Boy in the World,* by former Democratic campaign operative Andrew Tobias, which tracked the coming-out process of someone who was struggling to figure out where they fit in the big gay universe.

I would later steal from much of what Justin had told me during the dozens of similar come from Jesuses I'd end up having from the other side of the table—as you might imagine, being possibly the most visible gay Republican operative in America tends to lead to a lot of conversations with men who are struggling with the ramifications of coming out in their family, church, community, or friend circle. (Tip #1: Rip the Band-Aid off. Make a short list of the people that you feel need to hear from you directly. Tell them as quickly as possible. Then tell them to tell everyone else or post it on the 'gram.)

In the days after our chat, I tore through *The Best Little Boy in the World* and started to come to the completely obvious realization that I was not the first closet case in history who didn't think they conformed to the awful stereotype of gay people they had in their head. And it was during that *BLBITW* binge sesh that I received a final sign that I was on the right track from the gods of the political news cycle.

Republican senator Larry Craig, who had been nabbed going for a handy during a sting operation in a Minnesota airport bathroom (yikes), was trying to salvage his career. He agreed to an interview with NBC's Matt Lauer, which I watched in a Capitol Hill bachelor pad that had a mattress on the floor, a month's worth of dirty dishes in the sink, and only Maker's Mark and Goldfish in the cupboard. It was in that apartment I had spent the past few months alone, depressed, scrolling Craigslist M4M, but too afraid to do anything about it. Pretending to be something I wasn't. On my television was this sad old man trying to explain away that very same self-deception with a handsome, dour wife sitting next to him patting his leg.

In that moment everything clicked. *That* was the life I needed to be afraid of, not the openly gay ever-after I had been blocking out all these years. Larry Craig was the ghost of my closeted future. Justin was the ghost of my soon-to-be fabulous present. I could do this. I could stop this inexorable path toward becoming that sad, desperate man tapping his foot with a wide stance in a public restroom. I just needed to allow myself to see that there was another option, that my identity could be something other than what others had projected onto me and I had projected on myself. That it was okay to change.

Coming out was the best decision I ever made, by a landslide. If you happen to be reading this and are still on the fence, I'm telling you, you should do it. It improved my life in myriad ways, big and small. It widened the aperture through which I viewed the world and expanded my capacity for empathy. It saved me.

As a bonus, all the GOP colleagues who would disappoint me in the ensuing years over Trump were, to a person, wonderful when it came to my new life as a proud poofter. I will never forget when Grant Young, my former Iowa officemate, the most noncosmopolitan, brutish, 0.00 on the Kinsey scale het imaginable, called to say simply, "I heard the news, I'm with ya. Give me my talking points, in case anyone gives you trouble." Same as it ever was.

And yet, coming out still required me to unravel a mindfuck that was a quarter century in the making. The closet is omnipresent and omnipotent. It engulfs you. It makes everything you do a lie. Your clothes are a lie (I bought my first pair of "gay jeans" in Iowa during a mental trial run a year before I actually came out). Any comment that you make about the appearance of a human under the age of sixty-five contains a lie. Existing at a bar with friends at make-out o'clock is a lie. For some, the very manner in which they speak is a lie. Every single word. It's no wonder that so many gays go into PR. It was ingrained in us from the moment we had an inkling that something was different. To deal with all this, you build all these little Marie Kondo–esque separators and doors that let you block out anything that doesn't spark a safe, comfortable, unchallenging joy in your mind.

Throughout all this, I cultivated the very skill in both my personal and professional life that would come to mark how mainstream Republicans survived during the Trump era down the line: the power of compartmentalization. If you want to see championship-level compartmentalization in action, take a look at this interview I did with Kerry Eleveld for the LGBT magazine *The Advocate* a few years after I came out.

Eleveld asked how I felt watching an interview McCain did with Chris Matthews in the fall of 2006, after I knew I was likely to work for him but before I had officially joined the campaign.

McCain had long bucked the party's most harsh anti-gay partisans. Before his first presidential bid in 2000, the Republican mayor of Tempe, Arizona, a McCain ally, was outed as gay. When asked if he would denounce him by reporters McCain said, "He's a fine man. Who the hell cares if he is gay?" A middle finger to the bigoted assholes, not a comforting lie. We love to see it.

It was in this same spirit that he confronted a new question about the homosexuals, this time on the matter of gay marriage. The interview was being conducted in Ames, Iowa, just up the road from the office I was sharing with Young. "I think that gay marriage should be allowed, if there's a ceremony kind of thing, if you want to call it that. I don't have any problem with that," McCain said.

Hardball went to commercial break. McCain was nudged by an advisor who took the rare step of venturing from offstage to whisper something in the candidate's ear mid-interview. He told McCain that given the way he phrased the answer, it sounded as if he had just endorsed gay marriage. So, the next opportunity McCain got, he backtracked, offering a clarifying non sequitur at the end of a question about the farm bill from the Iowa State University College Republican chairman, Don McDowell.

"Could I just mention one other thing?" McCain said. "On the issue of the gay marriage, I believe that people want to have private ceremonies, that's fine. I do not believe that gay marriages should be legal."

Here is how I described my effed-up response to watching that exchange, when talking to Eleveld a few years later after I was out of the closet.

"At that point I remember thinking, I can't believe he just made that mistake. I wasn't really thinking about it that much from my personal perspective. I was interested in getting him elected. Iowa is a conservative place, and in order to win the caucus there, that's not really a tenable position," I said.

Yikes.

So let's pull back the layers of this mental onion together, shall we?

There I was, sitting in the basement of the Republican Party of Iowa headquarters in Des Moines, knowing that I was gay. I'm watching McCain give an interview with Chris Matthews in the state where I knew I was going to be managing his press. He goes off-script and says that he supports gays "having a ceremony kind of thing"—which is kind of nice and all, but not exactly a radical point of view in a free country. Hearing this, my reaction is to be *upset* that McCain is saying something that I perceive will hurt his campaign, rather than excited that I was planning to work with someone who doesn't want to deny me the ability to have a totally chill, off-the-books, man-man ceremony.

Then, after letting it settle in the old brain for a bit, I stop being upset about the politics of it and decide that this little gaffe is really a good thing, because my boss just kind of admitted that he secretly thinks I should be allowed to have a private garden party with a future lover that, in the moment, I am still too scared to even consider I might want.

This is not healthy! At the time, it didn't even faze me. When I gave this interview to *The Advocate*, I remember being a little embarrassed to admit out loud how calculating I was, but even at that point, a few years after I had come out, my mindset was still so twisted that I didn't have any second thoughts about that initial perspective, which I considered pretty rational, given my desire to be on a winning campaign.

Years later, this same impulse appeared when I was guilt-ridden after a series of right-wing bloggers and radio hosts attacked my then boss Jeb Bush based on a few of my pro-gay social media posts. To assuage that guilt, I offered to call Ralph fucking Reed, the homophobic former head of the Christian Coalition, to assure him that I would not turn Jeb into a pro-sodomy crusader. I couldn't even look my boyfriend in the eye after I hung up.

The only silver lining about this whole charade is that in revisiting this moment for the book, I must confess to getting a hearty laugh coming across a segment in which the porn addict turned reactionary Christian talk radio host Steve Deace rattled off the verboten gay parties I attended, which he uncovered while stalking my Facebook. "Homo/Sonic. SugarTit: A Dirty Polaroid New Year's Eve," he read in a grave tone.

The point is that my internalized contortions on this are a case study in how a person can convince themselves to make allowances for actions by the politicians they work for even if they are directly harmful to them.

In my case, it was even worse—I was actively rooting for my candidate to be more skilled at taking positions that would deny me the most fulfilling and important parts of my current life—my now husband and child.

If it's that easy to jettison something that directly impacts you, imagine how little willpower it takes to not worry yourself with matters that are going to only impact others. Or even more ephemerally, to block out things that may or may not impact others at some later date. Like, say, "mean tweets" or pretending an election was stolen to humor the president for a little while.

You just put those concerns off to the side in a box, subjugate them to whatever is convenient at the moment, to whatever you think benefits the team.

I had a brief window where I saw this clearly. I was in the liminal space between coming out of the closet and reentering campaign life when I had the chance to unfuck my brain. During that glorious intermission I was a flirty and fabulous political outsider, making out with boys on the beach, mocking the Palinized GOP, concerned about the rise of the Tea Party loonies, without any impulse to rationalize their actions or those of any other party or clique. It was all there.

Had I fully integrated my professional life with my personal awakening I may have trodden down a different path to a glorious and honest homosexual future. But my virtuoso compartmentalization capabilities hadn't fully abated. At the same time as I was seeing my personal life and the political environment so clearly, I had a day job managing astroturf groups for corporations that was still a full-time exercise in deceit. Meanwhile, my desire for the rush that comes from high-stakes politicking, from being in "the mix," was unquenched.

I was out of the closet but needed to get back in the game.

3

The Game

In close company, one bit of shorthand political operatives use to reference their line of work is "the Game." For those of us who worked primarily in campaigns or political jobs in D.C., "the Game" is what separates what we do from what the "wonks" or "careers" or lawyers do.

We specialize in strategy, tactics, messaging, advertising, opposition research. Slaying the enemy. Winning the race.

They undertake the mundane business of *governing*.

There's this weird kind of reverse power dynamic between those who have a role in the Game and those who focus on what happens when the campaigns fold up. An outsider might presume that the wonks would be in the higher social caste. They are the ones whose decisions impact how much people pay in taxes, what laws they have to abide by, and sometimes whether they live or die. But the preponderance of the wonks' work is boring and dreary. There aren't too many dramatic tell-all books or movies or HBO series being made on the behind-the-scenes story of how the COVID rescue package passed muster with the parliamentarian's reconciliation rules.

Outside of the foreign policy arena and the high-stakes world of diplomacy and international intrigue, there is not a lot of sex appeal in "governing." And there's especially little sex appeal in the waterlogged nongoverning that's been happening of late. Quick, name a staffer who was central to the Manchin/Sinema negotiations over the Build Back Better bill, which was set to pump trillions of dollars into the economy?

Got nothing? Me neither.

On the campaign side, things are quite different. Thanks to talk TV and the campaigns' HBO *Game Change* glow-ups, once relatively anonymous political strategists now have star power that had previously only been accessible to those at the tippy-top of the presidential strategist ladder, people like Lee Atwater or Karl Rove or James Carville or Paul Begala. By 2008 you had losing campaign managers like Steve Schmidt and younger Obama staffers like Jon Favreau and Robert Gibbs getting stopped for pictures at airports like they were LeBron or Aaron Rodgers.

Working on campaigns, there were various times that you could sense, or that the more brazen would admit, that staffers were imagining who would play them in the next movie. (Jay Baruchel for me; thanks for asking.) This D.C. celebrification was exacerbated by the increasing number of "political strategists" booked for shouty cable segments that used to be limited to *Crossfire* and *Hardball*, while Twitter even gave some lower-level staffers a notoriety that was a hair short of selfie status but significant enough to make them enamored with it. I used to joke that Jesus initially had only the twelve followers, while I had 8,000 (or whatever it was at the time). While that was meant as a joke, there was a discomfiting hint of truth in there. At times having such a following did make a person feel like they were somewhere on the path to veneration or crucifixion or both.

The strategery of the Game and the associated, niche "fame"

was not what drew me to politics initially. I had at least a flicker of youthful earnestness, but it is certainly how I got hooked.

Early in my political career, I remember visiting extended family in St. Louis for a wedding or funeral or some such. One of my cousins asked how I got into politics. As kids, he and I were both obsessed with sports, though neither of us were turning any heads with our athletic prowess (me especially). We filled that gap and sealed our bond by obsessing over trading cards and player stats and the decisions made by coaches and GMs. As we grew older, that evolved into fantasy sports and gambling. You know the type.

I confessed to him that politics offered me the same kind of competitive outlet that sports fandom had. In the very first campaign I worked on, for Colorado gubernatorial candidate Bill Owens, he won by 8,000 votes, or 0.7 percent. Owens was down most of Election Night and came roaring back late, with victory announced in the early morning hours. It was like a thrilling, two-minute game-winning drive. How could I not get addicted? From then on, I pored over the Charlie Cook race rankings and any polling data I could get my hands on. I scoured the candidate profiles on Politics1.com. I learned about the congressional districts' PVIs (Partisan Voting Index) rather than baseball players' RBIs.

This came to be referred to derisively as "horse race" politics. The horse race mindset, taken to its logical conclusion, makes ideology subordinate to gamesmanship. For those of us who engaged in it, the candidate's general political views mattered to a certain degree, but the actual impact of their policies took a backseat to the competition. This attitude was endemic among my campaign colleagues. My generation of political operatives' mindset was described aptly in the book *This Town*, the premier anthropological study of Washington, D.C., as "neopolitical junkies whose passions were ignited not by an inspirational candidate or officeholder, but by operatives on T.V., fictional or real. They were players in a thrilling screen game."

As we rose up the ranks in politics, everyone started to become a bit of a star in their own minds. As I was weighing jobs, I once even admitted out loud to my boyfriend that one thing that made me attracted to staying in politics was my craving for this bizarre type of fame had not yet subsided.

AHHHHHHH

AHHHHHHHH.

I can't believe I said that. And now I'm typing this in a book for other people to read!

Mortifying or not, it was our reality. Some preferred the instant gratification limelight of cable TV and the associated Facebook congratulations from acquaintances of yore. (There's nothing quite like the serotonin boost that comes from an "OMG I saw you on TV?!" alert from a person you haven't spoken to since chemistry class in 1999.) Others fancied themselves more of an enigmatic thimblerigger behind the curtain, avoiding the press unless it was dishing "on background" to reporters.

For those who aren't familiar, "on background" is a term of art for talking to reporters without having your name attached. It is intended to allow for whistle-blowers to share information anonymously or for reporters to get the true story from someone who might not be able to be fully candid with their name associated, without risk of losing their job.

These days, political reporters use it for a much broader range of things, including as a tool to curry favor with their "sources," allowing them to smear rivals without personal blowback. In the Trump White House, internal wars were waged with entirely "on background" material that was of questionable provenance and news value. Marco Rubio's 2016 campaign manager, Terry Sullivan, made OnBackground his Twitter handle. Subtle.

The shrouded Svengalis may not have cared about the cheap-calorie cable celebrity, but that didn't mean they weren't enamored with the drama. They loved to be whispered and gossiped about in the political press. To gain reputations as "killers." And on count-less occasions, I've heard powerful political admen and strategists boast about how they didn't worry about silly matters like "govern-ing." They were hacks through and through, adrenaline junkies who were in it for the fight.

No matter which role they were in, staffers began to see them-selves as tacticians in this made-for-TV blood sport rather than as functionaries in a system that is aimed to produce the best policy outcomes for their fellow citizens.

While being ensconced in this thrilling screen game that has little to do with actual outcomes for the public, the players still flat-tered themselves with a public "service" moniker, as if their work is on par with soldiers dodging IEDs in Fallujah. No matter your role in politics, you say you "served" your candidate or organization. "I served as deputy digital director for a super PAC" is something people in the Game say with a straight face even though their job was to send out emails tricking old people into giving five dollars from their fixed income to fund TV ads.

This service moniker carries with it none of the associated responsibilities that come with genuine public service, of course. Whether something was the right thing to do only mattered to the extent that it was also the right thing to do politically. When the strategy, politics, and policy impacts all aligned: great. But when they didn't, well, that was a concern for the wonks. Not our problem.

Something you didn't hear much from players in the Game was self-doubt over whether the political tactics they were employ-ing might hurt the people they were purporting to serve. So, the practitioners of politics could easily dismiss moralistic or technical concerns just by throwing down their trump card: "It's all part of the Game."

- Policy white paper doesn't actually add up? Who cares, part of the Game.
- Attack on your opponent isn't exactly in good faith? Part of the Game; make them defend it.
- Getting an endorsement from someone popular but repugnant? Game.
- Raising money from people you suspect to be corrupt? Game.
- Spam-emailing supporters with hysterical messages about how their five dollars is needed to prevent the evildoers from stealing everything that ever mattered to them? That's how the Game is played.

I could go on forever. These are just a few examples of how all ethical quandaries are completely excised from consideration. The human impact of one's work is not just inadvertently missing but actively mocked.

An example of how this manifests came from the person who taught me the ropes at the Republican National Committee's campaign school. He said the highest praise one political operative can give another is that they "get it." Raising concerns about downstream harm that might be caused by a proposed political gambit is one of the best signs that you don't "get it." And not getting it is a one-way ticket to the back office, where the wonks are slaving over white papers that nobody will read.

The only time real-world impact matters is when it changes your standing in the Game. It's okay to raise the notion that your boss might not want to do x, y, or z because it will lead to bad press or could backfire publicly.

For example, the RNC for years has been sending out unconscionable mailers to every elderly conservative in America. These letters are made up almost exclusively of hyperbole and ad hominem and conspiracies. They add absolutely zero to the political discourse. But they "work" in the sense that they are effective at keeping the olds upset so that they continue sending in their Social Security money.

For some reason, I was tasked with "approving" these mailers during my time at the committee, so I struck any lines that I thought would be embarrassing if it fell into the hands of a reporter. My cuts were apparently much more draconian than those of my predecessors, and this pissed off the fundraising team. One day I was summoned to the chief of staff's office, and we had a standoff over how much to cut, which the fundraisers won and I lost (of course). As long as the mailers were "working" and money was coming in, the boss figured there was no reason to rock the boat, unless I could prove that this was likely to yield bad press. I tucked my tail and rubber-stamped whatever nonsense they sent through, figuring that if it did become a controversy, I had already said my piece.

If you step back for a second, what is really alarming about this whole encounter is the fact that at no point in the dispute was there a discussion of whether we should be sending out a letter that was filled with lies and slander. Or the ethics of snaffling a few quid from the Greatest Generation. That was just the baseline. This letter was part of the Game. The only judgment call the chief of staff was asked to make was to balance whether the donations would be worth the potential embarrassment. And the answer was yes.

That was nearly a decade ago now. By all accounts, the degradation of the "service" mindset continues apace as more and more politicians cut the wonks out entirely, in favor of the performative elements of the Game.

Senators like Ted Cruz and congressmen like Matt Gaetz aspire to be multiplatform entertainers more than they care about governing. In the case of newly minted MAGA congressdude Madison Cawthorn, he "built his office around comms," not policy, ensuring that there will never be anyone around to harsh the vibe with the trifling concerns of constituents.

And oh, by the way, their most vocal constituents, the Republicans who turn out to vote in primaries, are slurping this up. Turns out they don't give a shit about incremental progress or the plight of their fellow man or a serious and nuanced response to a deadly pandemic anyway. *Boring.* They are only made upset if a politician *doesn't* satiate their desire to see hot-fire slams savaging their perceived enemies, further incentivizing the pols to prioritize this fight over all else.

The standoff I had with the RNC chief over fundraising tactics looks quaint in comparison to what is the standard operating procedure of basically every political campaign and committee in the country today—on both sides. They all just accept without hesitation that wheels-off missives about how the end is nigh if the other team wins are not just kosher but required.

As the insanity unfolded during the lead-up to the January 6th insurrection, I signed up for various Republican email and text lists to get a sense of what type of material people were getting. As a result, I was bombarded with dire warnings advancing the notion that the election had been stolen and the nation hung in the balance. Here's one example:

Alert: 1500 dead voters, 42,248 voted multiple times. Matt Schlapp here. I'm in Nevada and we have uncovered massive amounts of fraud. We're not going to let this stand. We are filing suit today in Nevada and I'm calling on you to help us. Will you donate $35 today to help our efforts and bring justice to President Trump in this election.

Here's another that came from the president of the United States himself (at least, that's what they want recipients to think).

TODAY. This is our LAST CHANCE.

We need to make sure you're aware of how important today is. Congress will vote this afternoon to certify, or object to, the Election results. **Over 100 Members of Congress have vowed to fight for President Trump and OBJECT TO the results because they are concerned about voting irregularities and potential fraud.** The stakes have NEVER been higher, Timothy. President Trump needs YOU to make a statement and publicly stand with him and **FIGHT BACK**.

Meanwhile, back at the various campaign HQs, the twenty-somethings drafting these emails and mailers and texts are no more inclined to revolution than the authors of the batty fundraising mailers I was tasked with approving a decade earlier. These are not coup guys. They are kids being charged with raising more money than they did the last quarter. They are pawns in a game that many of the people reading the messages didn't realize was being played.

Tell people that their country is being stolen from them long enough, and they take it seriously, even if most of the people writing and approving the text don't. And so it shouldn't have been much of a surprise that eventually some of those reading these end-times warnings would come to Washington with pitchforks and gallows.

We had long been laying the groundwork that led to such a result. And, for a time, I lapped it up.

• • •

By late 2010, I had been out of politics and the closet for three years and was itching to get back in the Game. I received a call asking if I would be interested in doing press for Jon Huntsman Jr.'s then-hypothetical presidential campaign. By that time, I was in a relationship with my now husband, who was a little sour on the prospect of me being a Republican spokesperson again, but eventually he relented. (Life lesson: always listen to your SO.)

The rationalization process on this one was pretty damn easy.

On paper, Huntsman and I were an exact political match. I'm not certain that there was a single political issue that we were on opposite sides of at the time, at least none of major consequence. He hewed to conservative orthodoxy on economic issues, education reform, and abortion. He held an internationalist view of foreign affairs, in which America had an important role to play in the world, but he had also responded rationally to the Iraq debacle and harbored doubts about the more militaristic strain of the GOP. He was willing to "go there" and argue that fiscal responsibility also meant paring back defense spending. He also recognized the areas where the GOP had gone wayward. He believed in climate change and thought we should do something about it. (Call him crazy!) He supported immigration reform and rejected the nativists and bigots in the party. He respected people from all faiths and cultures and had adopted two amazing daughters, from China and India, respectively. He was willing to work with the other side to such a degree that he served in the Obama administration as ambassador to China. He even supported civil unions openly, not secretly! This was my dream candidate and my dream job. I basically begged for it. I was excited about the prospect of reentering politics, working for someone who was a long shot but with whom I was completely aligned philosophically. I thought I could be part of the fight to bring the GOP back from the brink. It was about as pure in intent as a person can be when making a career decision.

Once I got the job, there was the less pure part of my brain that recognized this was my big break and that I needed to use it to prove myself. While I might have been a squishy moderate RINO on the issues, I needed to demonstrate I was a skilled knife fighter who could hang with the big boys. Part of the reason I had gotten the job was how I had proven my ability to drop colorful, killer "oppo" on opposing candidates on behalf of McCain four years prior.

My favorite "oppo hit" from that time was a front-page *Des Moines Register* story featuring the picture of a sad farmer who was devastated that Rudy Giuliani had canceled a campaign stop at her homestead because she was too poor to qualify for the estate tax. When the story dropped, I was absolutely giddy. Making family farmers angry at your opponent is as close as you can get to porn in Iowa campaigns, and that busty front-page pinup was featured prominently in my office until the day I packed up.

Using examples like this, I saw myself as someone who could channel the dark arts of politics to positive ends. If the more rational, reasonable, compassionate side of the party was going to win the battle for the soul of the GOP, we were going to have to do so as slash-and-burn executioners. We were also going to have to throw some elbows on behalf of the conservative base so they would know we had their back. At least, that was the story I told myself.

After I had been hired, but before Huntsman even had launched his campaign, I was sharpening my shiv and getting to work on this two-front war. My mind had easily warped the earnest ideological rationalization for getting back into politics into an excuse to be the Game's most dogged combatant. The two candidates we saw as standing in the way of any plausible path to victory were fellow center-right governors Mitt Romney of Massachusetts and Mitch Daniels of Indiana. Even though they were also, by far, the two best options in the field besides Huntsman, I began a merciless crusade to crush them.

With Daniels we had early success. I met with a few reporters and discussed some of his potential weaknesses as a candidate. Among them was an open secret about how his on-again, off-again marriage had left some hard feelings in its wake and the fact that his wife's ex-husband's other ex-wife (take a minute to diagram that) was aggrieved about the way everything had been handled. And she was not shy about airing those grievances, that I can tell you. Hoo, boy.

As a result, her contact info had been shared with our campaign, and I, in turn, hosted coffee meet-ups where I passed the digits along to select reporters who were vetting Daniels's potential run.

Following those handoffs, a handful of news outlets wrote some extremely tame takeouts on how Daniels's wife was reluctant to green-light the campaign, in part over a disinterest in having the country psychoanalyze their marriage. One of those stories noted that "a rival campaign" (us) had provided contact information "for the ex-wife of the man Cheri Daniels married in the years between her divorce and remarriage." Given that this was already an open secret, our view was that stories on this personal drama were inevitable if he ran and doing our part to push up the timeline a bit might further dissuade Daniels from entering a race that he was already squeamish about.

As far as political "dirty tricks" go, this one was rather mild. All we did was make sure reporters who were previewing a possible Daniels campaign had easily accessible info about something people in Indiana were already buzzing about. Shadily acquired laptops with pictures of the candidate's drug-addled son ripping lines in his tighty-whities it was not.

But it was still noticed. Daniels's staff tut-tutted in the press about the use of "such tactics." Soon after, he made it official that he wasn't going to take the plunge.

We were thrilled. I had no idea of the actual reason for his decision, but I considered it at the time to be my first scalp and figured my bosses would be impressed that it was executed so efficiently. We had succeeded at helping to clear our initial hurdle—making sure the center-right "lane" was as open as possible for Huntsman. (That lane turned out to be more of a narrow, precarious rocky shoulder on the side of a New Hampshire country road. Whoops.)

In recent years, Daniels's supporters have argued that this little bit of chicanery was the reason the American people were denied a Daniels presidency that would have united the nation and led us to the great technocratic conservative future.

While 2011 Tim is devilishly delighted by the prospect of having that kind of power . . . I'm deeply skeptical that that was actually the case. Daniels had to know that this kind of probe of his personal life was coming sooner or later if he wanted to be president. And anyone who chose not to run because of a quite vanilla press story didn't really have their heart in what was going to be a grueling nomination and general election battle in the first place. Not to mention the fact that wan, mild-mannered Mitch is not anywhere near a fit for the MAGA-fied GOP.

But for the purpose of this exercise, the "what if" counterfactual parlor games aren't really the point.

The reality is that I got reacquainted with the rush that came from being in the high-stakes PR game. Major news outlets were cryptically mentioning my coffee meetings! Social media would explode when a new Daniels shoe would drop, and I would get the satisfaction of knowing that I was behind it. Take that little serotonin boost you get when your social media post gets liked but multiply it exponentially. Everyone in politics was talking about something that my invisible hand was a part of. It was intoxicating.

In 2020, my friend Olivia Nuzzi wrote a *New York* magazine piece that profiled one of the anonymous leakers who continued working at the top levels of Republican politics throughout the Trump era while still loathing the man in private. One of this fellow's obnoxious explanations for his misbehavior stood out from the rest: how exhilarating it all was.

"I do remember the first time I leaked something. It was almost inadvertent," he said. "It ended up on the front page of a pretty big paper, and I remember thinking, Oh wow, you're playing with live bullets now. . . . It's fun."

I had reentered the Game with a doe-eyed desire to fight for one of the good guys and it had taken T minus two minutes for me to start ethering another one of the relative good guys without even taking a moment to consider any real-world repercussions.

I too have to admit, it was fun.

• • •

Romney was much more durable than Daniels. Since he had already taken a lot of the most potent daggers from me and the rest of the McCain team during the 2008 primary, there was much less salacious material to mine.

The 2008 barrage against Mitt was a political troublemaking masterpiece, and the pièce de résistance of our anti-Romney art angel was Seamus the dog. You must remember Seamus? The canine who sparked a thousand *New York Times* opinion columns? He has his own Wikipedia page now. It's titled "Mitt Romney dog incident."

Buried in a *Boston Globe* profile on the candidate was an anecdote shared by Romney's eldest son, Tagg, that the son must have found . . . charming? Humanizing? It's impossible to say. But Tagg told the reporter that their family dog Seamus would ride on the roof of the family's Chevy Caprice station wagon on the family's annual summer trip to Lake Huron—a twelve-hour drive from their home in Massachusetts. During one of the trips, Seamus had come down with irritable bowel syndrome and spewed diarrhea all over the car. Tagg, sitting in those cool rear-facing seats that they don't make anymore, had spotted the brown liquid excreta streaming down the back windshield.

I remember receiving an absolutely gleeful call from my boss on the McCain campaign after he first came across the Seamus saga. I can still imagine his face in my mind's eye: eyes lit up in playful, childlike wonder, cheeks reddened, laugh diabolical.

Our opponent had placed a family pet on the car roof. This was manna from the heavens.

When I look back on my time doing opposition research, this is the type of mischievous material that I can still regard with fondness. It was where I thrived. A political reporter at BuzzFeed described my style as "puckish" in a profile. Seamus allowed for such revelry. We were all so innocent then.

On the call, my boss had demanded that we locate dogs and dog costumes to hound Romney with at his upcoming events.

This "street theater" required a costume and staffing change from what I had been executing to date. Previously we had been dressing up a volunteer in a Flipper the Dolphin suit. Flipper would follow Romney around Iowa in various themes that highlighted his most recent flip-flops. In one of our most evocative iterations, the volunteer was dressed as Señor Flipper, replete with sombrero and mustache—which was probably in bad taste, given the benefit of hindsight. But Señor Flip became our team's coup de grâce, since he made it onto the front page of the *Washington Post*, paired with a story on a candidate cattle call.

Not all our hits on Romney were lighthearted busking. Around the same time, I recall someone unearthing a flyer showing that

Romney had marched in a gay rights parade (the horror!). I used that as oppo against him, pitching it to conservative blogs and religious groups in Iowa, once again compartmentalizing my role in advancing a narrative that demonized me.

With all the low-hanging fruit having been pitted and eaten in 2008, the 2012 effort would require a different approach—death by a thousand cuts. We planned to contrast Huntsman's more conservative governing record in Utah and perceived electability against Romney's flip-floplitude and paint him as a milksop who was too phony and stiff to take on the Obama juggernaut.

While our campaign may not have been running on all cylinders in other departments—we misspelled our candidate's first name on printed-out credentials during the announcement speech, for example—we put together a rapid response/oppo research shop that was the class of the field. So much so that we were simultaneously helping other, less organized campaigns take shots at Romney when the message might be more credible coming from them. When the Romney campaign started hammering Rick Perry for being too soft on immigration, I cajoled their team into taking our material so that their rejoinders were stronger. Meanwhile, my Twitter feed was that of a besotted Romney assassin. With encyclopedic knowledge of his past indiscretions, I would host a veritable *Mystery Science Theater 3000* performance on Twitter during his events.

As the campaign wound down, this began to look a little weird and pathetic, given that we were teetering around 1 percent in the national polls while Romney maintained pole position. But I was determined not to ever let up, and I sprinted through the tape. You won't be surprised to learn that a lot of the people in the Romney campaign hated me as a result and carried a grudge for years. His political director even shoved me in a debate spin room almost a half decade on!

But Game recognizes Game. Romney's campaign manager, Matt Rhoades, respected the fact that I got under his team's skin. So, when I went hat in hand begging for another job after we got our ass kicked in the New Hampshire primary, he didn't reject the idea.

A few months later, I was sitting in an office at the Republican National Committee with Rhoades and future *Dancing with the Stars* runner-up Sean Spicer. Rhoades said, "I figure if my people hate you this much, you must be pretty good." He gave Spicer his blessing to bring me on as his deputy at the RNC, with a focus on creating the same agita in Obama's high command that I had in Romney's.

Spicer, as was his style, lowballed me in offering a job as the RNC's deputy communications director. But that was just the fancy title. My real job was to be the party's anti-Obama hatchet man in the media. Despite the chintzy bid, I jumped on it.

In just eighteen months, I went from being on the sidelines, concerned about the trajectory of the GOP, to being the national party's hired gun and a rising star in GOP politics.

How did this make sense? Ambition and recognition.

As I saw it, from the RNC perch there would be a real avenue toward being a top spokesperson, maybe even the press secretary for the next Republican who made it to the White House. I could be the gay C. J. Cregg!

There was no way that I was going to return to a boring anonymous PR life and sacrifice the rush that had come from dropping oppo bombs on the presidential campaign trail, the status that had resulted from an incipient minor Beltway celebrity, and maybe, just maybe, a role in the White House.

When the offer came, I didn't hesitate for a second. I didn't stutter. I was on the fast track, and I wasn't getting off. In fact, I don't recall even contemplating the potential risks or downsides of being one of the public faces of a party that I had a few fundamental issues with, including the most obvious one.

My hire came just a few months before Joe Biden accidentally blurted out the Obama administration's support for gay marriage. It was certain that the issue would come to a head while I was at the committee. To the extent I did think about it, it was mostly to justify the decision by considering how being an openly gay man in the RNC might be a good thing. The fact that the chairman at the time, Reince Priebus, would put me in such a role and ignore the chattering Christians who whispered about their discomfort with having me there was a good sign, wasn't it? I could be a visible example for some of the closeted gay Republicans out in America. From that POV I was even kinda sorta still fighting the fight on behalf of the good guys. This is fine, right? Right?

It was Infrastructure Week in my brain.

4

Gay Traitor Degrading the Discourse

So, all that talk about being a knife fighter for the good guys?
Well, come 2013, I had put that notion into a fancy little jewelry box in the deep recesses of my cerebellum. My next job after the RNC was not, in fact, a noble effort to scrap for the soul of the party. Just the opposite. It was solidifying my reputation as a "pithy, slice and dice" political hit man who was one of the party's up-and-comers.

Following Romney's defeat, I launched what we hoped would be the Republican Party's preeminent opposition research organization, teaming up with Rhoades and RNC research director Joe Pounder. (Quick aside: Is there a better aptronym for a political hatchet man than "Pounder"? I don't believe so.)

The organization came to be known as America Rising, a chop shop that would specialize in mercilessly investigating and then eviscerating Democratic candidates and causes. Rising was an entrepreneurial endeavor on our part, and we saw it as an important step to level the playing field, since the Democrats had created a similar organization two years earlier, under the guidance of a fellow former Republican, David Brock. (Another quick aside: The Democrats often seem to turn to conservative expats like me, Brock, and the Lincoln Project to do their dirty work. I suspect it is in part due to a mercenary GOP consultant culture that attracts more shameless ball busters and in part due to Democrats' bed-wetting nature, which makes them perceive the right as being more ruthless.)

The publicly stated purpose of America Rising was "holding Democrats accountable" for their actions. We were planning on taking from Brock's model but expanding on it with a creative legal structure that would let us entrench ourselves more directly with Republican campaigns and committees. We would hire video trackers to hound Democratic politicians in every corner of the country. House a massive searchable repository of everything a Democratic politician in America had said so that we could expose any duplicity at a moment's notice. Seed negative stories about their candidates with news organizations. And maybe even build news-like platforms of our own.

We were in an information age, and in this vision we would be both supplier and corner store. Hillary Clinton once declared that Brock was part of a "vast right-wing conspiracy" that plotted in the shadows to take down her husband, Bill. America Rising was going to take that conspiracy into the digital age and conspire against her 2016 campaign right out in the open.

Four years later I would be voting for Hillary Clinton, the very person whom our group pledged to stop when we launched. Four years earlier I had just come out of the closet and felt alienated from the party that I feared was getting too extreme. Given that fact pattern, you might assume I would have had some pause about becoming a professional partisan axe thrower in service to these extremists.

Nope. Not a one. Honestly.

For starters, there was nobody in my social circle who challenged me to take into consideration any broad-vista questions about the nature of the GOP or what kind of impact a group such as this would have. To do so would have been a total affront to the D.C. culture.

Moving up the ol' career ladder was an unreserved good. You got a *Politico Playbook* shout-out and a round of congrats on Twitter no matter which team's jersey you had on. The D.C. swamp had Republicans and Democrats, and we tried to shiv each other from time to time, but there wasn't a moral component to it, really; it was all just part of a day's work.

To illustrate just how ingrained this mindset was in the D.C. bubble, despite having many friends "across the aisle" (cringe), I can only recall two instances in which Democrats confronted me on a personal level, rather than on a performative professional level, about my Republican oppo work. Both were relative strangers. One was a random acquaintance whom I had met a couple of times in Rehoboth Beach, Delaware, the preferred summer destination for D.C. gays. He posted on my Facebook wall, out of nowhere, about how America Rising was "degrading the discourse." The other was Obama campaign communications director Brent Colburn, whom I had never met before he remonstrated with me at a mutual friend's weeknight birthday happy hour in D.C.'s Adams Morgan neighborhood. I had sidled up to the bar and was waiting for my second bourbon drink when, out of nowhere, this dude I didn't recognize began shouting me down, belligerently asking how I could sleep at night over whitewashing the GOP's opposition to gay marriage. I had to ask around to figure out that it was Colburn and eventually left the revelry equal parts appalled and delighted at the prospect of triggering someone to such a degree with my mere presence. (A few years later, Colburn hired my consulting firm for a project, and we've since become Facebook friends. What a town.)

In both instances, the overwhelming feedback I got from D.C. friends and colleagues is that it was the critics who were the pricks. That it was beyond the pale to attack me in a public forum like they had.

There's one minor problem with that assessment.

The pricks were right!

America Rising was degrading the discourse. And I *was* white-washing the GOP's opposition to gay marriage. But the culture was such that it never occurred to a well-meaning friend to make these points in a way that might have made me reconsider my choices.

"Hey, Tim, buddy, I love you, but have you considered that you are actually a gay traitor who is exacerbating our political polarization and you should do something with your talent that isn't a net drag on our society" isn't the type of thing people tended to say at Tammy Haddad's garden party.

In *Losers*, his book about the 1996 presidential campaign, Michael Lewis wrote about the "rented strangers" who worked for Bob Dole and how they cared more about the "game of tactics" and their "putatively clever strategies" than they did about the policy differences they had with Bill Clinton, to the extent that they had them at all.

This mindset was endemic in Republican political circles by the time I came around. If you took a poll of all the Republican PR flacks' positions on the issues of the day, I would have almost certainly landed on the more moderate end of the spectrum, but I would have had plenty of company. In the quarter century from Dole to Romney, the campaign culture incentivized hiring clever assassins over ideologically rigid true believers. The inner sanctum of George W. Bush's presidential campaign was filled with former and future Democrats or Never Trumpers like Matt Dowd, Mark

McKinnon, Nicolle Wallace, Steve Schmidt, Reed Galen, and Stuart Stevens. Meghan McCain lamented that she and Sarah Palin are the only Republicans left from her dad's campaign (this was, I believe, intended as an insult to those in the non-Palin camp, though I'm not sure it landed).

A friend recently confided to me that he has never voted for a Republican for president in his life, despite being the mouthpiece for a Republican governor and state party! Now, I know there are disingenuous Democratic hacks for hire, too, but I would be hard-pressed to believe you could find one who was secretly casting their ballot for Bush and Trump. This behavior shows Trump voters were right about one thing, by the way. There was an unsustainable disconnect between those of us practicing Republican politics and voters who had different values and prioritized different issues, which makes it kinda crazy that this status quo went on as long as it did without a blowup.

Over the years, everyone became comfortable with this level of disingenuousness. Chris Matthews once compared Trump press secretary Sean Spicer to a public defender charged with advocating for a guilty client. Kind of a dick comment. But it was a mindset Spicer explicitly embraced. The problem with this analogy is that (1) there is no constitutional right for politicians to have representatives bullshit for them on cable, and (2) the PR flack is not assigned a client. They have free will and can work for anyone who will hire them.

As silly as the flack as public defender notion is, it isn't surprising that it resonated with my peers, because it sprouted out of a culture in which essentially all of the players—journalists, campaign hands, politicians—embraced that mindset as the norm.

We were rented professionals, working a job, no more and no less.

My job was verbal axe throwing. It was something I both enjoyed and was good at. (Actual axe throwing, not so much. If you haven't Google-imaged me yet, I have noodle arms.) Everyone around me encouraged it (who doesn't love flattery?). And I thought that with America Rising we were onto a strategy that I considered not just putatively clever but actually clever!

Plus, there was the fact that I was still more aligned with the GOP over the size, scope, and nature of our federal government than I was the Democrats. And after a stint as the RNC's rapid-response person, it is not as if I was going to be on a Democratic campaign's short list, even had I wanted to make the switch.

So, you take those rationalizations and combine them with the D.C. culture where this was the norm, and the notion that I should *not* become the head of the Republican oppo research arm didn't ever cross my mind. I was on the management track and inertia was propelling me forward.

Once we got going, there wasn't much opportunity to consider the alternative; we had a business to run. Pounder, Rhoades, and I spent the weeks following the organization's launch sitting outside a Cosi sandwich shop in Dupont Circle, next to street performers and panhandlers, plotting how we were going to fund our massive ambitions and make our new group work.

First, we did what we were good at: making the PR machine go brrr. Our rollout was, of course, a smash hit inside the political bubble. *Politico* gave us prime real estate. I was named a "rising star" by a political trade rag (what an honor!) and later one of the "most influential out Washingtonians of 2014." (My work for anti-gay candidates seemed to actually help my nomination. Reverse tokenization at work. Yay, Washington!)

After the wave of PR acclaim had crested, we began facing the type of challenges that any start-up runs into when making the balance sheet line up. For starters, the initial seed money was taking longer than we expected to come in. In the meantime, we "officed" out of Pounder's dad's one-bedroom condo in Ballston, a stale, suf-focating Virginia exurb. It was me alongside a half-dozen research nerds eating their disgusting hot lunches, licking their fingers, while they spent hours on LexisNexis dives. I wanted to go postal.

More critically, concerns over payroll were mounting. People to whom we had promised jobs weren't getting hired and were being forced to take other gigs.

That's when we got a call from a friend who was consulting on the only major, competitive campaign taking place that year—for governor of Virginia. We jumped on it. The Republican nominee for the job was Ken Cuccinelli. "Cooch" was a miasmic, anti-immigrant, anti-gay, Tea Party hard-liner. The type of Republican who, in any other context, would repulse me. The exact brand of Republican I had wanted to snuff out of the party when I reentered the game on behalf of Jon Huntsman. His opponent was Terry McAuliffe, who was better known at the time as Bill Clinton's best friend. (Just ask him, and he'll tell you.) McAuliffe is your proto-typical corporatist moderate Democrat. A little bit grimy, to my left on some things, but policy-wise he was going to be basically inoffensive to the centrist Chamber of Commerce set. On a per-sonal level, Terry's the kind of guy who is hard not to like, even if you are getting paid not to like him. After he won, he installed a kegerator in the governor's mansion. He once went on *Hardball* wearing a Hawaiian shirt and holding a bottle of rum like he had just got back from the pool in Cabo. Guy is a hoot.

During the campaign, I met Terry at one of those Georgetown cocktail parties you hear about that have mostly been taking place in the tony Kalorama neighborhood, near Dupont Circle, for quite some time now. I introduced myself to him at the bar, and he pro-ceeded to kibitz with me for half an hour, trash-talking about the race, poking fun at some of the other attendees at the party, and laughing a lot.

The next day, out of nowhere, a courier hand-delivered a copy of his memoir, *What a Party*, to the office. It was inscribed, "To Tim Miller: My favorite right-wing nut. Keep up the fight & always have fun." Say what you want about McAuliffe, that's good politicking.

It was quite the contrast with my client.

The only time I met Cuccinelli was during a debate prep session during which he dabbled in some jocular homophobia. He and one of his campaign staffers were lamenting that gay rights was an issue they had to prep for at all, given that—to their knowledge—there were so few homosexuals in the commonwealth. They suggested that bringing up Cooch's opposition to gay marriage was simply an attempt by the media to manufacture controversy and distract from the important issues like the economy and immigrant hating. As this conversation unfolded, the people close to the candidate all nodded in agreement. The handful who knew I was gay shot awkward glances at the back of the room, where I was privately praying away the topic.

A few minutes later, Cooch and I exchanged stilted pleasantries, then I went out to the spin room to troll McAuliffe for whatever nonsense we had planned to tag him with that day, schlepped a few hours back to D.C., and never talked to my client again.

Had I been a regular citizen of Virginia looking at the options in front of me, I would have almost certainly supported McAuliffe. Maybe I would have thrown my vote away on a libertarian candidate on account of his history of being elbow deep in Clinton sleaze, but there's no way in hell I was voting for Cuccinelli. He was by far the worst option available.

But the ability of my new business to succeed required me to continue running cover for him.

For the next few months, to help maintain my reputation as a "killer" and keep our fledgling company afloat, I continued to drop oppo and dunk on McAuliffe on Twitter over all manner of scandals real (GreenTech Automotive) and fabricated (he hasn't had a successful business since he paved driveways at age fifteen!).

Our work was being judged by other prospective clients. If we were doing a bad job, or had we chosen not to help Cuccinelli because he was a homophobic asshole, that was going to be noticed by the people we needed to hire us in the future.

Plus, given that McAuliffe was in league with the overwhelming front-runner to be the next Democratic nominee, this race was also serving as a bit of a stalking horse for our ultimate goal of taking Hillary out. Some of the research we were doing on McAuliffe included shady business deals with Hillary's brother. So our work served the dual purpose of testing out some of the same anticorruption messages that would be used against "Crooked Hillary" in the future and possibly even lead to fresh research that could hamper her campaign.

All of this goes to say that despite my revulsion at Ken Cuccinelli, it seemed to me that sitting this one out wasn't really an option, so I didn't reflect too deeply on my choices. To the extent that I thought about it along these lines at all, I concluded that this was an annoying but relatively unimportant sacrifice of my integrity in the grand scheme of things. As an added bonus, I figured that Cuccinelli was so noxious that he almost certainly wouldn't win anyway.

No harm, no foul. All "part of the Game" or the "price of doing business" or whatever else I needed to tell myself to justify doing terrible shit like working to elect racist, homophobic assholes in the year of our Lord 2013.

Ken Cuccinelli would lose that race, but it was a lot closer than many expected. He later leveraged his increased profile into a gig as one of Donald Trump's top henchmen in enacting that administration's unconscionable immigration regime. He has become a leading voice in limiting voting rights. He's a despicable twat.

Looking at it with the benefit of hindsight: Was being the

research arm that tried to help make this douchey bigot governor
of the commonwealth materially different from what Pounder and
my other colleagues would go on to do four years later, when they
took on Donald Trump as a client?

I think so. I can squint and find the red line between Donald
Trump becoming the president and making his immigration czar
a one-term Virginia governor. But it requires some high-level hair-
splitting.

Like Cuccinelli, Donald Trump was also so noxious that it was
widely presumed he was going to lose. Working for him was necessary for Pounder to keep the business going. (Can't exactly run
the Republican research shop and not support the party's leader.)
Trump's first opponent was similarly easy to demonize. And they
were merely a consultant providing a service, not part of the official "Trump team."

It's a lot more similar to my justifications than it is different,
that's for sure.

5

Centering the Comment Section

I was seated at a mahogany table in the "Breitbart Embassy" great room when a frowzy, triplicate-shirted Steve Bannon proposed that I join him on a trip to Laredo, Texas. With a roguish grin, he insisted that such an expedition would win me over to his side on the need for more draconian border security measures.

Listening to this pitch was one of those record-scratch, freeze-frame moments in life. Even as it was happening, I remember being taken aback by how absurd it was that I had found myself there. Steve Bannon was not yet "Evil Mastermind on the Cover of *Time* Steve Bannon," but Breitbart's ascension was well under way. The website was the home of the populist, nativist, culturally conservative #war against the old-line RINO elites. And there I was a gay, immigrant-loving, establishment Bushie discussing a postelection holiday with the wannabe revolutionary who was openly plotting to destroy all of the politicians I admired.

I would be lying if I denied giving serious consideration to accompanying him on this Rio Grande Dreamer Cruise for the sake of the story, the weird life experience, and, most importantly, the relationship. I figured he could be leveraged in service of my clients and candidates, a political consultant's core purpose. As such, I didn't contemplate the sacrifices such relationship building might require. My job was to use media contacts to buff up my clients and savage the competition. It's a job that often requires dealing with unsavory characters with questionable journalistic ethics. The line between dealing with Bannon and others seemed murky. Where was a professional PR man supposed to draw it? It was a question that required more reflection than I gave it.

In an email to Bannon following the meeting, I wrote, "I want to go to the border! Let's do it in November." He replied, "K . . . I will organize a trip for right after the elections . . . some guys go to the islands America Rising goes to laredo!!!" (Yes, Steve Bannon is a multiple-exclamation-point guy in emails. Now you know.)

Our Juarez fantasy never came to pass, but that meeting did kick off a multiyear informal working relationship whereby Bannon and I would collaborate on a story or issue in which we had common interests despite having deeply conflicting values and big-picture objectives. Sometimes our target was a Democrat, of course, but on other occasions there would be a Republican primary where Bannon would support the cryptofascist and I would back the moderate squish and we would make common cause by sullying the regular old Republican in the middle.

This was the case during the 2016 primary, when I became the Jeb campaign's liaison to Bannon, kinda by default. I don't think any of the other senior staff had ever talked to him, or if they had, they didn't have much interest in doing so again. As a result, my "relationship" paid some internal dividends. It allowed me to get early intel on the content in his colleague Peter Schweizer's upcoming anti-Jeb polemical e-book, "Bush's Bucks," which turned out to be a dud. It also gave me the ability to kneecap the candidates that I saw at the time as our rivals in the establishment "lane," such that it was, when they would find themselves afoul of the Breitbart base.

These exchanges were made possible by the time I had spent at the Breitbart Embassy, a town house in the Capitol Hill neighborhood of Washington, D.C., that served as the headquarters for the website, a gathering place for "anti-establishment" Republicans, a crash pad for Breitbart employees, and a party venue where they would host the very establishment types whom they pretended to hate but were actually obsessed with. The house's most distinguishing feature is a replica Lincoln Bedroom, just off the stairs on the second floor. It is said that Bannon slept, and maybe even lived there, for a while, but I never had the nerve to ask him if that was the case. His wrinkled garb that first afternoon certainly suggested that he might have just rolled out of bed, but then again, Trump dubbed him "Sloppy Steve" for a reason. My cousins would have called him a hoosier.

Our marriage of convenience was the culmination of my concerted multiyear effort to court "influencers" (cringe) in the conservative media ecosystem who might someday be useful.

Emblematic of the charm offensive was one of my first trips to the Embassy, for a party that fêted conservative commentator Greg Gutfeld on the occasion of his new book, *The Joy of Hate*, which, as it turns out, was a rather Sibylline title for the coming Trump GOP. Bannon had taken a shine to the Fox News anchor he considered a rising star. In a leaked private email, he said Gutfeld was a "brilliant cultural commentator who really got pop culture, the hipster scene, and advant [*sic*] garde."

At this party, Gutfeld demonstrated his keen eye for cultural commentary by hosting a petting zoo, which he hoped would trigger PETA. (It is unclear if that attempted triggering was successful.) Among the assembled animals was a brown alpaca, which Gutfeld dubbed an "alpaca of color" to contrast from its white counter-part. (With boundary-pushing "advant garde" racial comedy such as that, you can see why this man would go on to get a ratings-bonanza late-night variety show on Fox.)

I spent most of the evening milling about, networking with the conservative media types in attendance, trading tidbits about the upcoming election. When Gutfeld began his remarks, I snuck out the back to meet some friends on U Street, where the actual hipster scene was blossoming. These Embassy confabs were not exactly my idea of a good time; I just considered attendance to be a competitive advantage in the big game I perceived myself to be puppeteering. You see, most of the people who write for conservative media outlets are deeply socially awkward. Exhibit A is that Greg Gutfeld, a grating, affected Pomeranian wearing my grand-father's sweater vest, was considered the person in their ranks who was most in touch with the "hipster" scene. Republican PR flacks, meanwhile, tend to be either similarly socially awkward or sociable strivers who are more interested in earning the favor of the trendier mainstream media reporters, rather than the goobers who hung out at the Embassy. (Bear in mind we are grading on a massive goober curve here as we try to judge the relative coolness of those who inhabit a town where the signature social event of the year is dubbed "nerd prom" and features frumpy wonks salivating over C-list celebrities.)

So, between these parties and availing myself as a useful source, I cultivated a Rolodex of the ever-expanding conservative media landscape. America Rising would host bloggers for happy hours in our office and I'd help get their clips on the Drudge Report, which would drive massive traffic numbers for them and make their bosses happy. Matt Drudge was famously mercurial, but Rhoades was one of the few who had a long-term relationship with him and one of my friends had secretly stumbled into a job as one of his junior linkers-in-chief (this was an informal title). The ability to turn on this traffic hose for writers made us valuable and in certain circles added to our mystique.

I'd do other favors when I could. Toss them the personal email address of an important Republican strategist they needed to get in touch with. Help them land interviews with big-name politicians. Provide "exclusives"—all reporters want their story to be an "exclusive," no matter how meaningless the tip.

We also tried to ensure we were a key pipeline to the Fox News blowtorch. Around the time of the Gutfeld party, Rhoades and I went on a pilgrimage to New York for a meeting organized by Roger Ailes deputy Michael Clemente. Clemente oversaw daytime programming, while future Trump White House aide Bill Shine managed the prime-time talkers. I had overlapped with Clemente a little bit in past jobs and perceived him to be a totally rational, if party-line, Republican. We started to tell the Foxsuits about our new organization and how we could plug into their programming by providing the videos we planned to obtain from tracking Democratic politicians.

I remember being a bit taken back by the Q&A that followed. While they all made nice when it came to the idea of us providing clips of Democratic candidates making extreme or hypocritical statements, their real interest was in something else entirely: helping them confirm some of the crackpottiest right-wing conspiracy theories about Hillary Clinton.

Over the course of the afternoon, Rhoades would redirect those questions back to our work looking into genuine conflicts of interest plaguing the Clinton Global Initiative, but all Fox execs cared about was whether Hillary was secretly ill and if Huma Abedin was a foreign agent or lover of the candidate. It should have been a flashing siren, but I dismissed it as boomer brain rot that would be amusing fodder for my friends. I would come to find out that it was rot all the way down. Many of us who were serving it with a side of winks and grins were blind to just how powerful the forces we were unleashing would become.

• • •

As America Rising was gearing up, I would occasionally work out of a conference room at a PR firm in downtown D.C. run by establishment Republican bigwigs. Early on, one of the firm's partners brought me to a back-corner cubicle farm and introduced me to another millennial squatter with a start-up. Alex Skatell, a classically handsome former National Republican Senatorial Committee digital staffer, was incubating a digital news platform that he hoped would appeal to younger Republicans and culturally conservative independents.

A South Carolina native in his mid-twenties with the mien of a College of Charleston lacrosse team captain and a moderate political sensibility, Skatell was not your prototypical basement-dwelling conservative blogger. He had the energy of a cheerful VC bro, and, from the jump, I sensed that this was a person who might go on to big things. What I didn't sense at the time was that his hamartia would be a mirror of mine, from the media rather than campaign side of things.

By the time of that meeting, Skatell had already launched the *Conservative Daily* Facebook page, which featured a vintage head shot of Ronald Reagan in a cowboy hat as the avatar and boasted around 1.4 million followers. Together he and his partner, Bubba Atkinson, would build what was originally known as the *Independent Journal Review* on the back of redirects from this one Facebook account, turning a random side hustle into one of the best-trafficked news sites on the web in almost no time at all.

That first afternoon, Skatell eagerly showed off their makeshift war room, which revealed the secret sauce behind the traffic and engagement rocket ship. With a shit-eating grin, he ran through traffic data that sounded surreal (a million hits a day! how?!) and explained how they were testing and targeting different headlines and messages to different pages and audiences. His wide-eyed glee betrayed that the growth was even astonishing to him. Through instinct, testing, and trial-and-error, Atkinson and Skatell had stumbled on a gold mine—a powerful niche that mixed culturally conservative, Upworthy-style clickbait with gleeful mocking of the established mainstream media narratives and fact-based briefs on breaking news.

The *IJR* boys focused their public-facing "brand" on the uplifting stuff like: "These Lovable Therapy Dogs at Walter Reed Make Life Just a Bit Better for Wounded Vet" (14,000 shares!), but much of the site's best-trafficked material was a little darker. For every therapy dog meet-cute, there were several other examples of cruel clickbait that would be right at home in the Trump era. I recall one article that compared the supposedly "douchey effeminate Obamacare Pajama guy" to "post op Rachel Maddow" (referencing the Jack Antonoff–looking hipster man in pajamas who was featured on the Obama for America website promoting the Affordable Care Act). *BuzzFeed* reported on the site's massive engagement for their repeated promotion of the "knockout game," in which black youths were supposedly beating people to death at random. The site also specialized in countering the "social justice left" narrative following high-profile conflicts between blacks and police, beginning with that of Trayvon Martin.

By the 2020s, this type of content has become ubiquitous, so the value that was being provided might not be as clear to anyone for whom politics pre-Trump is a history lesson. But in 2013, *IJR* was first to the block. This was the meme-porn that the conservative tweakers were jonesing for.

At the time, the social web was still forming and most of the early online content creators who worked at the trendy, buzzy online news outlets lived in liberal coastal enclaves. They knew how to speak to college-educated twenty-somethings who were their peers but were missing the cultural flashpoints in huge swaths of the country. This left a gap in the marketplace for *IJR* and others to fill. The boomers who shared pics of John Kerry effeminately throwing a football via a FWD: FWD: FWD: email chain in the aughts yearned for Facebook content just as much as the next guy. *IJR* cooked it up for them.

Bubba built a team of content creators around the country who could speak to this disaffected audience, and, following the metrics, they provided a steady diet of waggish material that spoke to the conservative id, but also educated readers with a "on the one hand/on the other hand" look at the news of the day. His mindset on how to balance all these inputs borrowed from the USDA dietary guidelines. He described it to me this way: "If you give somebody vegetables—and that's like the jobs report—that has to be part of the meal. Then there's the meat and potatoes, and then there's all the way up to heroin. We thought we had to have a balanced diet of these things; we can't do heroin too much."

By 2014, the site had rocketed into the World Wide Web's stratosphere. At its peak, the traffic was outpacing even the more established big-name right-wing sites like Breitbart and Newsmax and absolutely swamping the fuddy-duddy old-guard periodicals like *National Review*. As the traffic and revenue grew, so did the founders' aspirations. They hired a cadre of staffers, dividing the team between "content" and "news" (the need for such a distinction should perhaps have been an early-warning sign). Over coffee one day at a new hipster joint in the gentrifying Shaw neighborhood of Washington, D.C., Skatell shared with me an aspiration for *IJR* to transcend the conservative clickbait world and become a credible, cheery, center-right counterweight to *Vox* and *BuzzFeed*.

Hosting a presidential debate was a dream of his and the first step toward that goal. I recommended some friends in the mainstream media world who could help them make that transition, and they successfully recruited Michelle Jaconi, a former *Meet the Press* and CNN bigwig who could bring some gravitas to the fratty start-up. With Jaconi on board, the first metric of success was met rather quickly. In 2016, thanks to a new rule that RNC communications director Sean Spicer had spearheaded in order to give his stubby liddle middle finger to the lamestream media, it was mandated that all GOP presidential primary debates include a conservative media cosponsor. The result was the ABC News/WMUR/*IJ Review* debate in New Hampshire that January. *IJR* blew it out, with a quirky video intro, questions from the "real people" who were the bread and butter of their audience, and viral yearbook throwbacks featuring the candidates. It was a massive victory for the site, and the promos around the event were legitimately funny and creative. In Manchester the morning of the debate, I bumped into a high-flying Skatell with his proud parents in a corner booth watching *Morning Joe* live at a downtown watering hole. In a lot of ways that morning was *IJR* and Skatell's peak. The clicks were flowing. The star was rising. The brand was being taken seriously on national news. The dream of a site that leveraged social media success and conservative politics to mainstream acclaim was becoming a reality.

But the underlying problems with the model were soon to be exposed. The balanced-diet content strategy became less appetizing in the Trump Steak era, and the transition from right-wing clickbait to an approach that balanced inflammatory "content" with hard news was rocky.

During the 2016 primary, tensions flared between the people who bought into the vision of the site as a real journalistic enterprise and the content farmers who wanted to focus on serving what the news side dismissively referred to as the "redneck army." This

divide was not too dissimilar to what was happening in the Republican primary at the time, norms-abiding Jebbies versus the MAGA
masses. The numbers favored the MAGAs. It was the redneck army
that drove the clicks, the revenue, the online engagement that
made the whole thing tick.

On the news side, Atkinson and Jaconi believed the model was
viable without the reliance on MAGA heroin, but never got the
opportunity to prove it under pressure to continue delivering the
horse. They both jumped ship during the 2016 election, to Axios
and the *Washington Post*, respectively, in order to build the mainstream digital video and events businesses that they had hoped *IJR*
would house.

Once Trump took the White House, with the "news" side of
the staff depleted, the wheels of the concept came completely off.
There was little joy left in the material. There was no more mocking those in power, because that would offend the Trump-adoring
readers. There was no balanced diet.

IJR bumped into the harsh reality that traffic-based "center-
right" news wasn't getting engagement on Facebook or anywhere
else online, partly due to choices the platforms themselves made to
surface the most controversial material, but also because Trumpier
players had joined in the culturally conservative social media game,
too. These other sites had eschewed the USDA approach, offering
even more digital heroin with less concern over whether what they
were selling was "true" or if their audience was getting any nutrients
in their news diet.

To keep up with the Joneses, *IJR* joined the race to the bottom. Their most well-known "reporter" became Benny Johnson, a
flamboyant conservative activist who had been fired from a previous journalism gig for plagiarism. Johnson fancies himself a social
media influencer and Liberace-esque entertainer for the college
Republican set, where the show was always more important than

the facts. His mindset was ascendant internally, since the sketchy material he was providing was driving the traffic.

Despite initially being a Rubio fan, when Trump won, Johnson was quick to adapt, turning into a full-time fluffer for the administration officials, making ostentatious videos about their brawn and brilliance. Benny would lash out at colleagues who bristled at this Trumpian brownnosing. A former *IJR* staffer told *Business Insider* that the site was "basically becoming a giant native ad for the Trump administration" because it's what they needed to do to survive in the new online ecosystem.

In just four years, a platform that we saw as an inventive way to reach center-right audiences had become just one of dozens telling conservatives only what they wanted to hear.

Orange God King Trump great. Immigrants and Black Crimers bad. "Democrat" Party evil. Etc. Etc. Etc.

Skatell wasn't the only conservative media entrepreneur who had aspirations for crossover success but who got stuck circling the crusty conservative drain. Ben Domenech, the founder of *The Federalist*, had pitched the site as a center-right alternative to *Slate* or *The Atlantic*, a serious journal of policy commentary. Tucker Carlson said he wanted to build "institutions like the *New York Times*" with his *Daily Caller* and early reports indicated he was determined to focus on investigative, shoe-leather reporting.

By late 2016, *IJR*, the *Daily Caller*, and *The Federalist* had all dropped their grand journalistic aspirations in favor of becoming Trumpian cum dumpsters. *The Federalist* now runs fantastical troll bait claiming that the worst Trumpian excesses never happened and that the election was stolen from him. Reading the *Daily Caller* on any given Tuesday is indistinguishable from a Donald Trump fan blog. This posture rejected crossover appeal and widespread legitimacy in favor of fan service. As Domenech would eventually put it, the LOL Nothing Matters Ethos had won out.

Unlike Carlson and Domenech, Skatell eventually pulled the plug on that transition. While the *Caller* and *Federalist* have completely turned themselves over to the deplorables, *IJR* has withered and died. Now when you search for "IJ Review" on Google the algorithm presumes you made a typo and serves up results from *IN Review* instead. Meanwhile, Tucker has a prime-time Fox show, Domenech was given a tryout for one of his own, and Skatell's former pup Benny Johnson is a prime-time host over on Newsmax, where he does a campy, down-market Carlson imitation.

Skatell, on the other hand, is out of the game entirely. He decamped back to Charleston with his new wife. When I caught up with him for the book, he sounded defeated. I asked what he was working on. In D.C., the clear unspoken subtext is that this is a professional query. He dodged, awkwardly, and indicated he was spending the preponderance of his time on a home remodel.

The concept he had envisioned was fundamentally flawed from the start, in the same way that the "conservative *Atlantic*" and "conservative *New York Times*" concepts were. They were based on the faulty notion that you could offer race-baiting MAGA propaganda heroin to draw people in and pair it with thoughtful policy-oriented scholarship (*Federalist*), serious investigative journalism (*Daily Caller*), or joyful middle-of-the-road memes (*IJR*) as the vegetables and then hope that the China White and the nutritious greens could live together on the same plate in harmony.

It was never going to work.

Shouldn't that have been obvious, by the way?

There's a reason there is no such term as a "functional heroinholic." Once the audience began to learn that hard drugs were an option, they weren't going to be interested in the meat or potatoes any longer. They wanted to chase the dragon and there were enough back-alley dealers willing to give it to them, even if Skatell had lost the stomach for it.

The *IJR* story is a microcosm for how the choices of the right-wing leaders, the incentives of digital media, and the pathologies of base voters have worked in concert to create an inescapable triangle of doom that degraded all the conservative institutions and ensconced Republican voters inside an apocalyptic media bubble with an ever-increasing cycle of radicalization. The only way to succeed in the triangle was to play along and give the people exactly what they want, principles or prudence be damned.

• • •

One guy who recognized that from the jump was Matt Boyle. Halfway through the 2016 primary, a friend pointed out to me that Boyle was the putative policy director for pretty much every other campaign besides ours. He did not carry this responsibility due to his industriousness as a pro bono expert who moonlighted for different candidates. In fact, technically speaking, he didn't work in policy at all.

His day job was as the top political reporter for Steve Bannon at Breitbart. And while he wasn't literally drafting policy for the other campaigns, the notion that his invisible hand was often at work was truer than it was fiction.

The son of a video rental store owner and deli clerk, Boyle had a middle-class upbringing. He bounced from Boise State to community college before finally landing at Flagler University in St. Augustine, Florida. He presents as a slovenly, awkward, pockmarked gamer. In a profile for the *Washingtonian*, his advisor at Flagler shared that in college he would mishandle basic human interactions and would often express frustration with lack of interest from women. This wasn't much different by the time I got to know him in his mid-twenties. He had a layer of sweetness underneath, but if you were just to judge a book by its cover, Boyle was a walking, talking incel meme. Ripping a pack of Marlboro Lights a day, chugging Mountain Dews, disheveled, stained, conspiratorial. He speaks in a sort of singsongy slur that is reminiscent of a grown-up Ralph Wiggum. Boyle is such a ludicrous character that if he had emanated from the imagination of a Hollywood liberal trying to cast a conservative blog boy in a movie, a fair observer would think the result was too over-the-top.

Boyle didn't make up for his sociability shortcomings by honing his craft and becoming a skilled writer or deft interviewer or subject matter specialist in the way that the many past awkward Washington journalists who have risen to career heights did. Instead he channeled the social rejection into a deep well of whinge that drove him to work insane hours and rely upon the special insight he did have—an understanding of the mindset of the soon-to-be-MAGA Republican base voter who shared his resentments.

This instinctive sense for the id of the conservative base separated him from his peers and was especially relevant to his time and place. He felt his readers' rage in his bones. He saw around the corner, sensing what these voters might be aggrieved by in the years ahead. In December 2012, Boyle's first article for Breitbart highlighted the excesses of the "social justice" left, a concept that most mainstream Republican staffers were completely oblivious to at the time but which would come to dominate the political discourse in the ensuing years. Reading it now, it makes for an eerily prescient preview of Trump's 2016 campaign message—if anything, a slightly upmarket version from the more childish Trumpian drivel.

> The political class in Washington has degraded America. Republicans and Democrats blame each other, and nothing gets done. The media exacerbates the problem, fans the flames and encourages false notions of "civility" and "objectivity." . . . While this charade perpetuates indefinitely, America grows

weaker. . . . The institutional left thrives in this declining environment. Record numbers of people are on the government
dole instead of being excited to work and succeed. So-called
"social justice" is implemented in place of real justice. Kids across
the country are fed "Occupy" propaganda in school after their
teachers take away their home-made lunches in place of "cafeteria nuggets. . . ." No matter what they tell you from their luxuri-
ous Washington, D.C., offices, they're out of touch with what the
American people really want.

This went straight to the heart of the populist anger that would
lead to Trump. Understanding it was Boyle's Unique Selling Proposition. He would turn this instinct, his website's astounding traffic
numbers and his lack of social graces into a puppeteer-like power
over campaigns.

He was shameless, relentless, and unabashed when it came to
horse-trading with flacks like me. He played the game well, providing carrots in the form of glowing, obsequious write-ups when
a candidate hewed the Breitbart party line and delivering the stick
of harsh rebukes if they broke from the desired orthodoxy. He
was brazen in asking uncomfortable questions to campaigns that
would force them into a political corner. Most of all, he was the
one who operationalized the innovation of Steve Bannon's that
most propelled Breitbart's success and supercharged the Republican Party's chaotic descent into mob rule.

Matt Boyle centered the commenters.

"Centering the commenters" meant elevating the issues that
most motivated core readers. Bannon would talk about the "hobbits" and "deplorables" who read Breitbart and how they powered
the campaigns of the site's favored anti-establishment candidates.
Boyle was a deplorable-hobbit citizen king. He was of them, and he
curried their favor.

Caring what one's readers think might not seem like that brilliant an insight, but it was a vast departure from how business had been done in the past. There is this haughty truism among political operatives and media types that went generally unchallenged and was utterly contrary to the Bannon/Boyle ethos: "Never Read The Comments."

The comments underneath a political article always contain the wheels-off views of the bridge-and-tunnel political obsessives. Conspiracy theories and verboten stances and mindless takes and fangirling and anti-Semitism and Godwin's law and weird porn and ad hominem and all of the things that eventually turn every unmoderated web forum into the dregs of interpersonal communication. It was widely accepted that spending time worrying about this flimflammery was a fool's errand.

However, those who challenge the unchallenged truths sometimes stumble on different or more powerful ones.

Bannon posited something so horrifying and so outlandish to the political elites that none of us dared contemplate it: What if you not only read the comments but listen to them and let their pathologies guide you? Using that principle as his north star, Bannon would enlist the hobbit army to overthrow the established order. While *IJR* was trying to come up with a balanced meal, Breitbart was saying, "Fuck it! Candy for dinner every night!"

The result of this consistent elevation of and advocacy for fringe views was that it forced the political campaigns to respond to the things that highly engaged voters cared about. In theory, this is a good thing. In practice, it led to madness. People care about a lot of crazy shit to begin with, and when they are being goaded and inflamed by a propaganda machine it leads to fresh concerns that resonate emotionally while being quite far afield from their daily lives. Boyle used this to direct the policy agenda of prospective presidents, and he was dogged in pressuring GOP campaigns to react to whatever claptrap was unearthed from the nether regions of his revanchist comment section.

While all the 2016 presidential campaigns fell into this trap, nobody was a thirstier sucker for the warm embrace of Breitbart's nativist love than Wisconsin governor Scott Walker. Walker was especially vulnerable because he had no idea why he wanted to be president in the first place, as I can testify based on his astonishingly hackneyed and childlike answer he gave when I asked him during a job interview before the campaign.

All Walker cared about was being president and making Republican regulars happy, not any of the niggling details. This made it easy for someone like Boyle to bait his short-lived 2016 campaign into taking a series of far-right positions that he didn't genuinely support nor give enough consideration to learn how to defend.

Take, for example, the time Boyle "interviewed" Walker and pushed him into a newer, butcher, anti-immigration policy plan. "EXCLU: SCOTT WALKER LAYS OUT PLAN TO SECURE BORDER, STOP IMMIGRATION INSANITY" screamed across the Breitbart main page. Despite how the headline looks, this wasn't a traditional campaign "policy rollout" or even an "interview" in any meaningful sense of the term.

There is a general cadence to how the announcement of "plans" usually works. The policy team works with the candidate to create a program. The comms shop then previews it with friendly reporters, pegs the announcement to a speech or a TV interview, and the result is a pretty package for the media that sums up for voters what type of policy a prospective president would want to implement on a given issue. I've done a million of these over the years.

But this "plan" didn't stem from Walker's policy shop. It stemmed from Boyle.

Here's how the rollout in reverse worked. Boyle pushes the "candidate" to take a Breitbart-friendly position by sending a series of leading questions for them to answer and then follows it up with a belly rub in the form of a news article announcing their "new platform" if they do it right. The result of these Boyle "interviews" don't read like a transcript of an actual human speaking extemporaneously about the topics, because it isn't. It's an email back-and-forth with a staffer offering sanitized talking points that the candidate may or may not have even read.

This was a standard tactic of Boyle and Bannon to curry favor with the campaigns, as I would know. Around the same time, on another matter, I sent them answers to three emailed questions speaking as "Jeb." In my case, the answers were utterly anodyne boilerplate ripped from our approved talking points and contained no news value whatsoever. But that wasn't the point. The "news" that was being made in this interview was that Jeb and Breitbart were playing ball together. The two parties saw it as a win/win situation. Breitbart gets to further cement their credibility by "landing" an interview with Jeb. Our campaign gets a free press release delivered to primary voters who are skeptical of our candidate, to say the least.

They posted the article unedited: "EXCLUSIVE—JEB BUSH INTERVIEWS WITH BREITBART NEWS" was the banner splash.

Bannon shot me a note just before the story ran that read: "Dude. Biggest lede we ever had. Coming soon."

Biggest lede *ever*? Was he being sarcastic? Buttering me up? Giddy he had co-opted a Bush? Trolling me? Some combination of all of them, I suspect. He's so full of shit, I'm not sure that he even knows sometimes. I recently watched Bannon conduct a twenty-minute interview with a crack addict turned pillow magnate who was claiming that long-dead Venezuelans had rigged our voting machines, while Bannon, barely suppressing a laugh, told him this could be the biggest story of the century. I suspect that back then he was giving me a similar treatment to less insane ends. But psychoanalyzing Bannon is less relevant than the slow co-opting that I missed.

I thought I was leveraging Bannon by earning a freebie puff piece for the ultimate establishment campaign. But in reality he had been gradually, over time, leveraging me.

There was no clearer evidence of this than in my relationship with another alt-right media figure, Chuck Johnson, publisher of GotNews. Chuck is an intense personality, probably a bit on the spectrum. He's thoroughly shameless in networking and inserting himself into situations that he thinks might make him rich and influential. He's a bit of a Forrest Gump for far-right politics, showing up in all types of weird places. He was Matt Gaetz's guest to the State of the Union. He somehow got a line into Julian Assange at WikiLeaks. He published the name and an incorrect photo of the woman who seemingly fabricated the *Rolling Stone*/UVA rape story. He framed the wrong person in the Charlottesville car attack that killed Heather Heyer. He sued Gawker for publishing a rumor that he had shit on the floor in college, and apparently won a settlement for it. And that's just the tip of the iceberg. Chuck has a rap sheet for pushing offensive, conspiratorial, and outright racist material that is eleventy miles long. I don't know half of what he got into, and I don't really wanna know, to be honest.

The specifics of how Chuck and I connected originally have faded from my memory, but I know it was he who first came to me. The basic gist of the arrangement he pitched was not that different from my setup with Bannon: You are an establishment guy. I'm an anti-establishment guy. We're going to be at odds at times, but when we have common foes, we can work together.

He could use my relationships and credibility with mainstream media outlets; I could take advantage of the fact that he could reach a readership that was not the type to like my more moderate candidates and corporate clients. It was a proposition that made

sense to me. Sure, it seemed kinda shady, but I was looking at it
through the prism of this being just another machination in our
big game, one that might give me an advantage over other flacks.

Chuck always cultivated weird gossip about political opponents
that would occasionally be true and useful but would just as often
fly over the cuckoo's nest. One stood out. For years he would hound
me about the supposed evidence he had gathered purporting to
prove that Chelsea Clinton was really the daughter of longtime
Clinton family friend Webster "Webb" Hubbell. He claimed to have
"people" who had dug through Chelsea's trash to get her hair follicles, which matched the follicles of Hubbell, a story that struck
me as intriguingly similar to a plot point in the children's movie
Ratatouille.

I tried to change the subject anytime he would raise it, which was
frequently, so I never did learn how he purported to have acquired
Hubbell's DNA. This might remain one of his many mysteries.
(One lesson here, for children of Democratic political candidates:
watch out for dumpster divers and keep your hairbrushes on your
person at all times.)

As is often the case with people who are a little bit crazy, Chuck
is also a kind of savant and would see opportunities where others wouldn't. So, we stayed in touch. Also, as a practical matter, I
would at times find the relationship useful. Many of the people I
worked for liked to have the ability to speak to "those voters" and
were impressed that I could make it happen. Chuck didn't want to
spend time actually writing, so when we had a client interest, he
would ask me to draft up the articles that he would put under his
name on GotNews. I justified this deceptive bit of ghostwriting
because nothing we ever sent through was false or bigoted like
some of the other material on the site. It was mostly attempts to
get the populist base voters riled up about boring shit that pro-
business normies cared about. For example, I sent him a story

about a rumored candidate for U.S. attorney who had previously attacked right-wingers in hopes it would help kill the appointment. Another about a provision in Obamacare a client wanted to stir outrage about. Another time I pitched him on an idea about how he might access a trove of Obama-era documents about antitrust review of tech companies and separately about how CEO Tim Cook had been lying about Apple's plans to build manufacturing plants in the United States. I wrote up some convoluted research about companies that Marco Rubio's family was invested in; upon reread-ing it for this book I couldn't even understand what I was arguing or why it would be scandalous. No wonder no actual journalists ran with it! I can only assume I sent it to Chuck because I had a boss on my ass to get this "hit" out the door and I wanted to check the box and get some empty-calorie brownie points.

This is the type of stuff you do to keep people happy as a paid hatchet man. It is the quotidian sausage-making of opposition re-search. We had clients who wanted to get information out to cer-tain audiences, he had a platform for reaching them, and I took advantage. In my head, this made sense. Putatively clever, but prac-tically crooked. And something I deeply, deeply regret.

When it came to manipulating the right-wing ecosystem for our clients' ends, my firm didn't stop there. After a while we started to ask ourselves, why are we giving away this valuable content to other conservative outlets rather than creating and managing it for ourselves? It started gradually, by turning the America Rising PAC webpage into one that looked more like a news site than a political action committee. I sent our designer *The New Republic*'s latest home page and told them to model our site after that. When our friends in conservative news orgs wouldn't publish a piece of research we had uncovered, we'd just write up a blurb ourselves, as if we were the "journalist."

My cofounder Joe Pounder built on this theme with the launch of the NTK Network. In 2016, *Politico* headlined an article about NTK as "GOP Researchers Get in the News Business." NTK, in our estimation, wasn't really different from many of the other conservative websites we dealt with. It put a news-like sheen onto anti-Democrat agitprop. We saw it as akin to a sports team's official site publishing news stories after a game. Everything is factual. You don't pretend as if the team won when they lost, but you also go out of your way to focus on the parts that make your team look good. The news is real without being real at all. The left has subsequently gotten into this business. One example came in 2019 when they launched Courier Newsroom, a series of local "news sites" funded by left-wing donors and run by a Democratic super PAC. Bloomberg called Courier a "liberal, digital spin on local news" when it launched. That's one way to put it! These days Courier "news" can be found running ads promoting their "articles" about how bad Republicans are to swing voters around election time. Sounds familiar.

Put everything together—relationship building with Bannon, Boyle, and Johnson, ghostwriting for conservative websites, creating news-adjacent sites of our own—we had created a full-service outrage generation machine right at the moment that the right-wing media ecosystem had become a surround sound of grievance peddling that instructed the audience on how to love hating the right people.

When you're in the thick of it, with your competitive juices flowing, with rationalizations of the hacky left-wing actors and the other industries that are doing similar things, it seems much more clever than problematic . . . at least to me it did. I felt like we were in control, and I comforted myself with the notion that we had lines we wouldn't cross. No conspiracies or fabrications or unfair personal attacks. Having those imaginary lines was nice and all, but as it turns out, I was still selling my soul and it didn't even work as intended. Our complicity only served to empower the more shame-less operators we were dealing with.

What Skatell and I eventually learned was that the only limiting principle on our crafty tactics was policing ourselves. But when you are dealing with unsavory characters, and money, influence, and political power are at stake, self-policing is about as likely to work as self-deportation.

While we were determining how to use these new outlets to our political advantage, serving a balanced meal, offering coded paeans to aggrieved audiences that only made them hunger for more, we missed the insight that Bannon and Boyle saw all along and that Donald Trump would use to seize the presidency the next fall. It was the commenters, the hobbits who had taken charge. And they were the ones dragging us along, no matter how we assured ourselves that we were in control.

• • •

By late 2020, we saw just how far these sacrifices to the mob would lead and the extent to which "normal" participants in this media ecosystem would go along with their mania. After Trump had been soundly schlonged in the election but before the Capitol had been stormed, I spent two days watching Newsmax, with hosts Sean Spicer and Benny Johnson, who had gotten a television glow-up since his blog boi days at *IJ Review*.

At the time, the Max had supplanted its predecessors in offer-ing the best blue meth around and I wanted to get a taste. Over the course of the two days, I watched the president's campaign lawyer call for the execution of Chris Krebs, a Republican Trump ap-pointee who oversaw election security at the Department of Home-land Security. I saw a host claim that if Biden were allowed to take office it would result in a war between the races. I saw repeated, hourly arguments that GOP state legislatures should overturn the election paired with fantastical stories of millions of votes being dropped off by Biden-Harris trucks in the dead of night. None of this was anywhere in the ballpark of reality, but it carried with it some vague authority since it was delivered by a guy in a suit at an anchor desk. Sometimes that's all it takes.

During that time, I wrote a lengthy diary for *The Bulwark* that railed against the dangerous fraud Newsmax was perpetrating on their audience. In response, one of the network's hosts, John Bachman, a guy around my age who I always perceived to be on the normal end of the spectrum, got a little butt hurt. He complained that I was calling him some sort of evil drug dealer.

He didn't see the problem with what they were doing. Newsmax's ratings were on the rise, their growth chart looking similar to the one Skatell had showed me in that back-corner cubicle seven years earlier. On Bachman's daytime show they were doing the "just asking questions" cha-cha slide while the prime-time Newsmax anchors stuck the "stop the steal" needle straight in the viewers' ocular cavity. From his perspective, they were offering a balanced diet of realish news with some of the hard stuff. It was audience service. He was taking the concerns of real Americans seriously. Centering the commenters.

Exactly one month after that complaint, the Capitol was stormed by people who were hooked on the smack his network was selling. Bachman hadn't seen it coming at all.

The appetite for vegetables had wilted. The mob needed their rage juice. Those who understood that and played to the audience were rewarded, at least for a time. Bannon would become chief strategist to a president. Skatell spent an early retirement refurbishing his open concept kitchen.

It all happened much faster than any of us imagined.

6

Red Meat for the Crocodiles

Anti-establishment right-wingers would often argue that people like me in the pre-Trump GOP consultant class were cloistered elites who were out of touch with the base and didn't understand what our own voters wanted.

This is one of those situations where the truth is even worse than the slander.

Yes, we tended to be more ideologically aligned with the college-educated suburban swing voters who decide general elections than we were with the base voters who are privately derided as "mouth breathers." But nobody with any sense in the so-called establishment was unaware of what tickled the base's collective pickle, least of all the political consulting class. We were the ones who spent our time poring over polls, attending focus groups, recruiting volunteers, and watching the responses that our candidates got on the stump. We knew exactly what GOP voters wanted. We understood who they were angry at, what issues riled them up, and which ones made them glaze over.

We just didn't care. Except to the extent that it helped us win elections.

Part of the reason for that is, unlike the Matt Boyles of the world, our awareness was a superficial one that papered over the source of the deep-seated worries and grievances that were driving our own voters' radicalization. We might have understood the zeroes and ones, the crosstabs, the trends, but we didn't feel the anger they felt in our bones. It wasn't visceral.

Most of us hadn't served on the front lines in interminable wars and those who did volunteered out of desire rather than necessity. We didn't spend our daily lives watching our way of life be replaced by a homogenized coastal culture that we were uncomfortable with. Our communities weren't being hollowed out and abandoned; we didn't live in places that were crushed by the housing crisis or the 2008 financial collapse. In fact, D.C. was a boomtown, and many of us were displacing a different hollowed-out community of color in the Chocolate City's urban core.

We weren't aggrieved over past slights committed by the elites; we were on the same meritocratic chairlift that kept climbing no matter how much we failed. We were inhabiting pockets of prosperity in the gilded city protected from these provincial concerns. This made it easy for us to understand and listen to the base voters' grievance without really hearing or feeling it.

As a result of this artificial awareness, our actions exacerbated the sense of alienation among many of "our" voters. Rather than trying to address their underlying concerns or channel their anger for good, which frankly may or may not have been possible, we chose instead to try to manage a raging fire, redirecting their resentment toward cheap culture war calories.

During campaign season we would make exaggerated promises that were never followed through on—in some cases because they were never possible to begin with and in others because, deep down, nobody actually wanted to do it.

None of this was done unconsciously. It was all just the accepted state of play. There is even a term of art for this type of political strategery: feeding "red meat" to the base.

During campaign season it was an all-you-can-eat buffet at the Sizzler, but when the whole business of governing came around, the steaks would be exsanguinated until the approval rating started to dip.

Those of us at the Republican National Committee, on the Hill, and throughout various GOP campaign high commands were under the impression that we were wise enough to be the self-imposed limit on the base voters' excesses. We could juggle keeping them energized, while governing prudently by deploying some rare sirloin when they needed to be fed.

They are mad about nation building in Iraq? We've got a bloody slab of Ground Zero Mosque Mania coming right up. They are pissed their community is turning into a putrescent ghost town? We've got a "Build the Wall" T-bone well done with a side of A-1. They are worried that the dominant white, Christian, patriarchal ethnoculture is being discarded? We are offering dog-whistle filets of "welfare reform" or forcing *uppity* athletes to stand for the damn flag.

The danger inherent in this strategy should have been apparent. History is replete with examples of mollification and appeasement gone awry. In his "House of Many Mansions" address, Winston Churchill identified the problem with this approach in one of Western civilization's most momentous mixed metaphors. "Each one hopes that if he feeds the crocodile enough, the crocodile will eat him last. All of them hope that the storm will pass before their turn comes to be devoured. But I fear greatly that the storm will not pass," he said. In Churchill's telling, the crocodiles not worth appeasing were, of course, the enemy fascists, while those of us in the Republican political class were simply charged with the appeasement of our own putative allies (and future Capitol rioters). The nature of the appeasement may have been different, but the lesson from the conceit is the same. In service to the crocs' ferocity, we would feed and fatten them, encouraging GOP candidates to make promises that they had no ability to keep, offering racially charged bromides that they were pretending to care about, and turning the Democrats from a rival party in a system that required comity to function into enemy combatants who threatened their Mayberry way of life.

Throughout it all, we felt that we were managing this fragile balance, when all we were doing was creating an increasingly rabid croc without actually satiating its appetite, hoping it's our competitor that gets devoured.

We were handing out little key bumps of cocaine, turning our own supporters into addicts, and then telling ourselves there wasn't a problem. They just need another bump to stay level. And another. And another.

• • •

On election night 2012, I was at the Romney "victory" party in Boston, tasked with spinning the media as the election returns rolled in. This is a rather silly tradition that every campaign participates in out of muscle memory even though the results are going to be the results and there's no real point in putting lipstick on a pig for a few hours. In a healthier system, we might all go out to the movies together while the counting happens and reconvene the next morning. But such is life.

In 2012, this exercise was made particularly fatuous thanks to our campaign's farcical inability to access any data that we could use to spin. The Romney campaign had spent weeks promoting Project ORCA, a purportedly high-fangled new web application that was supposed to help maximize voter turnout by identifying locations where some of our target voters hadn't shown up, so that resources and manpower could be deployed to harass them until they voted. It was also expected to give the campaign an early sense of how the results were looking, which made the salivating media hordes especially interested in hearing our "insight."

It turned out ORCA didn't work. At all. The system was overloaded with reports from the provinces. "ORCA is lying on the beach with a harpoon in it," a colleague said.

The media had been promised an early look at the returns, but the campaign knew less than anyone about how it was going. The massive bank of TVs that was supposed to be showing a whale of data loomed over the war room as a reminder of our campaign's incompetence and failure. For a few hours, I faked it till I made it, grabbing publicly available anecdotes from Twitter and passing them along to the press as special insights. Eventually word got out that ORCA had been beached, freeing me from the disinformation duties that were beginning to feel a little icky.

As the polls closed, I recognized quickly, based on the 2008/2012 county returns comparison chart that the *Huffington Post* was publishing, that Romney was on the road to a clear defeat. The losing trajectory was so obvious to me, I just presumed everyone else recognized it as well and was putting on a good face.

Apparently, that was a mistaken assumption.

As the rest of the staff continued gearing up for a long night, I made my way to the bar. On my way out of the war room, I whispered to *New York Times* star reporter Maggie Haberman that she could start prewriting her obit: we were cooked.

Before I could order up my first double bourbon and Coke, I received an urgent request to return to the battle stations. Karl Rove was having an on-air meltdown on Fox, ripping the media for misleading the public and arguing that Romney still had a chance to win. Some on the campaign were egging him on. This tantrum was a preview of Trump's 2020 offensive aimed at discrediting the notion that the media could call elections at all.

The only reason things didn't descend into madness in 2012 as they would in 2020 was that Romney wasn't deranged enough to play along.

While Rove was bellyaching on Fox, Rhoades told Romney that he didn't want to be a sore loser like John Kerry, who had refused to concede to George W. Bush on election night in 2004. The numbers weren't there and the responsible and dignified thing to do was accept defeat. Romney concurred. How quaint.

But consider the events of that moment.

- Rove's meltdown.
- Extensive discussion about "skewed polls" on the conservative blogs in the lead-up to election night, which proclaimed the pollsters were out to get the Republicans and that Romney was really winning.
- My colleagues' irrational exuberance about the possibility of a victory.
- The base's desire to delegitimize Obama in any way possible.

All of the ingredients for the madness to come eight years later were there that night. But it didn't feel urgent, because the "adults" were in charge. We ignored the warning signs and played our part in the show because we trusted the process. We thought we had the croc by the tail.

This mirage of control was on display after Romney's defeat, when I was sitting with the establishment GOP elites putting together what we thought was a way forward that blended the desires of the party base with what was best for both the country and winning swing voters. We branded it the Growth and Opportunity

Project (GOP, get it?). But if you know it at all, it's as the Republican Autopsy.

This project originated due to pressure that my boss at the time, RNC chairman Reince Priebus, was getting from donors and committee members to assess what had gone wrong, determine why the party had lost the popular vote in five of the last six elections, and figure out what needed to be done to win back the White House the next time around.

During the weeks that followed in the winter of the party's discontent, rather than plot a pathetic putsch to try to install Romney as an unelected soft dictator, party elites plotted ways to do better the next time.

Initially the "autopsy" that they discussed would focus solely on the mechanics of the campaigns. The GOP would gather the best-in-class experts to determine how to fix the polling and the ad-buying strategies, compete with the Democrats' nerd army on data and digital, up our game in online fundraising, and start copying the Obama "community organizer" ethos rather than mock it with racist overtones. This was all relatively safe turf that could solidify Priebus's hold over a party apparatus that was fracturing with the rise of competitors funded by the Koch Brothers and other bored billionaire conservatives who wanted to wield influence over it.

But Priebus and my colleagues on the RNC staff's desire to limit the review to campaign tactics kept butting up into the inescapable fact that the GOP's main problem wasn't the dearth of conservative hackers to make an ORCA that could actually swim. It was the reliance on older white men to win elections.

While the blocking-and-tackling sections of the report moved forward with little controversy or fanfare outside the parochial turf battles of any big organization when money is at stake, the question of how to handle the race and gender elephants in the room without angering the crocodiles became the biggest internal debate.

The players in this discussion represented basically every corner of what was then the establishment of the GOP and what could now be best described as the deeply ruptured former establishment. They were brought together by Priebus, who recognized that the autopsy would need to have outside "experts" to provide a sheen of objectivity. He first pulled in Henry Barbour, the national committeeman from Mississippi and former campaign manager for his uncle Haley's successful gubernatorial bid. A close ally of Priebus, Henry was a natural choice since he existed at the nexus of the consultant class and the grassroots members who make up the national committee. Together they identified a group of five to head up the project: Henry himself (in a Dick Cheney–esque fashion); Sally Bradshaw, the top strategist for Jeb Bush; former White House press secretary Ari Fleischer; Glenn McCall, a black national committeeman from South Carolina; and Zoraida Fonalledas, the committeewoman from Puerto Rico.

The outside committee couldn't be left to their own devices. So, they worked with a core group of staff from the RNC itself, led by Priebus, future insurrectionist congresswoman Elise Stefanik, future ballroom dancing phenom Sean Spicer, incoming chief of staff Mike Shields, RNC press secretary Kirsten Kukowski, and me. Stefanik was given the editor-in-chief role, having proven her ability to navigate the competing interests working on the GOP platform fight earlier that summer.

A decade on, the nine who came from the strategist class paint a complete picture of how the establishment reacted to the Trump takeover. Some were happy to become Trumpian throne sniffers (Priebus, Spicer), others were initially reluctant but came around when they realized how much was to be gained (Stefanik, Fleischer,

Shields), a smaller group became Never Trump stalwarts (Brad-shaw, myself), and the others tried to stay afloat in the party while cringing at what it was becoming (Barbour, Kukowski).

Despite the widely divergent ways in which each of us re-sponded when the next Republican Party presidential nominee used our recommendations as a wet wipe to remove his butterscotch bronzer, at the time all these players agreed on the right approach. We were only at loggerheads over how much of it to say out loud in the report.

None of us were "of" the populist movement that gave rise to Trump. None of us were policy heavyweights with contrarian views on the GOP's path forward. It was merely a cohort of political hacks with varying degrees of cosmopolitan values. The en vogue take that the party needed to diversify flattered our biases and we knew it would be received well in the press and the donor class. So, what congealed was a consensus outlook that the Republican Party needed to do a better job attracting minorities and women by re-skinning Bush's "compassionate conservatism" for the Obama era. That included (a) actually talking to marginalized groups and try-ing to earn their vote, (b) dumping politicians that said racist and sexist shit, and (c) tweaking some policies that might attract more voters of color, such as immigration and criminal justice reform.

Focusing on these areas was itself a bit of motivated reasoning. While there is no doubt it is true that over the long haul the GOP needed to diversify and it would be better for the country to have two dynamic, multicultural parties rather than one revanchist one, there was an alternate explanation for the loss that would have required addressing other GOP sacred cows. The ones that the Washington, D.C., smart set moos over: free-market "Ryanom-ics" at home and the mix of globalism and militarism that drove the established viewpoint on foreign affairs.

As a result, we totally ignored the concerns of the very voters who would be most turned off by this moderating tilt on cultural issues. No revisiting of the so-called forever wars. No reimagining of the supply-side economics or trade and globalization policies that had helped most Americans prosper, just not them.

These were the issues that hobbled Romney in Ohio and Pennsylvania and Wisconsin, not self-deportation. However, the notion that we should consider advocating for trashing the economic and foreign policy parts of the GOP's "three-legged-stool" was so verboten as to never have even come up during the autopsy's internal discussions.

All we offered was a sop on the cultural questions, while figuring we could just take out a flank steak to keep the base happy when we started to get pushback. As Henry Barbour said to me, "The thing that Trump got right, that we missed in the autopsy was getting the party back to being the party for working Americans and not having this country club, Wall Street mentality. That was something we missed, and that was a mistake that we made."

The ironic part of the whole thing is that it was Fleischer, the future *Hannity* regular who was the most adamant that the party focus on appealing to more urbane sensibilities, going so far as to hold a dinner at a Tribeca flat where Peggy Noonan and the monied elite provided their counsel with a dollop of Grey Poupon. While Bradshaw and Barbour worked on the less memorable sections of the autopsy, it was Fleischer who was charged with the "messaging" portion, which garnered all of the attention.

Throughout the process he was aggressive in pushing the notion that this could not just be weak-sauce lip service to the party's problems. It needed to include real, tangible change on issues that mattered to marginalized communities that were rejecting our candidates. Fleischer sent emails to the committee pushing for a change in the party's stance on gay rights and worked with outside advisors on memos calling for major overhauls in the way the RNC dealt with minorities, women, and the media. He even went so far as to raise the possibility of moderating the party's position on abortion, a notion that was anathema to the rank and file.

Some of the suggestions made in private memos that were not included in the final report would sound utterly preposterous in the Trump Party just a few years on. Here's a taste:

"Consider hosting the convention in a symbolic location like Puerto Rico." (*Rather than the balloon drop, it would feature a historic paper towel toss.*)

"Don't attack the media." (*The Enemy of the People shall be appeased!!!!*)

"Do something unexpected. Put up 'gay republicans' page on RNC site, do a 'green republicans' event." (*Orange would have been a better suggestion.*)

"Spanish lessons for all GOP staff." (*De-Baathification training would be more useful these days.*)

In the report itself, Fleischer's recommendations were framed with a quote from Jack Kemp. "No one cares what you know until they know you care." (*In Ari's defense, Donald Trump did prove the first part of the aphorism correct. It turns out that no one does care what you know.*)

He continues with various adages, advice, and exhortations that, read back now, sound as if they are from another century or another universe rather than just the last decade.

Here's a selection from just a single page.

"If Hispanic Americans perceive that a GOP nominee or candidate does not want them in the United States (i.e., self-deportation) they will not pay attention to the next sentence." (*The Republican Party wrote that! And then nominated a guy who said most of the immigrants from Mexico are rapists and criminals in his announcement speech.*)

It quotes former congressman Dick Armey: "You can't call someone ugly and expect them to go to prom with you." (*I'm not sure if there's a "calling someone's wife ugly" addendum to that little bit of folk wisdom, but if not, Ted Cruz must be the exception that proves the rule.*)

"We must embrace and champion comprehensive immigration reform." (*Priebus would later spin this to me as being vague enough to not be prescriptive, but in the context of the time, CIR was a stand-in for some type of "amnesty," which has zero purchase in Trump's party.*)

"If our party is not welcoming and inclusive, young people and increasingly other voters will tune us out." (*And by welcoming and inclusive we mean that you are excluded from using our restrooms if your genitalia do not match your gender identity.*)

"If we want ethnic minority voters to support Republicans, we have to engage them and show our sincerity." (*Nothing says sincere like the Trump Tower Taco Bowl. Just $24.99 plus tax and gratuity.*)

This final language was toned down from initial drafts that called for more bold change on a range of social issues. In the days before the release of the report, word had gotten out that Fleischer was pushing the scope outside the RNC's typical lane. Mitch Mc-Connell and John Boehner's teams had caught wind of the coming recommendations and wanted the RNC to leave policymaking to the policymakers. Meanwhile, those of us on the RNC comms side were worried about blowback from the conservative media, particularly anti-immigration outlets like Breitbart. And Reince didn't want his hard-line committee members to think he had gone soft.

So Reince and the RNC staff struck a few of the more specific recommendations with regards to immigration reform on the eve of the report's release, leaving the more generic choose-your-own-adventure "comprehensive immigration reform" pablum, which appeased Boehner and McConnell, and frustrated both Fleischer and Bradshaw. Reince also, I later learned, asked that language they had pushed for calling for softening the party posture on gay marriage be struck as well. On both counts Fleischer thought it was absolutely essential that any assessment of the party's failings include addressing these divisive racial and cultural issues that were preventing it from maximizing its support.

To be clear—all of the internal players who were objecting to this more forward-leaning language agreed with Fleischer on the merits (especially me!), but for various prudential reasons were concerned about whether or not we really needed to go there. Whether it was worth angering the crocs.

Reince, in particular, had his coalition to manage. He felt like the inclusion of comprehensive immigration reform was going to create enough problems for him on its own, so his disagreement on pushing further was merely a matter of stakeholder management, not substance.

In this instance, it was Fleischer who had the benefit of not having to worry about the Game or the feelings of the mob, because he was on the outside with a cable contract and high-retainer clients. It didn't bother him to ruffle a few feathers. Without being able to get inside his brain or heart, I believe that he was genuinely motivated by wanting this to be the best, most candid possible report, and had the future gone differently, had Marco Rubio become the Republican nominee in 2016 or had Fleischer refused to torch these beliefs in exchange for a few Donald Trump Jr. retweets, his advocacy would have a degree of prescience.

When all was said and done, every person involved with the autopsy was not only on board with the final recommendations wholeheartedly but was proud of it, especially Fleischer and Stefanik. More than a decade on, all of those who worked on the project and were willing to return my call felt that way still.

While we absolutely whiffed on the strategic opportunity to generate a surge in new white working-class voters as a plausible model for a Republican presidential candidate in 2016, the consensus was that in the long view we were basically correct that the path that the party was on would lead to disaster in the dynamic, diversifying, and growing parts of the country. It explains why Joe Biden won in places like Georgia and Arizona, why the Democrats would take back full control of Washington seven years later, and why the Republicans have mostly ceded the fight on gay marriage in the interim.

After the disagreements over the policy particulars in the report were resolved, the whole team gathered at the National Press Club to officially roll out the autopsy to the media. Reince, feeling the need to throw Fleischer a bone, gave in when the latter requested that Zoraida Fonalledas, who had nominal involvement in actually putting together the report, provide a performative reading of the document summary in Spanish to Reince, as if he a) didn't already know what was in it, and b) could understand what she was saying, given that his time in Miami for law school and scattered Rosetta Stone sessions left him well short of fluency in Español.

Fleischer felt this *Veep*-esque nod to the Spanish-language press was a critical part of the announcement and would send a message that this party was serious about making changes.

So there we all were, dolled up in our suits and ties and dresses, listening to the pro-statehood for Puerto Rico committeewoman deliver a Spanish reading of the report that we had all settled on, which called for a party to be more welcoming, more diverse, more friendly to immigrants.

It may have been phony as all get-out, but at least our hearts were in the right place.

We had all wanted to reform the Grand Old Party in our image, or at least in the image we saw in our mind's eye. It was the path forward we thought to be right strategically and morally while also, just by coincidence, confirming our ideological priors.

But the crocs didn't like the meal we tried to feed them. In the wake of this ship wedging itself into the Suez Canal of America's political psyche, I would become the face of an anti-Trump super PAC. Spicer would become the face of Donald Trump's lies. Stefanik would become the face of the GOP rising stars' complete submission to nativism and conspiracism.

Bradshaw would leave politics altogether, opening a bookstore in Tallahassee and marking her wrist with a SPEAK TRUTH tattoo that serves as a daily reminder to not give an inch. Rather than be devoured or let the storm pass or walk away, Fleischer, Priebus, and Shields just gave in to their animal impulses as the price of playing the game.

What within each of us was at the root of that crack-up?

How could a group that had been so aligned respond to the wholesale rejection of our vision in such dramatically different ways?

7

The Breakup

For me the divergence began with a phone call.

A few days after Jeb was routed in the South Carolina primary, I returned to Miami and decided to partake in one element of South Florida life that I had missed, being so immersed in the race. I woke up, got a cold brew from Panther Coffee, and drove across the bridge to South Beach armed with a towel, a coming-of-age novel, and a bubbly water. It was a scene that I intended to repeat every day for a few weeks. My now husband, then boyfriend, was stuck working in D.C., but he understood my delayed return. It had been a long year. I had put my whole heart into campaigning for a man I truly believed was best suited to be president and was rewarded with the hourly indignity of getting schlonged by Biff from *Back to the Future* in front of the whole world. So, I required a bit of the so-called self-care that has become fashionable with my fellow millennial coastal elites.

I was only about two hours into this intended life of leisure when the call came in. My skin had not tanned. The bildungs-roman's protagonist hadn't even reached his first setback.

The man on the other end of the line had a proposition. He

was interested in making me the front man for a super PAC trying to stop Donald Trump from winning the nomination. They had engaged in some low-profile advertising in Iowa but new money was rolling in. It was time to turn up the heat. The clock was ticking. If I wanted in, I needed to act fast.

I would be lying if I said my heart didn't skip a beat. Yes, I was tired. But I'm a certain kind of junky, and this was my fix.

Before I lay out what came next, I need to fess up to the fact that in considering this proposal, my mindset was colored by something that might not make sense given the events of the ensuing half decade. I know that you, dear reader, have come to this book hoping to get insight from a supposed political expert, a grizzled campaign veteran who can rely on a deep reservoir of experience to see which way the political winds are going to blow.

But I swear, hand to God, that even at that late a date, even after Trump had won the New Hampshire and South Carolina primaries and dispatched my former boss—son to one president and brother to another—I still didn't truly believe that this manifest incompetent would be the Republican Party's nominee. And I sure as shit didn't think there was any chance he could actually become *president*. People were really going to elect the *Apprentice* guy? C'mon. This bigoted, barmy, bargain-basement Berlusconi could not possibly win. My brain just refused to allow for the possibility.

I cannot deny that this misguided expectation of Trump's demise was one of a few contributing factors that made me intrigued by the prospect that was presented. Over the next twenty-four hours, I was surprised to find out how many people did not share my irrational confidence on this point. None of the old wise men I called *wanted* Trump to win. There was no secret reservoir of support for him somewhere inside the Republican elite. But while these friends and mentors all said they would support any decision I made, they also warned me about taking a career and maybe even personal safety risk by crossing an unstable madman who could actually win the big one.

Not only did I completely reject their advice, I barely even took it seriously.

My overriding concern about taking the gig was about how it would reflect on Jeb, who I thought might be in need of some self-care of his own following such a brutal loss. I figured that trashing Trump on TV as a "former Jeb Bush spokesman" would surely be a headache for a guy I admired and who had been through a lot already. But when I shared this worry with him, he echoed the same concerns others had about the wisdom of my career choice. I needn't be concerned about him, he said. Jeb is a good egg.

Given that feedback, my decision came down to this: I thought all the people cautioning me about Trump's possible victory were batshit, and the outside prospect of Donald Trump as president was unacceptable in every imaginable sense. If those cautioning me were right and he really did have a chance, then it would be even more important for me to get in the arena and try to kick his ass.

And so it began. As *GQ* wrote, my job was to "basically go on TV and talk shit about Donald Trump. That's incredible and he's very good at it." Indeed it was incredible. Thanks, *GQ*.

For a few weeks at least, I was having the best time of my life. I spent my days trolling research books and the interwebs for anti-Trump nuggets while sitting poolside at my apartment in Miami. Then, every few hours, a cable network would send a car to pick me up and take me to a studio, where I would parry with a Trumper for the entertainment and educational benefit of their viewers.

Among the highlights: mocking former *Apprentice* contestant and shrimpy Trump surrogate Andy Dean Litinsky for sitting in a "booster seat" live on-air so he would look taller when he sat next to me; navigating a minor hangover and spring cold, I vomited in a TV studio bathroom exactly thirty seconds before shouting myself hoarse at another Trump surrogate over their candidate's refusal to release his taxes; getting my dander up every Friday night as the Alan Colmes–style foil for Fox News host Eric Bolling, who would yell at me and question my manhood when he sat in for Bill O'Reilly.

It was all invigorating . . . for a while.

The weight of what was coming and the devastating loss I was going to experience didn't really start to hit amid all the trash-talking. But eventually reality began to set in. By April, Our Principles PAC (OPP) had crashed and burned, functionally shutting down after Trump won the Indiana primary. But that wasn't the part that really stung.

Are you ready for this?

Despite the fact that the PAC that had hired me had bestowed itself the righteous name "Our Principles," every senior person involved in the organization went on to work for a *pro*–Donald Trump PAC called Future 45 during the general election, except me and the executive director, Katie Packer Becson.

Every single person! What the fuck?!

Later that summer, the same guy who interrupted my beach respite put me on speakerphone with Todd Ricketts, a trust fund grown-up who had used his father's largesse to launch OPP. They were taking the Acela train from New York to D.C. for a meeting of the minds and wanted to once again try to recruit me, this time for the pro-Trump PAC they were launching.

They pitched me on "getting the gang back together," like this was some make-believe *Ocean's Twelve* shit, not a megalomaniac taking over the world's essential nation. I swear to God I thought it was a prank call. You couldn't make it up. "Principles" was right there in the name! Our *Principles* PAC.

I declined.

By the time Trump accepted the nomination, I was in a pretty dark place. I skipped a planned trip to the convention to drive to Richmond, Virginia, to go see the Arcs, an indie-blues-rock band, with Romney confidants Will and Kelli Ritter and some other RINO operative friends.

That evening, the nightmare I never imagined could come to pass started to become very real, very fast. To try to ward off this intense feeling of impending doom, we banned discussion of Trump. I had pledged to myself that I would stay off my phone and enjoy the guitar solos in blissful ignorance. But I'm a weak man. I couldn't help but look. The images of this sociopathic, nativist monster were too much to bear. The drinks and cigs started flowing. By the time the band came on, I was in a full blackout. It's not exactly clear how and when I got back to my friends' house. I have a vague recollection of shutting down the bar adjacent to the venue that night. Eventually I wound up back in the guest's quarters, just down the hall from their bedroom. Lying there, I tried in vain to punish myself with news about Trump's speech but couldn't manage to read anything, thanks to a freshman year dorm room case of the spins. Eventually I realized the moment required vomit. The only bathroom upstairs was right outside my friends' door and I didn't want to suffer the indignity of knowing Kelli could hear me violently chundering in her toilet. So I stumbled down to their basement and spent the night on the cold concrete floor. My career and political identity were in tatters. Donald Trump was the party's nominee. Things had gotten very real indeed.

Despite it all, my mind couldn't, wouldn't fully accept the idea that Trump as *president* could *actually* happen, so I continued with the self-delusion. I did an interview with *Politico*'s Glenn Thrush in which I stated confidently that Hillary would beat Trump even if she were in jail—a headline that haunts my Google-fu to this day. I made the rounds on television, making equally brash and obnoxious predictions about Trump's expiry that were later featured in gleeful YouTube mash-ups circulated by his supporters.

On election day, I revealed on a NowThis News livestream that I had voted for Hillary, the very person I had launched a PAC to stop three years earlier. It was a crossover so drastic that almost none of my compatriots joined me, preferring instead to throw their vote away for a third-party candidate or a random write-in. But my fear and loathing of Trump had grown to overwhelm any vestigial Clinton animus. For me, it wasn't a close call. And there was no amount of rationalizing that could have gotten me there.

That afternoon I took the Acela to New York to do the talking-head deal. On the ride up I sat next to a political reporter who got a call from Katie Walsh, the RNC chief of staff. Walsh and Spicer, on behalf of Priebus, were providing a pre-autopsy to reporters about the impending loss for Trump, making the case that the RNC had done their job, but the unstable candidate and his ineffectual campaign had cost the party the White House. So, I wasn't the only insider who had it wrong.

I was set to be a panelist on the late-night shift at CNN, but, well . . . you know what happened. Long before I was set to be on-air, the result was clear. I slumped into an Uber, called the producer, and said I wasn't going to do the hit. They were pissed. I said that I wasn't going to cry on-air for free, told them to make Ana Navarro bite the bullet, and hung up.

I cabbed straight back to the hotel and had what can only be described as a full-on panic attack, during which I took several sleeping pills to try to force my brain to stop reeling. The following morning, I went to church, the only time I had done so for a reason other than pleasing my mother in years, possibly decades.

Outsiders to Republican Washington might think my reaction was an outlier, and it was certainly on the more extreme end, but it wasn't just us Never Trumpers who were shook.

Down in D.C. at the America Rising, RNC, and conservative media parties there were some whose mood was not too dissimilar, while others resorted to a detached posture of macabre and nihilistic amusement, simultaneously enjoying the demise of the Clintons while feeling uneasy about what would come next.

A friend who was sitting in the same third-floor RNC conference room where we had gleefully watched the returns during Scott Walker's successful defeat of a recall in Wisconsin described the mood as quite different from what we had experienced, despite the fact that the GOP was taking the presidency and both houses of Congress.

"You could see the demeanor of the room change to a nervous excitement. It was a mix between that and others being like 'what the fuck is happening' and, speaking for myself, it started to be like 'what have we done,'" he said. "Looking around trying to make eye contact there was a soulless 'what is happening' stare. And there were people that cried . . . Not of joy."

Trump's future executive assistant Madeleine Westerhout was among the criers. According to Tim Alberta's *American Carnage*, Westerhout "broke down crying on Election Night, inconsolable over Trump's victory." Friends say the tears also flowed for Katie Walsh, who a few hours earlier had been trying to save face over the expected loss.

Over at the America Rising "victory" party, my colleagues weren't in much better shape. They had rented a room at a now-extinct downtown D.C. bar where staff who were on call hunched over laptops analyzing the returns while clients and family and others mingled over hors d'oeuvres and cocktails. Following a few surprise early wins for GOP Senate candidates, the room exploded in cheers and revelry, as one might expect. Soon after, the mood started to shift. The savvier ones realized that if the swing-state Senate candidates were winning, someone else might win, too.

A friend who was there recalls that the entire place went from "jubilant to subdued, quietly staring at their screen." He goes on: "Don't get me wrong, there were some people there who absolutely loved the idea of a Trump presidency. But I would describe the vast majority of the people at the party as 'deeply concerned.' There were definitely people crying in the bathroom—a combination of the looming result and beer tears."

One might think an election result that brought panic attacks, feelings of complicity, deep concern, and tears might have been the thing to force a little self-reflection in the Republican governing class.

Nah.

• • •

By Thanksgiving, the very people who had been weeping on election night had started to find reasons to give Trump a chance. Many friends who had confided their private horror and deep distaste for the president-elect ended up taking jobs throughout the administration and associated Republican apparatus.

The decision to enable a manifestly unfit incoming regime took different forms in different people, but over time, surrounded by others employing similar self-trickery to reach the same result, the group's justifications began to congeal. The mental superstructures required to overcome the concerns were built. The narratives they invented to make such service not just defensible but maybe even honorable took shape.

The enablers I am referring to here are not the pure-hearted bigots or QAnon kooks or Trumpian superfans who make up the core MAGA rally base. In the wake of Trump's victory, slithery Stephen Miller and his sleep chamber, Foghorn Leghorn Jeff Sessions and his lust for the blood of immigrant children, and their ilk, bathed in deluded grandeur.

Those ghouls were necessary, but not sufficient elements to Trump's rise and reign.

In order for Trump to amass the power that led our democracy to the brink, he needed to win over the reluctant, the striving but skeptical. These individuals were all, at some point, to varying degrees . . . like me. Maybe if you went issue by issue they weren't as squishy and moderate. Maybe they didn't have a full-on panic attack on election night. But when it came to their judgment of the president-elect and the mob that had rallied behind him, every single one of them at some point said to themselves . . . Ew, no. I can't.

Now, to a person, they were jumping on board. They weren't doing it because they really believed Donald Trump would "grow into the job" (lol). It was because somewhere inside their brain they had found a way to tell themselves a story that justified coming to the aid and comfort of a man they knew full well was an incompetent menace.

This was, to me, the most demoralizing part of the whole experience. Despite not really believing such a caricature of cretinous cruelty could win the presidency, I had lived through the Palin and Gingrich and Bachmann and Cain boomlets. I knew that my party might someday nominate an extremist or kook. What I didn't expect is how my friends and mentors would respond to this aberrantly dangerous one.

I had knock-down drag-outs with them over their choices. One night during the transition, I went to dinner with one of my best friends at the time, a double date to meet the boy she was starting to get serious with. I was nervous about how it was going to go. She had just taken a job working in a senior administration role, and we hadn't yet discussed it. We danced around the topic for a while, focusing instead on life updates and get-to-know-yous.

Before I said anything, she volunteered a preemptive defense for her "service." She told us how the job came to pass then asked rhetorically, "What was I supposed to do when a cabinet official calls and asks to meet? Turn them down?"

"YESSSSS," I blurted out a little too loudly in the middle of a French bistro, spittling into the rabbit stew as a Harry Potter vein bulged from my temple. Yes! That's exactly what you do. Just don't take the call! My face reddened, chest harrumphed, and eyes rolled.

Things got a bit awkward from there.

But that night I had reached my breaking point. I couldn't believe that literally everyone in my life was going along with this. I was flabbergasted by the unanimity. Despondent over my deteriorating friendships.

This was Donald motherfucking Trump! It wasn't a close call!

I tried to explain to them how crazy it would be to go work for this wretched shit stain affixed to our collective drawers.

He contained not a single honorable attribute they would want their child to emulate. He had an empty set of virtues. Throughout his entire life, at every opportunity, he had screwed the people who worked with him. He had bilked the innocent victims who had signed up for his myriad scams, only to be left bankrupt. And he did it in order to fill the bottomless black hole within him that required boundless validation and indulgence for sustenance. He was constitutionally incapable of shame or self-reflection. Even his biggest apologists admitted that the best way to get him to do the right thing was to prey on his insecurities. No matter how much anyone who considered working for a man such as this might have agreed with the "policy" they guessed he might implement or believed in their ability to nudge things in the right direction, it was inevitable that he would tarnish it with his all-enveloping stank.

Signing up to work for Trump was asking for certain humiliation and a lifetime of association with all manner of horrors that they could not yet even predict. They would go in trying to make him clean, but he would be the one to make them dirty. There were decades of evidence that made certain this was the case.

Donald Trump was the snake. Everyone knew he was the snake. He told us he was the snake. Yet when the snake offered his spoiled fruit, these otherwise intelligent people took from the tree and ate it.

When the phone rang, they picked it up.

Why was he getting through to them? Why wasn't I?

• • •

There are plenty of answers to those questions bandied about by the left-wing commentariat. It was for the money! They were always evil Trumpians in disguise! They have no soul! White supremacy!

Sure, it was some of those things. People do like money and fancy titles. Some of my old colleagues did purchase beach houses. Many were blinded by privilege. There were certainly a handful of secret racists who finally were given the excuse to let their confederate freak flag fly. But none of those answers proved wholly satisfying.

Every week, bewildered liberals would ask me on TV or Twitter or at the coffee shop some version of the same questions: Do they believe all this? Is it just a charade? Or, as I had been chastised by that drunken Obama staffer a half decade prior: How do they sleep at night?

Understanding the real answer to that question is critical to learning from this. Why wasn't their ambition or desire for financial success offset by their inner Jiminy Crickets? Why didn't they see the land mines? Where was the line? Is there a line?

It's easy to paint with a broad brush. To decry them all as no different from the worst, the most sociopathic among them. But in reality, humans are much more complicated than that.

There were thousands of people who at some level complied with Trump who weighed the costs. Who knew the dangers. Who could have gone in my direction and not his if their circumstance was just a little different. If the story they told themselves came from another vantage point. If they could have imagined a different, more fulfilling future for themselves.

Part of understanding why they succumbed requires recognizing how we let it get so out of hand in the first place, how we fed a mob that we lost control of, and how that made it easier to go along with what came next.

But that next step . . . to Trump . . . still felt like a pretty big jump! Why would person after person turn to the leader of the mob that had displaced them and say, "Thank you, sir, may I have another?"

Over the next four years, the answer to that question started to come into focus. I endeavored to create a bit of a field guide that laid out how it happened here. How my complicit former compatriots' actions connect to all the little sacrifices I was a party to in the decade prior and the syzygy between my rationalizations then and theirs now.

Before I get to them, I first have to explain myself, one last time.

8

Inertia

Nobody on planet earth was more horrified by the notion of Donald Trump as president than I was. As much as you think you loathe him, I loathe him infinity-to-the-nth-degree more. You know the famous picture of the gobsmacked Obama staffers watching in abject horror as the baton was passed peacefully to their successor? I was all of them in one. A complete emotional wreck.

My career was a shambles. I felt alone, despondent.

I literally couldn't even drive past the White House on the way to work in the morning without being physically sickened, so I began taking a longer route. I didn't go out to dinner, for fear of how I would react when I bumped into former colleagues who had gotten aboard the Trump train.

In Washington, Christmas parties are where the networking happens, and I had once been a formidable yuletide hopper. In 2016, I attended just two parties. The first was for the Republican Attorneys General Association, one of my clients. I had about half a drink before my friend and patron strode forty yards across the ballroom, leaned into my ear, and asked if I was all right. He thought I looked equal parts disgusted and physically ill. Somehow I managed to be both flush with rage and peaked with horror, being surrounded by merriment in Trump's Washington. I left without talking to anyone else.

At the party my own colleagues hosted, I became so incandescent at everyone who came up to me—some worried about my career, others making snide remarks, the "good ones" whispering that they were with me in secret—that I stormed out and walked home alone, whimpering and chain-smoking. I spent the actual Christmas holiday back home in Denver, reading the saddest fiction I could get my hands on, mewling privately in my parents' guest bedroom as I devoured Hanya Yanagihara's *A Little Life* before being admonished by my brother for petulantly avoiding my mother's attempts to draw me into the Christmas spirit.

I felt like everything I ever knew and believed about my country, my career, my colleagues were a lie. The Americans I most despised had taken over the country I loved, bringing almost everyone I had once looked up to along with them. Like Yanagihara's Jude St. Francis, I felt that I had "become lost to the world, in which I otherwise wasted so much time."

Despite all of that emoting, when I got a call asking if I would provide consulting for those whom I detested, the very people I rued wasting so much time serving, I said yes, one last time.

You read that correctly.

Between tears and tantrums and self-loathing and resentment and apocalyptic night terrors, I decided to fit in some PR advice for someone who needed help reaching their goal of serving the very devil whose ascension tormented me.

I didn't have any illusions about what I was signing up for. I just didn't know what else to do. This was my life. I started working in Republican politics at age sixteen. I was a late bloomer, so in that first job, I hadn't yet finished puberty and looked like I was twelve;

everyone asked me where my parents were when I went into the office for my internship. I spent the next eighteen years in and out of campaigns working eighty-hour weeks, obsessing over politics, breathing it, defining myself through it.

At a time when I felt like everything around me was collapsing, I was offered a lifeline, something that would ease my mind by focusing it on a task that I knew I could execute.

Scott Pruitt needed my help ensuring he was confirmed as Donald Trump's Environmental Protection Agency administrator.

It was a life preserver. And I grabbed it. I didn't know what else to do.

Fuck me dead.

• • •

I got to know Pruitt a bit in 2015 when as attorney general of Oklahoma he had endorsed Jeb's presidential campaign. Jeb's endorsers came in a few stripes—the true believers, the obligated, the calculating—and Pruitt had been one of the thirstier. It seemed he mostly wanted to leverage the campaign to build his own national profile, so I would hear from him with disproportionate frequency, given that I was the line into the media.

When he was nominated for the Trump administration job, and our firm was recommended to help deal with public relations, it made sense for me to run point on the project, given that relationship. Or, well, it didn't completely "make sense," given my maniacal disposition toward his soon-to-be boss, but we just glossed over that little inconvenience.

The transition period was chaotic, and while Trump is vengeful, he is also unorganized and easily flattered. So, politicians who hadn't endorsed him were able to get into the good graces of his team if they humiliated themselves and played their cards right.

Pruitt was happy to oblige. He was an unrepentant and shameless groveler when need be.

This MAGA redemption path did have one caveat, though. Amnesty was not granted to those who committed the lone high crime against Trumpism, criticizing him on the telly-telly, where he would see it, given that he managed to watch more cable news than a catatonic nonagenarian whose wheelchair is permanently stationed two feet from the tube in the Villages' rec room. This was a crime I had been committing every day and twice on Sunday for the past year, something Trump was well aware of. (Anyone so intimately familiar with the constellation of low-rated daytime cable pundits that they are able to recognize me immediately—as Trump did when he shouted me down during a post-debate spin room altercation—should be discussing their TV news habit with a professional psychotherapist, not ascending to the presidency.)

In order to keep Pruitt out of trouble with his new daddy, I kept a low profile and managed the war room communications behind the scenes, bringing on others to interface with the Trump team directly. They, of course, sniffed out this not-so-clever plan, and eventually I was forced to have one unpleasant phone call with a D-list goombah-cum-spokesperson named Bryan Lanza. I assured him that he didn't have to worry about my being some Never Trump fifth column, I was simply here to help Pruitt and would be a good boy. Afterward, I wanted to shoot disinfectant into my veins, get light inside the body as almost a cleaning. Instead I tried to block it out, distracting myself with some fresh gay lit that was rife with heartbreak.

The distance I maintained from the Trump team somehow made me feel a little bit better about everything. I guess? I wasn't going to actually go into the administration, like the friend I had lit into at dinner. I was just a hired stranger helping this one guy get appointed to a random agency whose main job was going to be getting rid of the oppressive Waters of the United States rule (which was dumb, I swear) and other wasteful regulations. Maybe this was not the *best* rationalization, but it was a trying time and I was desperate.

Things eventually got busy. We had to build a website, and I coordinated the "rapid response" to the various attacks that came his way. I spent an inordinate amount of time on the phone with Pruitt's closest advisor, with whom I bonded over a shared adoption story. I learned all about Scott Pruitt's CV, his peccadilloes, past controversies, and successes. We gamed out scenarios. I put out mini fires. The old political strategery muscles were getting warmed back up. It felt good. It distracted me from our dystopian reality and my deep despair over what I was going to do with my life. I wasn't useless. My career might go on. This is fine, right?

Pruitt got confirmed. It was bittersweet, but it felt nice to get a "win" again. The EPA gave my firm a contract for media-monitoring services. We would compile the news clips and send them to the staff. There was nothing particularly scandalous about this project. The previous administration had used some other company that was gouging them, so we could say we'd saved the taxpayers some cash. Still, technically speaking, I was on the Trump administration payroll, which was icky, at best.

Pruitt would call from time to time for advice on how to deal with this controversy or that. When I started writing this section of the book, I jotted down, as a hold, that after a "few weeks" I got to the point where my personal hostility and public anti-Trump commentary made me feel too conflicted to continue with this free counsel. But when I went back to look at my texts and emails, my heart sank into my stomach. It wasn't a few weeks; it was somewhere just shy of an annum. I can't pinpoint the exact date. The emails dissipate by the fall of Trump's first year. But there's a trickle through the winter. I couldn't track down exactly when, but at some stage I told Pruitt's communications director to tell his boss that he had to stop calling me unless he was planning on agreeing to the only advice I could provide in good conscience: he should resign. Not only did Pruitt ignore that helpful suggestion, he did the opposite, engaging in the most obsequious, pathetic lobbying campaign imaginable to replace Jeff Sessions as attorney general, pitching himself to Trump as someone who would be a more loyal top cop than Sessions amid the probe being led by former FBI director Robert Mueller into possible pro-Trump Russian interference in the 2016 campaign. This gambit was nauseating, corrupt, and mind-bogglingly megalomaniacal.

But this time his suck-up sessions didn't work, and the job went, temporarily, to another former America Rising client: Matt Whitaker, who, in a feat of such world-historic grandeur that the people of Guinness should confirm it as a peerless achievement, managed to present himself as even more toadying than Pruitt and thus more controllable to a corrupt president who needed a bitch at the Justice Department.

In the following months, Pruitt went deeper and deeper down the dark Trump sinkhole. The job brought out every demon he had inside: self-importance, avarice. We never talked again, and I later learned he had a falling-out with the longtime advisor I had bonded with on the project over his behavior.

But for that brief period of time, I had succumbed to the very temptations that trapped all the other enablers. The ambition doesn't just disappear.

Having walked away from America Rising for no compensation over Trump, I didn't have any other paid political work, so I pivoted to the corporate opposition research side of things and didn't miss a beat. I compartmentalized all my concerns about the state of the country as a political matter, and when I had my corporate hat on, barreled forth trafficking in that same old fake-news adjacent, oppo work that I had been a party to in the pre-Trump era. Now it was just for companies instead of politicians.

The reflection that I had been doing about how our politics had gotten off the rails didn't extend to my own career . . . again. I wanted to have my cake and eat it, too, savaging the Trumpified GOP in the media while letting inertia take hold with my day job.

Amid all this I earned widespread liberal plaudits for my advocacy, especially after I endorsed Democrat Doug Jones in his Alabama U.S. Senate campaign against the despicable Roy Moore. I was invited on left-wing media outlets and gained a strange new respect from thousands of randoms on Twitter, all while maintaining my role as a corporate hit man for hire.

Some clients wanted to leverage my familiarity with the EPA. Others wanted basic, inoffensive PR work addressing issues they faced in Washington. Still others wanted to get their message to the far-right media members I had cultivated relationships with. This felt like such lower stakes than the presidential malversation I had been righteously criticizing that there wasn't any reason to self-immolate over it. I was just another PR flunky doing a job. Why not continue doing a little Beltway gay-for-pay routine when so many others are complicit in so much worse?

At least that's what I told myself.

In reality, the inherent conflict between my public advocacy and client work was untenable, and it ended up being my support for Jones that sparked a bizarre chain of events that finally dislodged me from this too-cute two-step.

Why opposing Roy Moore—a creepy homophobic ephebophile who shouldn't be within one hundred miles of Congress, or a middle school—made such waves in the media, I will never know. But it did. A tweet I sent announcing my donation to Jones went ultraviral, garnering 15,300 retweets and three million impressions. A National Public Radio stringer who lived near my home in Oakland came by to do a segment with the local Republican specimen as if I were an albino Inuit pickleball prodigy. I participated in a series of interviews about the party's cowardice in going along with a pervert bigot like Moore and did a stand-up bit on a comedy podcast mocking the whole charade. This caught the attention of Trump's chief of staff, John Kelly, and the chairman of the RNC Ronna "Don't Call Me Romney" McDaniel, who were quite displeased and tried to leverage my business partners to force me to shut up.

Now, you'd think that the Trump White House chief of staff would have some more pressing business than a minor Twitter celebrity's opposition to Roy Moore, but apparently not! The calls shook my partners a bit, which pissed me off, so we met and agreed to start gaming out an exit strategy that would allow me to spread my wings and fly away from a business that I was no longer a fit for.

I didn't know at the time that I had pissed off more than Ronna McRomney. Like every drug dealer in every movie, I was about to get pinched right at the moment I thought I was getting out.

The tenuous quasi-secret relationship I had maintained over the years with the nativist assholes in the far-right media blew up in my face, Chuck Johnson and Steve Bannon had turned on me (shocker, who could have seen that coming!), and they spent the fall of 2017 spreading the lie that one of the women who accused Moore of improper sexual conduct was fabricating the charge, and that I was behind this bit of trickery.

Moore called me out by name on the stump the weekend before the election, claiming I trumped up the allegations. In *The Fourth Estate*, a documentary about the *New York Times*, you can see Bannon mouth "Tim Miller" to one of the *Times*' reporters, trying in vain to pin his pedo client's sins on me. He made the accusation explicit in a panel at a *Financial Times* conference after Moore lost.

None of this was true, of course. Moore's accusers weren't fabricating anything. And it turned out that Bannon's calumny was, as usual, merely projection. It was he and Matt Boyle who were trying to fabricate a lie about this incident. After the campaign ended, the *Daily Beast* reported that Moore supporters had plotted with Breitbart to try to bribe one of the accusers' lawyers, hoping to get them to backtrack and testify that she had made the whole thing up. During an in-person meeting where they tried to seal the deal, Boyle and another Breitbart "reporter" were present and encouraged the accuser's lawyer to go along with the scheme, to no avail. Breitbart denies the specifics of this report, but from my perspective this little bit of botched palm-greasing marked the final step in Breitbart's devolution from centering the commenters to manipulating campaigns to becoming a straight fake-news propaganda arm for their chosen candidates.

Their smear campaign against me never landed, but not long after, another opportunity for payback fell in their lap. The *New York Times* was working on a story about the work that the company I was exiting had been doing for Facebook and how, among other things, we had pitched a research document to a few reporters that laid out how George Soros and other left-wing donors were likely funding anti-Facebook front groups. The paper's original charge was, in my opinion, a bit overheated. I understand the sensitivity around any accusations that mention Soros, given the unconscionable anti-Semitic slander of which he is often a victim. But this research document was such a nothing-burger that I had never even seen it before the *Times* called, it had never amounted to anything public, and a year later, the *Times* reported that there was, in fact, a group of prominent liberal donors funding anti-Facebook efforts (for good reason, by the way!). Today, Soros's foundation is unapologetic about their work funding nonprofits whose aim is to break up Facebook and other big tech companies. But given the context of the time and the cause célèbre target, the controversy ballooned. As a result, the *Times* reported a follow-up story that went into greater detail about all our firm's activities, much of which was genuinely damning.

The key source the reporter talked to for that follow-up story was none other than Chuck Johnson, who was happy to burn me, thanks to his bitterness over my attacks on Roy Moore. He leaked everything about our past dealings and detailed how I had drafted articles on behalf of my clients for GotNews. When the story broke, my short-lived newfound respect in liberal environs was rightly revoked. At the time, I had a token contributorship to Crooked Media, home of *Pod Save America*, which was terminated, and everyone who had ever held a grudge against me spent a week gleefully tomahawk-dunking as I suffered the indignity of becoming Twitter's unfortunate main character.

As usual in an internet pile-on, some of these charges against me weren't exactly fair, but what I came to realize after a healthy stint in therapy was that in the grand scheme of things, that doesn't really matter. Overheated or not, the real question was, why the fuck was I still doing this shit at all? What value was I serving by trying to smoke out the enemies of Facebook? Why was I heading up a PR firm that was exacerbating the polarization in the country by doling out daily oppo drops that fed people's anger?

I began to stare at my own work through a different light. Not the PR kingpin and badass dark artist engaging in shrewd subterfuge. But the putz who was being used by some of the forces that contributed to the latest wave of white nationalism in America and the election of a truly evil man. I was favor-trading with people who were causing real-world harm so I could get a pat on the head from some client who wanted self-serving scuttlebutt fed to the rubes. To what end? Shouldn't I be doing something more productive and virtuous with my skills?

I was making all the same mistakes that had gotten me and the party in trouble in the first place. I was compartmentalizing my bad actions and only focusing on the positives. I was not acting with the integrity I was demanding of others. I wasn't taking the ramifications of my work seriously, but rather was cashing checks and acting as if it was all part of some big game devoid of real-world consequences.

From Pruitt to Facebook to pitching nonsense to Chuck Johnson, I was reactivating the muscle memory that got me back into the same old public relations patterns I was comfortable in. Identify a problem, work to solve it, and in the meantime, put the best possible face on it, truth be damned. Use whatever levers I have to get information out that makes my side look favorable and the other side look bad, even if it's skeevy or dishonest.

This is not just a Republican politics thing, by the way.

How many of the biggest, most corrupting scandals in recent memory have been, at their core, a tale of face-saving PR and rationalization? Police unions covering up for vigilante killings to protect their own. The film *The Social Dilemma* features tech executives coming to terms with the ways they've covered up how their products turn kids into attention zombies who require the endorphin rush that comes with every engagement.

During the Bush administration, the Republican National Committee put out "Iraq Facts" highlighting any positive tale they could tell from the roiling catastrophe they had unleashed. I was reminded of this watching the Biden administration attempt to spin their way out of the humanitarian nightmare in Afghanistan, talking only of those whom they ferried to a sweltering, shit-filled hangar in Qatar and deflecting questions about those being left to the whims of our barbaric foe.

All of these failures and countless others are based on the intrinsic human desire to justify and defend one's honor. To protect our tribesmen from outside threats. To judge ourselves by our "best intentions" and our opponents by their "worst examples," as former President Bush put it. We are hardwired to activate this survival instinct.

There's nothing inherently wrong with that or with the notion of "public relations."

The problems arise when it comes with no self-examination. No reflection about the underlying problems you are papering over. No willingness to walk away when the person or group you are defending becomes indefensible or in conflict with your own integrity. No questioning if any particular outcome is worthy of justifying the corruption, dishonesty, or insanity you have to wade through to reach it.

They arise when you convince yourself that since you, personally, don't harbor racial animus, it's okay to be in league with avowed racists who are stoking that hatred, because you are merely one player in a game, so complicity in their actions is not a professional red line that one must not cross.

A fellow Never Trumper, Ben Howe, wrote about how he reckoned with needing to change how he looked at his political work: "Some people just need a tap on the shoulder to change. Others need a slap in the face. Me? I've often needed a piano dropped on my head. The piano fell years ago, but I suppose I'm still crawling out from under the wreckage in some ways. I'm better than I've been. And I intend to be better than I am."

When Trump became president, the piano fell on the entire Republican establishment. Some of us crawled out from the wreckage and, in fits and starts, slowly dislodged ourselves from the corrupting game we'd been playing that got us there.

I'm sure many of my critics would argue that I'm still very much playing it, just for a different team. There might be something to that. Politics remains a competition, after all, so there is no path to total purity if you are a participant, only to an awareness of how you can be corrupted by the contest and a willingness to say no if lines are crossed.

If the people you are working alongside are not well intentioned.

If you can't defend those who you are paid to support with probity. If you don't describe them in public in a similar way you would in private. If you are providing cover for someone you know in your heart of hearts is probably kind of evil.

A lot of my former friends in Republican Washington still seem to be a long way from acting with this minimal level of awareness and intention.

• • •

There is one fun little postscript to this story of personal growth dotted with setbacks.

Tara Westover wrote that "vindication has no power over guilt." That is something that resonated with me while I was writing this. I don't know that I'll ever fully shake my guilt, but I have to admit that little vindications do bring me some pleasure.

Months after Trump had lost in 2020, I received a message from Chuck Johnson, that one-eyed wonder weasel I never should have talked to in the first place.

He wanted to reconnect.

"You were right about all things Trump," he sent via Signal. "My sincere apologies. I know it's late, but better late than never. Doing my part to pursue the various criminals as best I can. And spies."

Lol.

Who knows what his real angle was? I did what I should have done from day one: ignored him. It's too bad it took all those pianos falling on my head to get me there. But there is one thing about his note that I found particularly gratifying.

If even someone like Chuck, one of the sharts of humanity, eventually saw Trump for the malevolent con man that he is, what does that say about the rest who still excuse him?

9

The Enablers

As a gay man who contorted himself into defending homophobes and a Trump abhorrer who didn't hesitate when
asked to spin for a Trump lover, I am more than capable of inhabiting the mind of the enabler.

I have had more drinks where reluctant-MAGA and MAGA-
adjacent professional Republicans spilled their guts than I would
care to count. I've heard the lengthy laments from members of the
2 percent about how they've got bills to pay, a college fund to fill.
Regiments of the "privately concerned" have shared their worries,
as have the professionally depressed.

I've listened to men bemoan the fact that they can no longer
talk politics with their wives and feel judged by their friends. Been
shaken down by the guilt-ridden who wanted to see how they could
help our efforts to take down Trump behind the scenes but were
never quite willing to put their name on anything. Been filled with
assurances by insiders about how they are needed to keep things
on the rails because of all the horrible things I wouldn't believe
they'd prevented, but that they weren't at liberty to detail.

When you are a prominent Never Trumper and not a total

prick, you attract these types of conversations. Obviously, I'm not the person they pick up the phone to call when they've had a work success that made them proud. People tend to tell you what you want to hear if they have that option available. In moments of frustration or doubt, they would find me. They weren't all that dissimilar from the coming-out-of-the-closet convos I'd had over the years. People dealing with their internalized shame. However, in these instances there was one important difference: the realization that they brought the shame upon themselves.

These conversations became formalized late in the Trump term, once I began writing for *Rolling Stone* as a sort-of anthropologist to the Trumpists for the boomer Piketty set. My task was somewhat akin to a *National Geographic* adventure journalist who embedded themselves in a remote Amazonian rain forest to report back to the mainland about the culture of previously uncontacted tribes. Except the tribesmen were my former colleagues, and the readers shouldn't have required a middleman's lingua franca to understand their perspective, because they were unknowingly standing next to them in the Whole Foods checkout line the entire time.

Throughout these informal and professional exchanges, over time, I began to build a reservoir of understanding as to what was going on in the interior lives of the men and women who succumbed to the MAGA wiles. Their hopes and fears and loathings and animal desires.

They all had internalized what they thought were the lessons of the previous decade. The "political reality" meant that the crocs, commenters, and hobbits must be appeased and managed. A groupthink emerged whereby this "reality" came to be treated as if it were delivered from on high. And the Truth mustn't be reflected upon without the whole game being jeopardized.

When I dug deeper beneath this cozy conventional wisdom, what I found were real choices made by individuals who all fell back on a few phyla of rationalization that reveal why they did what they did.

The result? This binder full of complicity . . . if you will.

Some of the categories reflect universal, human failings replicated across industries and societies and ideologies. Others are unique to the creatures of the Washington swamp or the contaminated right-wing political ecosystem that sustained the Mango Monstrosity.

They all turned out to be much more powerful than I had anticipated.

I'd divide them into these buckets:

- Messiahs and Junior Messiahs
- Demonizers
- LOL Nothing Matters Republicans
- Tribalist Trolls
- Strivers
- Little Mixes
- Peter Principle Disprovers
- Nerd Revengers
- The Inert Team Players
- The Compartmentalizers
- Cartel Cashers

First among equals were those with the **Messiah Complex**. The Jesuses walking among us in their crowns of *Apprentice* thorns. The messiahs' self-regard was such that somehow the most grandiloquent leak during the presidency of the world's most bombastic individual did not actually flatter the narcissist-in-chief himself, but rather the self-appointed messiahs who went to work for a man whose manifest unfitness made them afraid and whose grotesque personality they detested.

In August of Trump's first year, *Axios*'s Jim VandeHei and Mike Allen announced the "Committee to Save America," a "loose alliance" of generals, cabinet officials, and high-level staff who took it upon themselves to protect the country from disaster. Among them were National Security Advisor H. R. McMaster, Secretary of Defense Jim Mattis, economic advisors Gary Cohn and Dina Powell, and John Kelly, the man who oversaw the implementation of the Muslim Ban from his perch running the Department of Homeland Security before being promoted to White House chief of staff. These self-appointed supermen and wonder women saw themselves mostly in terms of "bad decisions prevented" rather than successes, according to *Axios*.

You don't say.

The committee members felt that taking on this oh-so-altruistic act on behalf of America meant that they didn't have to publicly reckon with the moral compromise of working for someone like Trump. Somehow this justification persisted even after they no longer worked for him and were using their access to make it rain in the private sector. Convenient!

Not a single one of the brave warriors on the Committee to Save America endorsed the only person who could actually save America from Trump—his opponent in the 2020 election.

Despite this logical incongruence, it was the self-flattering messiahs who won the argument among Republicans in D.C. Their demand that "good people" do everything in their power to protect the country from the horrific realities of the president eventually extended not just to those in the national security apparatus but to midlevel political offices throughout town.

From their wake emerged their messianic junior partners who worked as Trump aides and Hill staffers and campaign flacks. They may not have convinced themselves they were saving the world exactly but were justified in the knowledge that if they did not take a glamorous White House job or continue working for a white-bread rational senator, the country would be saddled with someone far worse. Maybe even a white nationalist! Who's to say? (The fact that a white nationalist might be their replacement did not seem to strike many of the juniors as something that required reflection on the nature of their employment.)

These **Junior Messiahs** told themselves they were patriots, sacrificing on behalf of the American people, who deserved dedicated public servants like them. This belief was buttressed by the fact that they often had a point: the staffer who would replace them or the politician who would upend their boss in a primary *was* almost assuredly more terrible. In Trump's GOP, entropy was taking hold. From the cabinet to the Senate to the school board, the stodgy erudite men of yesteryear were being replaced by ambitious MAGA-fakers who were in turn being replaced by psychotic true believers, giving credence to the conceit that they used to comfort themselves anytime doubt crept in.

The **Demonizers** were the quickest to drink the Trumpian orangeade as a chaser to liberal tears. For some this was a dogmatic response to any signs of Democratic hostility to people of faith or the free market (or both, for those with the in-home Milton Friedman shrine). For others, it was cultural, a rejection of the liberal pieties that ground their gears, a discomfort with how fast the script around gender and race was changing. For still others it seemed more personal, emanating from a bitterness over the snooty know-it-allism of the liberals in their life.

Some clung to anger over the way the left and the media had treated decent Republicans over the years; they concluded that if Mitt Romney and John McCain were going to be tarred as sexist, racist warmongers, then they had no choice but to throw in with the real sexists and racists. Some, I assume, were good people with genuine deeply held policy disagreements reinforced by the various ways in which the Democratic Party has drifted left in the past three decades.

Whatever the underlying reason, these Demonizers have decided that the left, the media, the Lincoln Project, the big-tech oligarchs, the social justice warriors, the people who put *they/them* pronouns in their email signature, the parents who take their kids to drag queen story hour, the Black Lives Matter protesters, and the wokes who want to make stolen land acknowledgments at the start of meetings are all so evil that there is no need to even grapple with the log in their own eye. Trump was a human fuck-you to the bastards they thought were out to get them. Once you've decided that the other side are the baddies, everything else falls into place rather quickly.

Then you had the **LOL Nothing Matters Republicans**. This cadre gained steam over the years, especially among my former peers in the campaign set. It is a comforting ethos if you are professionally obligated to defend the indefensible day in and day out. Their arguments no longer needed to have merit or be consistent because, LOL, nothing matters. Right? The founder of the Trumpy right-wing website *The Federalist*, Ben Domenech is, I believe, the one who coined it. He said the LOLNMRs were "inherently fatalist," believing that the most "apocalyptic predictions about right and left are happening no matter what and that the lights will go down in the West." Now, from my vantage point, that's a rather ostentatious way of describing the standard-issue prep school manchild of privilege contrarian cynicism that has been memorialized in teen cinema for ages . . . but you get the point. The LOLNMRs had decided that if someone like Trump could win, then everything that everyone does in politics is meaningless. So they became nihilists. Some eventually took jobs working for Trump; others flipped from center-right normie game players to MAGAfied populist warriors in a flash; still others gave themselves a cocoon of protection working for the Mitch McConnells of the world, staying Trump adjacent so as to not have to challenge their newly developing worldview. But all of them avoided any of the hard questions of the era, wrapping themselves in the comfortably smug sense of self-satisfaction that comes with a lack of concern for consequences.

The professional **Tribalist Trolls** overlap in their tactics with the Nothing Matters crowd but are different in that they at least have an ethos. Whatever is good for their side is good. And whatever is bad for the other side is good. Simple as that. In the early social media era, I was attracted to this mindset, and for a time when the stakes seemed lower, I was even a member of their ranks. But during the Trump years, I became aghast as it spread like a virus to people's parents and friends and well . . . some days it feels like pretty much everyone? Or at least everyone who is part of the online political discourse.

If you want to know if you are a Tribalist Troll, ask yourself this—when something horrible happens in the news, does your mind impulsively hope someone from the other tribe is responsible? Nobody wants to admit that they do this. But social media has laid bare our darker angels, and we can now see in real time that a large swath of the participants in our civic dialogue have reduced themselves to the most base type of Tribalist. Veterans of the very online Washington wars have warped themselves to such a degree that every news item, every action, is not something that requires a real-world solution that mitigates the suffering, but is just the latest data point in our online forever war. Many people believe the bullshit they are being sold about their opponents to such a degree that there is an internet culture adage—Poe's law, which indicates that no matter how over-the-top your parody may be of your political opponent, some of your followers will believe it to be real because they've been so conditioned to hear the other side's awfulness. This insidious Weltanschauung has infected everything from sports message boards to recipe websites to online gaming, which are all now consumed by politicized power users who want to turn every corner of our society into their battlefield. This has created a reinforcing feedback loop up to the politicians and media personalities who are rewarded for constantly embiggening their troll game and expanding the remit outside the bounds of campaign politics. I've seen decent people become so warped by this imaginary battle that they began to appreciate Trump's skill at trolling it even if they were personally repulsed by him. Of all the categories of enablement, this might be the most pernicious and inexpiable.

Naturally, in Washington there are those who don't need complex ideological justifications for their actions because they are pure old-fashioned **Strivers**. Some, especially the politicians, are motivated by a blind ambition that is just frankly not that interesting. The fact that pols want to attain higher office so they contort themselves to the whims of the crowd is not a new or unique phenomenon, nor does it merit much deep examination. It's the first subcategory to the world's oldest profession. But there's a uniquely Washington class of Striver that was drawn to Trump like moths to an orange flame. This species doesn't necessarily want to move up the career ladder for ambition's sake, but instead, they crave merely the possibility of being "in the mix."

Every Striver city has a drug that best suits its residents. In New York it's money . . . and coke. In Los Angeles it's fame . . . and coke. In Silicon Valley it's the chance to be a revered disruptor, changer of worlds . . . and microdosing. In D.C. the drug of choice is a little more down-market. All political staffers really want is to be *in the mix*. It's not even the power itself that they crave. That would be less pathetic, frankly. It's the proximity to power. For these **Little Mixes**, it's the ability to tell your friends back home that you were "in the room where it happened." (If it's possible for an entire body to cringe while typing, that's what mine did when I wrote "in the room where it happened.")

Lindsey Graham is the prototypical example of this animal. More than anything, he just wanted to be on the golf cart next to Trump. To be able to pass along a message. To be on the right hand of the father. Whether or not Trump did as Graham asked was merely icing on the cake. He could be denied for months on end to no effect, but if once, just once, he was able to say to his dinner mate that he talked the president into or out of doing something, his heart was made full. He was officially in the mix and no one could take that from him. Washington is full of Little Mixes who don't get anywhere near the president's golf cart but are nonetheless omnipresent, sitting in a conference room with Sarah Sanders or being in the back row of a meeting with a cabinet official or staffing a principal in a television greenroom that also contained "the Mooch" or Gloria Borger or some other minor celebrity. Through this access, they get the thrill up their leg that comes with having a story they can share when they go back home over Thanksgiving, about the private moment they saw or heard that makes them feel important. It turns out that's all they need in life, and it doesn't matter who the source of power is.

Another Striver subcategory was unique to the Trump orbit: the **Peter Principle Disprover**. For the uninitiated, the Peter Principle is the business management concept that people in a hierarchy rise to their maximum level of incompetence. In practice, it means a person will be promoted up and until the point where a new skill is required that they do not have. An example is the engineer who becomes a suit and fails because they have to manage relationships and payroll when all they are actually good at is maximizing widget output. Trump's administration was filled with ambitious Strivers who were punching way, way, way, way, way, way above their weight. People who were promoted three or nine or eleventy million rungs higher than their maximum level of incompetence.

These hacks and maroons would have been nowhere near the Oval Office in any other administration, so they were not going to miss their opportunity to experience the heights of American power and governance just because a malignant ass pimple was behind the Resolute Desk. To understand just how far beyond the Peter Principle the Trump White House had gotten: a man whose previous job was working as a golf caddy was empowered to create international incidents without any management oversight. The White House's "external relations" director was a twenty-year-old Instagram influencer named Camryn Kinsey, who said in an interview, "Only in Trump's America could I go from working in a gym to working in the White House." Hard to argue with that, Camryn! Camryn and the caddy mirrored the quality of staff throughout much of the federal bureaucracy, with scores of other enterprising back-row kids taking jobs just because they were not throwin' away their shot.

The view into the mind of these dolts was captured by Stephanie Grisham, who "served" as Trump's third press secretary, if you can call her that, given that she never actually held a press briefing. In a jarringly candid interview with *New York* magazine's Olivia Nuzzi, during which she acknowledged being part of something "unusually evil," Grisham said, "My lack of confidence in myself as a single mother and someone who has made mistakes in my past, I thought, well, this is my only shot. Nobody's gonna ever want me, really, but these people did." Grisham's sense of inadequacy was compounded by bitterness toward those who were saying all the things she knew were true about herself and her boss. "You have this sick sense of pride," she says. "All the people who told you how terrible he was? You're like, Oh? He's the [president], buddy!"

The White House was littered with other disprovers who

shared Grisham's combination of ineptitude, imposter syndrome, self-loathing, and bitterness toward their critics but who haven't acquired the distance from the exhilarating madness to see it clearly.

The PP Disprover had a marginally more capable counterpart: the **Nerd Revenger.** You can't really understand Washington without familiarizing yourself with this prototype. The entire city is made up of sociable wannabes who aspired to sit at the cool kids' table in high school but were too awkward or unlikable to get the invite. When they got to D.C., things changed. All the time spent obsessing over political redistricting as a teen because their lack of social aptitude left few options for getting laid was finally rewarded. They got to spend their twenties and thirties reaching the pinnacle of influence in Hollywood for Average-Looking People. (N.B.: we upgraded from the old moniker of Hollywood for Ugly People during the Obama years.) Now the Revengers got invited to nerd prom parties, flirted with by moderately attractive strangers, and recognized on the street by interns and tourists. They landed jobs that seemed more interesting than those held by the classmates they had been jealous of and now their younger selves' dorky little dream was becoming reality. When these poindexters got the opportunity to secure positions in Trump's Washington that would yield even more invites, more acclaim (within certain circles), and better content for Instagram, some of them jumped at the chance. It was one big "look at me now" to everyone who had negged them in the lunchroom of life.

Then there were the **Inert Team Players**, who lacked the imagination to conjure what else they could do with their lives. Company men and women couldn't fathom another option besides taking the next step up the political ladder. Many are so wrapped up in their identity as a Republican that the idea of being anything besides that is inconceivable. They had been college Republicans and they go to Republican bars, they have Republican LinkedIn handles, and, hell, some even have Republican tattoos. I know *multiple* people in GOP politics who named their daughters Reagan. For many people in Washington, their party is more a part of their identity than their ethnicity, religion, or personal history. It's how they see themselves and how everyone in their social network defines them. Shedding an ingrained identity that others use to define you takes courage, even if that identity is toxic and self-destructive. All of this makes the bar for removing "Republican operative" from a person's identity pretty hard.

Throw on top of that the fact that Republican politics is how they made a living and they still opposed tax hikes and abortion and you can see why people were reluctant to cut bait.

If they were going to envision a new identity for themselves, they needed a Larry Craig tapping his foot in the bathroom moment. Something that let them see it was the current path they should fear, not the fresh one. Most were in too deep and their thinking was too rigid to recognize that their escape hatch was through Trump's wide stance.

Instead, these Team Players kept their day jobs, but unlike the Strivers, their distaste for the president resulted in receding a bit from the social scene. Scaling back their ambitions. Over time, the sharpness of the moral sacrifice dulls. They consider themselves one of the "good Republicans." And as the years go by, they become increasingly less and less likely to make a dramatic identity-altering gesture. Then, one day, they are editing a press release that expresses concerns about the electoral count in Pennsylvania and wondering what the hell they are doing with their life.

But they still had kids and mortgages and would end up reverting to what they know, like a midlevel oilman who trudges back into the office the day after a spill. What else am I supposed to do, they would ask me? (I would proceed to make a series of suggestions that were rebuffed.)

The **Compartmentalizers** were the Inerts' more anxiety-riddled peers. As the onetime Compartmentalizer-in-chief, I can grok these folks' motives the most clearly. Many of them agonized over sticking around. They would tuck bad Trump thoughts in a box in the corner of their brain somewhere and go on with their duties, clocking in and clocking out as required. Work that had once enlivened them had become a miserable chore, with sporadic bouts of gratification. They cut back on news consumption, trying to mentally check out as much as possible. Some picked up new passions away from work; for others the new passion was an alarming increase in their intake of wine, an old passion. Anything to keep the moral quandary of providing aid, however indirectly, to Trump from emerging from their hippocampus. Every other month or so the bad thoughts would spring from the dark recesses of their brain. "Very fine people on both sides." *Bang.* "Helsinki." *Bang.* "Send them back." *Bang.* And each time their self-loathing would eke out for a day or a week before it got sent back to the lockbox, and they reverted to their old habits.

Finally, I would be remiss to ignore the most common and obvious motivator for this or any ethically dubious endeavor: money. One big misconception about Washington is that money is the straw that stirs the drink. Activist types always demand we look to the money! Sometimes they are right, but the driving motivator for most during the Trump era was not a desire for riches. This town is not filled with Gordon Gekkos. More often, it's the other, more egocentric motivators that drive nefarious actions in D.C. Raising money remains important, but fundraising is really about status and power. Yet there were a handful of entrepreneurial Republicans whom most people have never heard of who did enrich themselves beyond their wildest imaginations during the Trump years. These **Cartel Cashers** now spend time designing their Caribbean compounds while the slightly less successful among them are merely making modest additions to their Bethany Beach, Delaware, home away from home. The Trump years were good for the greedy and the grifty, no matter how much swamp draining he claimed to undertake.

• • •

Most people don't fit neatly into a single category. Some had a little from column A and a little from column C. There was a jumble of rationalization blended in with their best intentions and their shadow wants. But you know a type when you see it.

Consider Chris Christie: a Little Mix and Team Player and Junior Messiah all wrapped up in Costco Club packaging. Christie is a Churchill in his own mind but was turned by Trump into a sniveling church mouse.

For years Trump demeaned and diminished Christie at every turn. He threw away the transition plan he wrote after the election, passed him over for jobs, and made him into the family's personal gimp, to be summoned from his shackles on command.

You might think that someone with Christie's ego would eventually have walked away from this type of torment. But no. Ever the glutton for being in the mix, he kept coming back for more.

Toward the end of the 2020 campaign, at the height of the COVID-19 pandemic, Trump unshackled him one more time, demanding he play the role of Biden in the president's debate prep. Months later it was revealed that the president had tested positive for COVID before these sessions began, but kept it a secret, holding Christie captive in close quarters for days, brazenly spittling diseased airborne droplets all over him.

Soon after, the sub contracted his dom's virus and spent a few harrowing days in the intensive care unit, where he genuinely feared he might die. When Trump called Christie in the hospital, as he lay on death's door, Trump's only concern was whether the little mouse would have the courage to publicly blame the sickness on him before election day or would keep running cover for his master.

The depraved indifference! The collaring! How does a man accept such despicable treatment and maintain even a modicum of self-respect?

Unlike the millions of others who were not so lucky, Christie managed to come out the other side. But that doesn't change the fact that Donald Trump nearly killed him with the same abject, megalomaniacal recklessness he had subjected upon the entire country with his management of the pandemic. The president was so hell-bent on minimizing the threat of COVID-19 and demonstrating his imagined ubermensch virility that he put Christie and the hundreds of others he encountered while contagious at risk.

And yet when Christie returned from the hospital, rather than stand up for himself, rather than get angry, he waddled right back into the clutches of his patient zero, supporting his reelection campaign.

At the time of this writing he continues to maintain that he has not ruled out going back into the breach for Trump one more time should the latter run for president again in 2024.

That shows you how powerful the complexes that afflict these enablers are. They persist even in the face of a near-miss visit to St. Peter at the Pearly Gates.

Christie's particular motivations, and those of my other former colleagues who knew better, might be somewhat different, but all roads led to the same Trumpian hell.

10

The Little Mix

A classic midwestern pleaser, Reince Priebus rose through the ranks of the Republican Party with a skill for making everyone from the tricornered-hat-donning Tea Party loony to the Brooks Brothers–clad, deep-pocketed donor feel like he was going to do what *they* thought was best.

From the cradle, Priebus was a natural networker. In high school, he dressed like Alex P. Keaton and sauntered into school, briefcase in tow, peacocking for his teachers. As a young striver he worked to impress the other Badger State up-and-comers like Paul Ryan, who would come in handy down the line. At law school in Miami, he was such a presence on campus that as a second-year he managed to receive 4 percent of the vote in their 1996 presidential straw poll, finishing just a hair behind the actual GOP nominee that year, Bob Dole. (Whether Priebus lobbied for these write-in votes or was just the beneficiary of a grassroots campaign of obstreperous campus Republicans remains a mystery.)

After law school, Priebus returned home, where he took on clients at a law firm for his day job while volunteering in politics as a side hustle. He made his bones, and the contacts that would serve

him in the future, as chairman of the 1st Congressional District
GOP, a seat held at the time by Ryan. He then tried his hand at becoming a candidate himself in a failed campaign against an incum-
bent Democratic state senator. After that flopped, he refocused on
the things he was good at: glad-handing, organizing, and kissing
up to other influencers, resulting in his election as chairman of
the Wisconsin Republican Party, the youngest in the party's history.

Now, being a state party chairman can be important as far as
local politics go, but generally it isn't a stepping-stone to national
fame. Climbing the greasy pole from Madison to the penthouse of
the national Republican Party was not an easy task. The RNC top
job is generally acquired in two ways, and very few who attempt
Priebus's approach pull it off. The first is being appointed top-
down by elites in Washington, D.C. These chairmen usually have
the job bestowed on them by a president who wants an ally at the
party. The other path is bottom-up from the states. These chairmen succeed by buttering up enough committee members to fill a
void when a party is out of power.

Priebus did the latter, networking with grassroots leaders in
other states, which he first leveraged to help Michael Steele in his
successful campaign to be the party's first black chairman in 2009,
selling an inclusive vision for the GOP. Priebus went on to serve as
Steele's consigliere and general counsel, before turning on him
and running for the office himself.

The chairmanship was a job that suited his skill set and his high
key desire to be loved by all. He was naturally adroit when it came
to keeping the elites happy but was able to pair that with a keen
awareness of how to manage the rank and file. He had an ear for
complaints that would come from the Breitbart crowd and would
make sure to take in feedback from the local Wisconsin officials
who were more in touch with "the people."

When I was prepping Reince for any event that would have a

GOP audience—a TV hit on *Hannity* or a speech at the Conservative Political Action Conference (CPAC)—he would zero in on what
he could say that would rile up the base, always hoping to find a
zinger that would tingle the erogenous zones of the party loyalists.
So, he had experience dipping his toe in the water when it came
to many of the controversial and conspiratorial issues that Trump
would take head-on. The question was always whether this was a
necessary part of achieving his political ends or if he was just living
for the applause.

I remember an early sign of the troubles ahead during my
time at the committee when Reince embroiled us in a minor ker-
fuffle amid the Scott Walker recall election. During a local radio
interview he had this to say when it came to the possibility of "voter
fraud" in his home state: "I'm always concerned about voter fraud,
you know, being from Kenosha, and quite frankly having lived
through seeing some of it happen." He added that Republicans
"need to do a point or two better" in Wisconsin because they have
to overcome it.

A point or two better? This was obvious nonsense and not anything the comms team had prepped him with, but he was adamant
that the line was a winner. Some of us tried to push back and at
least direct him to be more specific in his criticisms of the election
management, but he'd roll his eyes, then tell us we didn't know
what he knew about Wisconsin and that putting the pressure on
the local Democratic officials was part of the job. It was his way
of both working the refs and telling the rank-and-file what they
wanted to hear to earn their trust and their praise.

That trust paid off when the autopsy turned out to appeal less
to base desires and more to the entrenched establishment that
would decide the fate of Priebus's chairmanship. And as far as
Reince's career was concerned—the process worked perfectly. He
was reelected without a challenge despite the party's failures at the

ballot box that year. He solidified his position in 2014 on the heels of a successful GOP midterm and charged into the 2016 presidential cycle confident that the GOP could win the White House and he would be crowned for the changes he had implemented in the Growth and Opportunity Project.

Then along came Donald Trump.

One might have thought that someone as screwy as Trump would challenge Priebus's ability (or desire) to juggle the competing interests within the party. Too anti-establishment, too contrary to the recommendations that had been put forth, frankly, too Hollywood for a kid from Kenosha. Maybe he'd go back home and run for office in Paul Ryan's footsteps. Or go get the big payout awaiting a former party chair on K Street. The opposite was true. In Trump's rise, Priebus saw even greater opportunity to insert himself into the middle of the mix. During the primary, as party elites' consternation grew over the possibility Trump might lose and then sandbag them by running as an Independent, Priebus worked his future boss over and convinced him to declare an elephant blood oath during a television extravaganza that Priebus schlepped to *Apprentice* HQ for.

As a result, Trump and Priebus had all eyes on them when the candidate signed an "official document" promising that he would support the Republican Party nominee even if it were not him. This led to a different type of consternation for Reince to manage— from mouthy staffers like yours truly who wondered why he was a) giving this type of credibility to a bigoted dotard, b) trusting that a world-renowned contractor-stiffing, contract-breaking scam artist would honor some phony-baloney ad hoc pledge, and c) not providing the same white-glove, VIP treatment to the other candidates.

Months after the press conference, following some public criticism I leveled at Reince on these counts, he called late one evening, exasperated, to explain himself. He tried to push the blame onto

senior staffers from the various campaigns, including purportedly some of my colleagues who he claimed had asked him to get
Trump to sign the oath.

Is that true? Maybe! Campaigns are unwieldy. It's certainly possible that some in Jeb's orbit disagreed with my assessment that it
was maddening and absurd that a party chairman would get on a
train to lick the boot of the most dangerous presidential candidate
on the roster rather than do what he could to isolate him. They may
have considered this nonbinding piece of paper important protection against Trump playing the spoiler to the coming Jebessaince
and shared that view with the chairman. Who the hell knows? At
this point it's all academic.

What is telling is that Reince was so committed to herding all of
these unherdable cats and ensuring they all were pleased with his
gentle crook that long after the deed was done, he was still desperately trying to win me over on this point rather than doing bedtime
with the kids or watching reruns of *Everybody Loves Raymond* or
tending to his fish or whatever else he did after dark on a school
night. He couldn't let one ball go by. He needed to have everyone
on board. And despite having the most polarizing presidential candidate in history on his hands, for a while he managed to do it.

The next spring, at the very moment when it was clear that
concerns about Trump tanking the GOP had been warranted not
because he was going to run as a third-party spoiler, but because he
would be the standard-bearer, I bumped into Reince at a douchey,
decadent RNC donor soiree inside a South Beach hotel in Miami.
The event followed the final presidential debate before the Florida
primary. That evening a flagging Marco Rubio, the GOP mainstream's last best hope, passed on his final chance to take Trump
head-on, choosing instead to pliantly present himself to the Donald, officially marking the establishment's final whimper before
full MAGA penetration.

That night, horrified and panicked over the Trump nomination that was beginning to look like an inevitability, I walked up to Reince at the makeshift bar, leaned in, and whispered that I needed to talk to him in private. We retreated into an exterior hallway, far enough from the slurring bleached-blonde cougars and their frumpy husbands to ensure nobody would overhear. Sitting at a high-top table, I made a last-ditch pitch for him to walk away from his chairmanship.

Now, I was, I will admit, a tad overserved and vulnerable in this moment, so it's possible he didn't take me as seriously as he might have in another circumstance. But I was deadly serious. I looked him square in the eye and told him that as a friend, I thought that this was his opportunity to get out and let Trump put his own people at the committee so that he would avoid being tarnished by the unknown horrors to come.

He replied at first with nervous laughter and conflict avoidance, as was his style. "Oh, come on, pal." But I became increasingly severe, reiterating several times that my counsel was for his own good, that he would regret staying the rest of his life, and that I was trying to look out for him.

Ever the apple polisher, he recognized what I wanted from him and began to change his tone. He patted my shoulder, told me he appreciated the concern and would give it some thought, but the reality was he wasn't going to quit. He thought it was too important that good people be at the helm if things went awry. There needed to be a "reasonable guy" at the table.

It was the exact same argument he had made to me three years earlier, in a different context. At the end of the autopsy process, just before I was going to announce my departure and the formation of America Rising, Reince had summoned me to his office. I sat across from him, next to the infamous "empty chair" from Clint Eastwood's Republican National Convention speech, and he pitched me on staying at the RNC. He was ready to move on from Spicer, who was communications director at the time, and wanted to groom me to take his job.

It was a flattering offer, but I had my mind set against it. For starters, I wanted to build something new and was excited about the entrepreneurial opportunity before me with America Rising. But more than that, I had decided that I didn't want to be at the Republican National Committee when the Supreme Court ruling on gay marriage came down. I had been at the RNC the day that then-president Obama announced he had "evolved" on the matter. I desperately wanted to slough off my work duties and go revel in victory with my gays. Our moment had arrived! Instead, I had to participate in discussions about how the RNC would "message" Obama's flip-flop. After a few hours of pain, with the cringey statement about how Obama was "playing politics" drafted, I snuck out of the office and sat alone in the back corner of a Capitol Hill bar drinking a Captain Crunch–flavored comfort shake.

When I explained this to Reince, he was surprised by how deeply I felt about it all. After mulling over my perspective for a moment, he made a contrarian pitch in trying to persuade me to reconsider. He thought it would be *better* for me to be at the RNC when SCOTUS decreed that I could marry the person I loved. That the party's messaging would improve if I, as an openly gay man, were involved. He felt he had credibility on this point since he had fully supported me coming on board despite complaints from some committee members about my preference for peen. In other words, he thought that I might be the "reasonable gay at the table."

I declined because I knew there was a limit to the impact I could have on the party's posture, and that limit was above my threshold for pain. That evening in Miami, Reince made the opposite bet.

His tolerance for pain was high. He cared more about being in the room and nudging things in the right direction than he did being tarnished by the sleaze. He was betting on his own ability to make friends and influence people. An ability that had served him so well it improbably led him to the chairmanship of the entire Republican Party. On this point he was so irrationally exuberant that I honestly believe that he even convinced himself that Reince Priebus of Kenosha, Wisconsin, could be the one voice that made Donald J. Trump something he wasn't, however implausible that sounded to the rest of us.

It was a sucker's wager, but I couldn't convince him otherwise.

Before we parted, he did make one promise. He said that if things "went too far," if they got as bad as I said they would—he would take a stand to protect the party, just as he had when the RNC dumped Missouri senate candidate Todd Akin after he waxed on a few years earlier about how the body has a way of taking care of things if a woman suffers a "legitimate rape."

I told him that was never going to happen. That this was his one opportunity to get out with a clean slate. It would have been natural to let an outsider nominee choose his own chairman. He could have decamped to Wisconsin with minimal brushback and been an outside "advisor" to the committee. Went on with his life. But if he was going to do it, he would have to do it then. Once inside the bunker it would be too deep to pitch out of. He would feel compelled to ride the Trump Train into the abyss.

On the midnight ride he went.

A few months later, after Trump encouraged rally-goers to punch protesters and offered to cover their legal expenses, after he refused to disavow former Ku Klux Klan grandmaster David Duke, after he tarred Heidi Cruz as ugly, after he made the explicitly racist claim that a judge couldn't do his job because of his Mexican heritage, after he slandered Gold Star parents, Reince Priebus was still in the job, herding cats, waiting for the moment just over the horizon when things would go too far.

This was on display when Reince had lunch late in the campaign with a mutual friend, who subsequently told me all about it. They were sitting at Talay Thai, a midmarket mom-and-pop joint on Capitol Hill in D.C. that sat between the RNC and Subway, and the chairman was miserable, but knew he no longer had the option to quit.

After all, he was the key man, the reasonable guy at the table. The party needed people like him. If he left, everything would go to shit. Still, he wished he didn't have to carry this burden.

In TV interviews, he was denying that this was the case. He told CNN's Jamie Gangel that he was "having fun" and wasn't "pouring Baileys in my cereal," a weird line that only made people wonder if he was in fact doing that. Stephen Colbert noted this was "a very specific reference for something you are not doing."

At Talay Thai, the chairman's curry was Baileys-free, but he was very much not having fun. There he revealed that he was privately as tormented as everyone suspected, confiding that he was so miserable juggling all the Trump nonsense that he was praying he would have a heart attack. My friend gave an awkward laugh and tried to determine where on the continuum this fell between a joke and a confession when Reince expanded on the point, showing that he had played this cardiac fantasy out in his mind and was already a few moves down the board. He said that he hoped the heart attack would be just serious enough to allow him to quit his job without seeming like a traitor to the cause but also just mild enough so he wouldn't have any long-term health effects and could continue being involved in politics. He still had young kids, after all.

The myocardial infarction of his dreams never came. Reince soldiered on. But the opportunity to live up to the promise he made me did present itself one last time.

A few weeks after that lunch, the infamous "Grab Them by the Pussy" *Access Hollywood* tape was leaked. Back at Trump Tower, the nominee's high command held a meeting to discuss the path forward. There, Priebus told Trump that he could either "drop out right now or lose by the biggest landslide in American political history," a pitch not that dissimilar from the one I had presented to Reince in South Beach.

Or, at least, that's what the newspapers *said* that he said.

The quote always rang a little false with me. Reince was never that direct in his criticism of someone. He got his point across in different ways to stay in everyone's good graces. Gentle shepherd's crook, remember.

As it turns out, my gut was right, and the leaks missed a key part of the exchange. Reince didn't volunteer that *he* thought Trump should drop out. Quite the contrary, he didn't think it was legally possible for the nominee to be replaced at that late date and had come to terms with the fact that they were stuck together come hell or high water.

Here's what actually happened. Reince gave that threatening answer in response to a question that Trump, ever the narcissist, asked of him often. "What are people saying about me?" And so, in his most storied moment of defiance, it turns out Reince was merely reporting what he was hearing, what the swampy chattering class was saying. He was still in the mix!

Reince knew Trump wasn't getting out; he just hoped this troubling report from the gossip mill might help nudge his future boss toward better behavior and get him to take seriously the peril his campaign was in. Meanwhile, across the room, the suck-up son-in-law and "Sloppy Steve" Satan on Trump's shoulder were assuring him all was well and plotting to "change the narrative" by escorting his opponent's husband's former mistresses to the next debate as a distraction.

That was a plan Trump could get behind. He pressed forward with Bannon's forty minutes of hell approach and ignored the midwestern schoolmarm who wanted him to spend the final few weeks acting more prim and proper.

No stand was taken. No landslide occurred.

Trump grabbed Reince by the pussy, Charon's ferry glided on, and the chairman's acquiescence was rewarded.

After Trump won he needed to keep a guy like Reince around, someone who was in the middle of everything, who could tell him what people in town were saying about him. Reince once again convinced himself that a reasonable guy was needed to protect not just the party but now the country from worse options.

On inauguration day, while former president George W. Bush looked on, flabbergasted by the "weird shit" that had taken place, back in Kenosha a group of Priebus's friends and family gathered at a local watering hole dressed in GOP red.

Underneath the big screen that aired Trump's American Carnage address was a blue placard with yellow writing that said "Hail to the Chief (of staff) Reince Priebus."

The kid had done it. He had brownnosed his way to the top. The Young Republican who carried a briefcase to class, the guy with the weird name nobody could pronounce, the man who orchestrated back-to-back-to-back-to-back successful national party chairmanship races, got his payoff.

He got the most in-the-mix job in all the world, in service to a country he loved. Just as he had always wanted.

I sent him a note with the subject line "Congrats—Praying for You." The body of the message was a continuation of the advice he had long since rejected. "The most important thing you will have to say going forward is, 'no.' Be strong."

He thanked me. And that was that. When we reconnected, long after he'd left the White House, he claimed that he had done what I had asked. He dubbed himself "Mr. No" and prevented untold horrors from being visited on our land. He makes a similar pitch to others anytime he is outside MAGA-friendly environs. Leaks from the paid speaking circuit reveal that Reince would play to the audience and flatter himself by cryptically promising that for all the crazy stuff we saw in the news, behind the scenes there was fifty times that amount of craziness that we didn't see. He's echoed a similar line when speaking privately to mutual Never Trumper friends.

Fifty times worse than we knew but not worth doing anything about. It's an interesting pitch.

In the days after January 6th, he told one of the friends who were pressing him to come forward that it would make no difference. Nobody cares what little old Reince thinks. He sent a single tweet that morning criticizing those who attacked the Capitol but said nothing about the man who sent them there. Doing so, he reasoned, would be pointless. It wouldn't have stopped anything and if he did walk away, he would lose his influence within the party, given that Trump may very well run again. And if he does, Reince is surely planning to be sitting shotgun.

All of that is hard to square, obviously.

How can a person be utterly inconsequential in speaking out against Trump, while undeniably essential in convincing him to behave better?

How can what happened behind the scenes have been exponentially worse than the horrific reality we all saw, and yet the crazed maniac should regain power?

For Reince these are not circles that require squaring. They are separate but equal arguments that are to be deployed when convenient to serve the arguer's ultimate end. When he thinks his audience wants to hear that he was one of the messiahs who protected the country from Trump's excesses, he presents himself as one. When he needs to be a loyal soldier to stay in the mix, he salutes.

Donald Trump's errand boy, Chris Christie, has enough self-awareness to explain the compulsions of this mindset better than

Reince ever could. In an interview with *The Dispatch*, aimed at re-
suscitating his political career, the Republicans' Reek relayed a
piece of advice that he had given to a fellow governor who was
approaching the end of their term.

> I said to him, "Look, one of the things you need to know is,
> the music stops. Like you watch your [successor] get sworn in,
> the troopers take you back to your house, you wake up the next
> morning, and they're gone. And the cameras are gone. And the
> phone calls stop, and the music stops. And you got to figure out
> that okay, what do I substitute in for that?"

To understand what it is that motivates the Little Mixes you
must understand what "that" is.

"That" thing he was missing wasn't his ability to serve constituents. It wasn't the desire to pass True Conservative policies. "That"
thing Christie and Priebus so desperately needed was their little fix.
Getting calls. Feeling important. Remaining relevant. Being In The
Mix. Once you've already determined that "that" is the objective,
the justifications only need to match the desired outcome. And so
Little Mixes like Christie and Priebus find themselves wrapped in
a pretzel of their own rationalizations.

Reince may have perceived himself as "Mr. No," and I'm sure
he said "no" from time to time, but the truth is he was never going to be a "No Man." A real "no" man would have had the self-
assuredness that comes from being comfortable knowing that
every rejection of the tyrant's demands might be his last. That isn't
Reince. He desired too deeply to be in the middle of it all. He had
stumbled improbably into a job that let him have everything he had
ever dreamed if only he could manage one little problem: a boss
who was both the leader of the free world and certifiably insane.

I don't know anyone who thought that was a task he was up for, except Reince himself. Even his friends who pushed him into the job knew it was a fool's errand but figured it was better him than Bannon, or worse. But Reince thought he could handle it, at least for a while.

He had flattered and managed and coaxed crazy egomaniacs to political ends for his whole life. He had sucked his way up to the top. He had worked everyone over, including me.

It turned out that assurance he gave me in South Beach was just one little twerk in his ever-evolving Little Mix dance. Reince was trying to stay in everyone's good graces while the world around him unraveled. He merely told me what I wanted to hear, because he told most everyone what they wanted to hear; it's what had gotten him into the big chair.

A mere fourteen months after we sat at the Miami high-top table, Reince Priebus's bill came due, his promise to me unfulfilled.

The Chief (of staff) was sitting in a black SUV on an airport tarmac, thinking he was about to join a presidential motorcade, when he was dismissed by the president via tweet. He had been on the phone with Trump three minutes prior to the digital pink slip. They had been planning a golf outing at his Bedminster, New Jersey, club where the two would discuss when Priebus might move on to his next job.

Trump hadn't given him any warning the tweet was coming.

He was in the mix until the end.

11

The Nerd-Revenging
Team Player

Attending Connecticut College, a liberal, liberal arts school on the Atlantic coast, Sean Spicer wasn't exactly the most popular guy on campus. His freshman-year roommate, Dave Bry, recalled that he was not well liked but also not hated. He tried to be pleasant and befriend his classmates but just "wasn't so good at it."

"He would walk into the room, and everyone would kind of go: 'Ugh, Spicer.'"

This interpersonal disfavor didn't hinder the young man's campus political aspirations. Spicer campaigned for class president each of his four years running as an unapologetic Republican and never won. During one of those campaign clunkers, the *College Voice*, the school paper, summed up his reputation with a sobriquet snafu. The paper referred to its subject as "Sean Sphincter" in print, a staff in-joke for the perennial loser that they hadn't intended to publish but which slipped through the cracks.

Spicer presumed it was an intentional slight by the Campus Fake News. The paper insisted it was a private gibe gone awry.

Based on the one weekend I spent with a friend on the New London campus, Occam's razor would indicate that the *Voice*'s editor probably took a few too many rips on the old bong before the copy went to print.

Spicer did not accept their explanation, writing a scathing letter to the editor in response, claiming that such a smear went "beyond the bounds of free speech." He wanted accountability. An apology. For someone to be canceled.

He got none of it.

Instead, the nickname just spread like wildfire across campus, giving the glad-hander no choice but to accept it. While the widespread admiration he tried to attract at school never materialized, Sphincter figured out other ways to be seen. From the jump, he knew that he was a Republican and knew he needed to find a crew, so he picked two and dove in.

He joined the sailing team and Bry recalled Spicer talking about "how that kind of provided this automatic little social circle for him because all the sailors had to get up really early to go to practice." Spicer would end up captaining the team his senior year and taking on the role of de facto player-coach for a group that performed better than anticipated, a point of pride. A New England Bill Russell in miniature. In addition to the core group of seamen, he also linked up with the College Republicans, continuing a passion that he had cultivated by volunteering for GOP campaigns as a teen in Rhode Island.

For some of us, our college selves are a youthful departure from the people we grow to become, but for Spicer, this social dynamic neatly reflected his adult life. He transitioned from the collegiate sailing posse into a more serious Navy Reserve unit where he'd earn the rank of commander. He continued climbing the elephant trunk as a try-hard political communications staffer who craved attention from the new cool kids on campus—the media types who

covered the politicians he worked for and other members of the
D.C. glitterati.

These attempts to rub elbows with fame didn't always work for
him. Spicer wasn't above being left standing outside in the rain at
a White House Correspondents' Association party hoping to befriend, assuage, or guilt-trip the gatekeepers. As a result, many of
those he was buttering up in the more celebrated D.C. in-group
often found themselves echoing, "Ugh, Spicer."

But he tried his damnedest and was always able to fall back on
the establishment GOP clique that he had entrenched himself in
from the beginning of his career. For his first decade or so in town,
Spicer hadn't exactly been on the fast track in political communications circles, but he was lumbering along making a life for himself.
For years he was a loyal functionary, a man in decent standing,
holding relatively important midlevel jobs. On the social circuit, he
was a running partner for the guy who threw the signature Republican Christmas Party, which always featured as a special guest the
type of D-list celeb that Spicer would himself eventually become.
(Full disclosure: One year the guest was Dennis Haskins, or as you
probably know him, Mr. Belding from *Saved by the Bell*. Belding and
I chatted it up and subsequently I rented him for an arm-wrestling
contest against my BFF during his LA bachelor party. Belding to
this day believes I stiffed him for that engagement; I'm certain that
I paid the agreed-upon amount. Now that a few years have passed
and my stubbornness and costly online poker habit have abated,
I feel bad about the misunderstanding. So if one of Belding's pals
is out there reading this, please let him know I would like to make
him whole.)

Spicer leveraged relationships he built while working the holiday happy-hour circuit and after years of trying to force his way
into this established club, in 2011, on the cusp of his fortieth birthday, he earned the title that finally made him bona fide: RNC

Communications Director. It was a surprise selection, but the chief of staff at the time was impressed by how eager Spicer was for the role and the amount of work and dedication he indicated he'd put into it.

It was in this spot that Spicer finally got to become the man he always thought he should be. At long last he would be the one whom other aspiring party functionaries needed to befriend if they wanted a seat at his table, rather than the other way around. It was a role reversal from which he derived great pleasure. To his credit, he did his best to bring along the other not-so-cool kids, throwing contracts and odd jobs to people from his past who hadn't been as successful at working the inside game. He empathized with their hardship.

He also knew how to leverage the role to draw in the beau monde, whose attention he had long craved. During the autopsy, while the rest of the crew focused on the policy or the party-building brass tacks, Spicer volunteered himself to handle the debate calendar, ensuring that the TV network executives would have to come to *him* to negotiate the details of their highly rated quadrennial events. This was a job worth holding on to, and he planned to never let it go.

To get a sense for just how much Spicer began to revel in this new role at the beating center of the Republican establishment and how much he wanted to nestle himself in the party bloodstream, try this on for size. During the height of the 2012 presidential campaign, Spicer directed junior staffers to spend time sending personal requests for two copies of signed paraphernalia to the office of every former Republican presidential nominee. Amid another rather important undertaking—the intense daily combat with the Obama juggernaut we were embroiled in—it was this project that would make Spicer the most animated. From time to time I would step into his office and find him giddily opening FedEx boxes filled with the latest Republican regalia that he considered his spoils.

Once the set was complete, Spicer directed the staffers to get the items framed. The first batch went to the shrine he had created to himself and the Republican Party in the basement of his Northern Virginia home. The second hung on the wall in the RNC headquarters. Underneath the autographed placards he had his employees affix a small bronze plaquette that read: "These signs have been graciously loaned to the RNC by Sean M. Spicer."

Through these historic mementos, Spicer wanted to ensure that his name would be emblazoned on the committee's walls long after he was gone. Graciously.

Sadly, I recently discovered that while the campaign signs still ornament the committee's walls, his plaquette has been removed. I couldn't uncover the backstory on this unceremonious excision, but it pleases me greatly that I can do my part to ensure Spicer's graciousness will be forever memorialized.

This project paired nicely with another undertaking he spearheaded while at the committee. Spicer endeavored to create a complete history of those who had "served" as RNC communications directors, a fabled list that grew on his whiteboard in a prideful attempt to give an air of history to this pedestrian office. (Danny Diaz, 2008! Doug Heye, 2010! And congrats to the latest entrant, Donald Trump's man in Capitol South, Michael Ahrens, 2019–20!)

Such a distinguished position was not so absorbing that it didn't allow time for Spicer to engage in a Republican-themed side hustle, though. Entrepreneurship is ingrained in the very fabric of the Republican ethos, and Spicer took that maxim literally in attempting to launch an elephant-themed necktie brand featuring the committee's trademarked pachyderm.

These exceptionally thicc silk monstrosities were offered

in either pukey lime green or royal blue. Spicer offered staff members—many of whom were asked to provide pro bono services to this burgeoning company—an opportunity to get involved via an ad hoc multilevel marketing scheme in which they would earn a cut of any sales they secured. Sadly, this project hit the skids before it could get off the ground.

Being a department head at the RNC does have its perks, but it does not give a person carte blanche over the committee's various trademarks, nor the ability to force underlings to provide unpaid labor for outside business efforts. Unfortunately for Spicer, these rules still apply even if you had graciously donated some historic placards. As a result, the intrepid communications director was slapped down by the legal department, and his career as a conservative cravat magnate was cut short.

All of this is to say that Spicer is nothing if not a party man through and through. He was the type of person who would take the job of White House press secretary from literally anyone who was a Republican and offered it, and in a weird way Donald Trump might have been the most likely person in the world to be that meal ticket.

Despite the fact that Spicer came from the party's establishment wing and was a prototypical swamp creature, even though he acknowledged Trump's insanity to RNC colleagues in private, he and his future boss were a match made in heaven. For starters, they had both failed at retailing phenomenally hideous ties that would only appeal to people with no sartorial eye. They also share an utter shamelessness when it comes to self-promotion, as evidenced by their shared foray into the world of prime-time reality television. Neither was immune to some casual workplace harassment. After I left the committee, he targeted one of his direct reports with a running "joke" of sorts about how, in his oh-so-discerning eye, she turned out to be much less attractive in person than the picture on her profile. He even went so far as to put up a "MISS-ING" poster designed as a milk carton, implying that the more attractive woman in the picture could not be found on his staff. You can see how he and Donald got along.

They weren't just simpatico in their piggish behavior toward women.

As communicators, both were graceless blunt-force instruments with a carnival barker's disposition, completely unmoored from the compunction that makes other mortals hew toward facts or reality. Both were more interested in the dramatic gesture than in staying within the traditional bounds of political discourse.

When asked by Jimmy Kimmel about his dogged willingness to spew disinformation on behalf of Trump, Spicer explained his job this way: "I've never had a boss I represented where one hundred percent I agree with what they believe. That's not the job you sign up for. You're not saying I'm going to agree with you. You're saying I'll do the best job I can communicating the thoughts and ideas and beliefs that you have."

From Spicer's stated vantage point, if Trump believed that men should not be legally held to account for assaulting women as long as they have a minimum level of fame, he saw his job as merely putting the best shine on that cad apple. He didn't see anything wrong with that. All part of the game.

In 2014, Spicer provided a *Veep*-esque preview of the Trump administration to come when he provided my friend Peter Hamby a behind-the-scenes look at the new RNC "comms college," which had sprouted from the autopsy's suggestion that the Republican Party help its candidates avoid more embarrassing moments like Akin's "legitimate rape" remark. The college, for which I was a guest professor, was going to train spokespeople how to stay "on message," among other basic tasks of a campaign press secretary.

During Spicer's interview with Hamby about the importance of message discipline, he proceeded to extol many of the other virtues of the program, including access to the "database of surrogates." Demonstrating the power of the database, Spicer offered some hypothetical use cases: "How many Asians do you have? How many Jews? You wanna do a Rosh Hashanah thing?" he hypothesized.

This was a bit cringeworthy given that nothing says "on message" like creating lists of Jews. So, the morning after the story came out, with Spicer taking some heat on Twitter over his trapper-keeper full of Hebrews comments, he exploded at his staff. At first he pretended that the quote might have been fabricated—the very same claim that Trump initially made to his staff when reports of the *Access Hollywood* tape surfaced two years later—and demanded that an underling berate Hamby and pressure him to remove the embarrassing quotes from the story.

Alas, Spicer had been caught on tape, and CNN had the receipts.

Once in the White House, colleagues told me that his Trumpian tendencies were exacerbated. He became preoccupied with the accoutrements of the office, demanding that he sit in key meetings with principles, taking selfies with fans outside of rallies, absconding with various White House mementos. His short-lived tenure ended not because he reflected with any seriousness on the actions being taken by the White House he was serving. Nothing Donald Trump did ever met Spicer's ire. For him the final straw was when he was "layered over" and told to report to Anthony "the Mooch" Scaramucci, costing him the direct-to-Trump privileges he had enjoyed. (Little did he know that he only would have had to suffer the indignity of working for Mr. Mooch for eleven days, before the new boss was also shown the door.)

This resignation gets to the heart of why Spicer went along with all the lunacy in the first place. It was over an affront to *status* that he called it quits. You see, Spicer wasn't fazed by being ordered to humiliate himself on television with obvious crowd-size lies. He was happy to oblige when asked to spin the despicable implementation of Steve Bannon's Muslim Ban.

It was once again being made to feel as if he were on the outside of the club that was a bridge too far. Sphincter wasn't going to let Mooch, the eighties teen movie rich kid bully, get one over on him, so he took his toys and went home.

After the White House, most press secretaries take high-paying corporate gigs, which is a practice that has its own grotesqueries. Obama's trio of spokesbros went on to McDonald's, Amazon, and United Airlines, respectively. But that option wasn't in the cards for a man who was best known for spending his first day on the job trying to tell the entire world not to believe their lying eyes. That type of blatant deception is generally frowned upon in the corporate world. Or at least, being perceived as being the type of company that commits blatant deceptions is frowned upon. The goal is to deceive deftly.

A blunt-force instrument like Spicer didn't do deft. He had to blaze a different trail. First, he attempted a crossover into mainstream celebrity. He visited twice with Kimmel. Attended a few red carpets. And famously turned his lime-green ties into a similarly shaded ruffled blouse for *Dancing with the Stars*, hoping that leprechaun pirate might be the new look for the 2010s.

But as much as Hollywood may love an antihero, Spicer's combination of MAGA sins and negative charisma offset the benefits that come from recognizability. Once again, he was desperately trying to be loved, but the cool kids were left saying, "Ugh, Spicer."

You can imagine how this gnawed at him. After years of clawing for recognition and being denied it, he had reached the highest imaginable heights. He wanted to walk out of the White House, jump on top of the school cafeteria table, and shout, "I WIN." Like Martin Prince, he dreamed of having more friends and more allies come to his new pool, so he could bask in their adoration and be named Queen of Summer. But the snotty stoners at the school paper still saw right through it. Even when he was invited to play their reindeer games, he was still at his core the red-nosed Sean Sphincter.

So he went elsewhere for validation, finding his fame in the right-wing sewer, parlaying the fan base he had cultivated by lying for the cause into a career as sort of a public avatar of hackneyed Trumpism. When a daytime tabloid show hosted by Belding's *Saved by the Bell* colleague A.C. Slater wanted someone to do glow-up puff pieces on minor MAGA celebs, Spicer was their man. When Cameo offered the ability for parvenus to send messages to their fans, he jumped on it, donating the proceeds to charity: "If you have a birthday, Columbus Day, Groundhogs Day . . . let me know," he pitched his prospective donors. In the MAGAverse, Spicer was omnipresent. If a Trump superfan was in the market for someone to put on a red hat, orange makeup, and make Build the Wall balloon animals for their kids' kindergarten graduation party, Spicer might very well turn up.

These gigs built on one another until eventually he landed a role as a prime-time anchor for Newsmax, a very non-prime-time outlet (you can find it on Comcast Xfinity, channel 1115). Newsmax had spent years languishing on the outskirts of the media landscape, but Spicer arrived just at the moment when it was poised for its insurrectionist glow-up.

For the first few months of his show, *Spicer & Co.* was garnering a paltry 58,000 views a night in prime time. But after Biden schlonged Trump at the polls, the numbers increased twentyfold.

What explained such a surge? It was not Spicer's unsightly ties. It was the network's brazen lies. After the 2020 election, Newsmax saw an opportunity to outflank its bigger brother and snatched it, offering 24/7 election-fraud mass hysteria. Fox tried to play the Trump coup attempt straightish, giving a bit of oxygen to his election-fraud hallucinations while mixing in a dose of reality from their "hard news" anchors. They avoided booking the more unhinged Kraken-spouting Trump surrogates and tempered the fantasy that the greatest fraud in history had been perpetrated on the public.

The mob didn't like these news vegetables, so they went shopping for some fresh treats. They needed an outlet that would be happy to feed the Big Lie straight into their pulmonary veins and Newsmax was drawing up the syringe. By the eve of the January 6th riot, Spicer was bringing in one million viewers a night with bat guano guests diarrheaing hysterical nonsense about illicit late-night dumps all over the screen.

Spicer knew better, of course. He would try to redirect the conversations back toward more "legitimate" concerns about how various states managed their elections in a pandemic. But the viewers weren't registering the tepid attempts at nuance.

Spicer's celebrity was on the rise again. And despite this transition to "journalism," at heart he was still just a flack doing a job. Communicating the thoughts of the leader to an audience that had no interest in being challenged. It was a skill he had honed for decades that had allowed him to get the requited affirmation.

Like so many Washington types, Spicer craved the recognition he never got in his youth. He became a loyal party man in part because he shared the ideology, but also because he wanted a table to sit at. With the Republican Party he had found it, and with Trump he became not just another member of the clique but one of its stars, asked to do a paso doble for those who were lower on the totem pole, where he had once been stuck.

As a result Spicer didn't ever feel the need to rationalize his choices the way Priebus, his former boss, had. He had no illusions that he was providing some unique public service or that he was the reasonable guy at the table. He is a replacement-level spokes-person and he knows it full well.

Spicer took the job as Trump's spinmeister because there was never a chance he would do anything else.

He would be loyal to the team. He would avenge those who sneered. He would have his name in lights and engraved in bronze. He would be recognized, remembered, maybe even revered as a man who contributed to the team and did so graciously.

His plaque may no longer adorn the walls of the RNC. He may not ever be loved by the jerks at the school paper. But little ol' Sean Sphincter will always have risen to the position of White House press secretary for a Republican president.

He got nearly everything he ever wanted.

And you'd better believe he'd do it all over again.

12

The Strivers

In late October 2016, Congresswoman Elise Stefanik rushed off the stage at SUNY Adirondack after the second debate of her reelection campaign, lucky to have been wearing a sensible heel. In hot pursuit was a gaggle of upstate New York reporters, all trying to get an answer to a matter that she had been eliding throughout the campaign.

The shaky CBS6 news footage of this confrontation shows Stefanik ducking behind a step-and-repeat backdrop, then disappearing down a dark hallway, the camera's focus reemerging only to reveal a phalanx of Republican staff bros in blousy checkered dress shirts blocking the view of their boss as she escapes into a dimly lit parking lot.

In the voice-over, a severe-sounding correspondent says Stefanik "took off running from our camera" and closes the segment with a live stand-up from the SUNY campus, ominously noting that the congresswoman does have "one more scheduled debate" where she will have to address the issue.

Generally speaking, when the local *Live at Five* newscast resorts to grainy footage of a hightailing politician, something is deeply amiss. Maybe the pol has been caught at the home of a lover who is not their spouse? Or revealed to have been a party to some unseemly graft? Or been lying to the public about a matter of grave concern? But on this night in Queensbury, there was no scandal of that sort embroiling Stefanik.

The reporters simply wanted to know who she would be voting for on the presidential line. They had been asking for months, to no avail.

In fact, Stefanik felt so uncomfortable with the notion of Donald Trump as president that during her reelection campaign, she couldn't even bring herself to say the man's name. Anytime she was cornered by a journalist, she would reply simply that she would back the "nominee of my party," which is not exactly a ringing endorsement and is possibly even a sign of Trump Derangement Syndrome, though I am not a licensed doctor.

By debate night, that evasiveness had caught up to her thanks in part to the fallout from a tape in which "The Nominee of Her Party™" admitted to enjoying the perks of his fame, such as the ability to commit serial sexual assault without repercussion. Some of the other Republican rats were jumping off ship, so the press was no longer satisfied with Stefanik's non-answers. They wanted to know once and for all, would she vote for a man she was so grossed out by that she couldn't even spit out the word "Donald"?

Anyone who knew Elise casually, as I had, understood her reluctance with regards to He Who Shall Not Be Named. She was a person whose predilections were about as far from the Nominee of Her Party™ as one could get. And a simple look at her résumé revealed that Elise's path to power was a parody version of a striving Bush-era establishment Republican.

Her first foray into politics came as an undergrad at Harvard, that populist bastion in Cambridge, Massachusetts. There she was chosen among her peers to help run a weekly study group for Ted

Sorensen, the famed former speechwriter for John F. Kennedy. From Harvard she took the meritocratic path through the GOP elite, "serving" as a liaison to important Bush administration officials, up to Chief of Staff Joshua Bolten. After leaving the Bush administration, she started a blog—American Maggie—named for Thatcher, natch, the goal of which was to elevate the voices of GOP women. She signed to her board prominent Bush-era voices like Dana Perino as well as squishy centrists like the pro-choice former New Jersey governor Christine Todd Whitman.

In the 2012 presidential primary, she hitched her wagon to the mulleted moderate Tim Pawlenty. Following his face-plant, she went on to work on the RNC platform and then prep Paul Ryan for his debates with Joe Biden. Her CV also included a stint at the Foreign Policy Initiative—a think tank launched by neocon godfathers Robert Kagan and Bill Kristol. It was during her time at FPI that friends say she was a frequent hanger-on at Kristol's magazine *The Weekly Standard*, which has since been shuttered by its owners over its lack of fealty to the Orange God King. At a few of these stops, she buddied up with Dan Senor, a Manhattan political operative turned management consultant, who was the key man for Paul Singer, patron of the American Opportunity Alliance (AOA) fundraising juggernaut, which would eventually catapult Stefanik to Congress.

These names may not mean much to those who aren't consumed by the turf wars of the interminably online conservative political set, but to the attuned Super MAGAs they are a cast of characters that embody the moderate, open-borders, neoconservative, pro-Israel establishment that Trump promised to overthrow. An establishment of which Stefanik was a key cog.

If that experience wasn't enough to demonstrate her anti-MAGA bona fides, there was also, of course, the autopsy. Stefanik had "the pen" on the document that was set to launch the party into a *Weekly Standard*/Paul Ryan/Christine Todd Whitman RINO future. Having "the pen" meant, mostly, that Stefanik was charged with marrying the language provided by Barbour, Fleischer, and Bradshaw with the desires of those of us on the RNC staff. She had earned this trusted slot having successfully managed the contentious platform committee goat rodeo for Priebus at the GOP convention. While Stefanik herself wasn't originating the language, she fought tooth and nail with staffers who wanted to water down some of the moderating suggestions that came from Fleischer. She fully embraced the GOP pivot laid out in the autopsy and didn't spend any of her time in the catbird's seat trying to mold the recommendations toward the party's Trumpy future.

Her move from RNC staff to candidate was met with surprise by those who worked with her on the project. I must admit, I didn't see it coming, though, to be honest, I already had one foot out the door and have the solipsist's deficit of not always noticing what doesn't impact me directly. A colleague said Stefanik caught him off guard in confiding her plans to take the unconventional step from the RNC to Congress during one of the stops on Priebus's nationwide autopsy roadshow.

Just as I had used the recommendations that we drafted to justify the need for America Rising, Stefanik saw the document's focus on expanding the GOP's appeal with college-educated women as a launching pad for her own campaign. She propelled herself from autopsy editor-in-chief to congressional candidate in no time, husbanding support from all the establishment Republicans she had networked with, from the Bush White House to the American Maggie blog to the Pawlenty and Romney/Ryan campaigns to the RNC, which proved crucial in a primary race against a self-funding Republican businessman. American Crossroads, the super PAC run by Karl Rove, pumped in seven figures, even though they generally stayed out of competitive primaries and saved their resources for beating Democrats in the general election. The same story was true for Singer's AOA network, which used its vast financial resources to fund Stefanik's primary as part of their "Winning Women" program.

In both cases, those involved tell me that Stefanik stood out as worthy of this unique type of investment because she embodied everything deep-pocketed donors and Bush-era strategists wanted for the future of the party. Singer, who later became one of the primary funders of the anti-Trump Our Principles (lol) PAC, which I fronted, was attracted to Republican candidates who shared his pro-Israel, soft-on-immigration, pro-gay views, and on those scores, Elise was top of the pops.

The man who was described as the "strategic mastermind" of her winning campaign was Phil Musser, the *IJ Review* figurehead whom she had worked with on Pawlenty's 2012 presidential bid. Musser put together a team of young staffers with moderate sensibilities who were excited to work for a like-minded candidate who might go on to be the youngest woman ever elected to Congress. He described the mindset of the campaign as that of a "future-minded conservative" who "got it on climate" and "got it on social value questions surrounding the changing demographics in our country," two platform planks that no current Republican in good standing would say out loud. According to one of her OG advisors, this 2014 effort was a "feel-good campaign" that was the "best I've been a part of" and represented what they thought was "good about America."

They weren't in their feels for long.

During the 2016 presidential primary, Stefanik stuck with this independent-minded approach saying Trump had disqualified himself with untruthful statements. "I think he has been insulting to women," she said in a local radio interview. She said Trump had "hurt" the effort to reach out to women that she had spearheaded within the party. She called his pussy-grabbing comments "offensive" and "just wrong," no matter the context. As for the Muslim Ban, she lambasted it, saying that that's "not who we are as a country."

Soon she would come to find out that banning Muslims and fanny snatching *was exactly* who Republican voters in her district were. In the meantime, she faced a challenging balancing act trying to figure out how to be true to her "forward-looking" conservative promise without clipping the wings of her ambition. During this period, she held out hope that the craziness would just blow over, while using all the tried-and-true tactics of the anti-anti-Trumper: Hiding from reporters. Focusing her critiques on the left's excesses. Performatively attacking the media for having the gall to wonder what she thought about the leader of her party.

For a while after Trump won, she managed to maintain her Tim Miller–approved, Jon Huntsmany policy platform, joining the "Tuesday Group," which represented the moderate wing of the House GOP caucus. She opposed Trump's tax cuts because they punished people in high-tax blue states and she gave a thumbs-down to the phony "national emergency" Trump concocted to seize money for his unerected border wall. She initially supported the Equality Act, which prohibited discrimination against gays in employment, but later backtracked. One mutual friend who was a vocal Never Trumper told me that during this time she even tried to recruit them to run for Congress as part of an effort to get more people willing to buck the president in the Republican caucus!

But then her behavior started to dramatically change. I wanted to give my former colleague the chance to explain these changes for herself, but she wouldn't go there. Her last email to me was a sarcastic dig about my "epic" Twitter feed. My repeated attempts to get her to bare her soul for this book were rebuffed.

Yet the answer doesn't seem to be too far from the surface. I had many conversations with her friends and colleagues on the matter and they all went the same way.

Me: "So, I'd like to hear your perspective on what happened with Elise."

Them:

- Deep sigh
- Perfunctory "I don't know"
- Lamentation about how hard it is to watch
- Sounding resigned: "I guess she just did what she had to. She is doing what her district wants."

That final sentence was the pat answer from friend and former friend alike. She was just doing what the district wants. She has no other choice! Right? Right?

You would think this ethos might have some limits. If the district wanted her to be a Marxist who distributes wealth based on race science, would she make their case on the House floor carrying her new pair of calipers? If a colony of nudist absolutists migrated to Lake Placid, would she defend to the death their right to shake their frigid fun bags in the Olympic Village? Seems unlikely, but figuring out how far this principle extends proved elusive.

The more you talked to her compatriots, the more the reason for that slipperiness became clear. The "in my district" excuse was a feint. A cover.

Stefanik actually had a bit more ability to get distance from Trump than some of her colleagues. She lives in a rather safe district in upstate New York that was increasingly Trumpy, yes, but not radically so. If she wanted to continue bucking the president when it was called for, there's good reason to believe she would have been just fine. In fact, John Katko, who represents a nearby New York district, did exactly that and maintained his seat. If that calculus proved wrong and she hadn't survived, a Harvard-educated former congresswoman with a massive Rolodex would have had plenty of other opportunities at her disposal. It's not as if it was either Congress or the coal mines.

The truth isn't that she's a mindless slave to her constituents. That's just a thing for her pals to say to avoid having to face the much darker reality. A reality where Elise made a conscious choice to go all-in with her own personal Voldemort because she came to recognize that her popularity, fundraising, and ability to rise within the party would benefit if she evolved from an "independent," "forward-looking," moderate to a forceful Trumper.

So that's exactly what the Striver did.

Former congressional colleagues directed me to an inflection point in spring of 2018 that led Stefanik to take the red pill and open her mind to the great MAGA future. It began when she started working with the White House on a traditional, old-school, neocon Republican priority—a military funding bill that would help her district. During that process she recognized that getting something out of the White House required that she be on her best behavior when it came to criticizing the head man, so she zipped her lips.

Around the same time, she noticed that those who she thought were in her clique were falling by the wayside. In April, her former boss and the Speaker of the House Paul Ryan announced he was abdicating his seat. For all Ryan's spineless abetment of Trump, in the early days of the administration he had at least offered some air cover for those in the caucus who wanted to maintain independence from the president. By the time he exited stage right, the conventional wisdom was beginning to congeal—arm's-length Trumpism was a path to early retirement.

In August, Stefanik got to experience the benefits of succumbing up close and personal. The president had signed the bill she was pushing for and accepted an invitation to her district.

Standing on stage at Fort Drum, he singled out Representative "Steff uh nick" for her leadership, bungling the pronunciation of her name. But colleagues suggested to me that the raucous cheers caught her attention more than the slight. It was the type of reception she had never gotten for the pragmatic rhetoric she'd been employing to date.

This tracks with the experience of other Trump-skeptical but striving GOP pols. Going from the Stefanik town hall to the monster-truck rally that is a Trump event influences a person. Particularly one who craves the spotlight or who correctly calculates that their power is derived from the enthusiasm of the cheerers. They start to recognize that if they are striving to maximize their influence, they need to arouse these sorts of passions as well, and the only way to do that in the modern GOP is to go full bore.

This instinct was confirmed for Stefanik that fall when many of her closest allies in Congress went the way of Ryan, having been euthanized by voters who demanded fealty and a president who wielded his Twitter feed to ensure it. Her peers—the "winning women" and young aspirational moderates from the 2014 congressional class—people like Barbara Comstock, Will Hurd, Carlos Curbelo, Mia Love—all got crossways with Trump and either lost or narrowly avoided defeat in the 2018 midterm. By 2021 all of them were out on their ass.

That could have been Elise, and she knew it.

When the first Trump impeachment came along in 2019, Stefanik used her perch on the House Intelligence Committee to lay down a marker. She wasn't going to throw in the towel like the conquered cucks in her class. She wanted the brass ring. And she would do what it took to get it.

The throughline in her résumé might have been neocon centrism, but the throughline of her life story was ambition. Stefanik wasn't just doing what her constituents wanted; she was doing what was required to get the next buzz. Ambition was the drug for her.

To understand just how dramatic the shift in her behavior was, all you need to do is look at her personal Twitter feed. From Donald Trump's campaign launch in 2015 until her invitation to Fort Drum in 2018, Congresswoman Elise Stefanik tweeted the word "Trump" zero times.

ZERO. Nada. Nil. Zilch. Zipola.

Trump had been the biggest story in politics for three years and she hadn't even been able to Say His Name.

But during his first impeachment, she steeled herself and not only named Trump but became the Republican House caucus's most shameless and slavish spinmeister in defense of the then president's ham-handed, tinpot dictator-esque attempt to bully our vulnerable Ukrainian ally into investigating his political opponent. She turned her defense of Trump's shakedown into an online fundraising bonanza beyond her wildest imaginations and earned the praise of a president who went from calling her Steff uh nick to deeming her a "star."

With that star turn, she was off to the races. "Trump" was no longer a verboten word. And she quickly saw the spoils of her integrity's sacrifice at his altar.

While many of her fellow RINOs had become extinct, she has since become a member of the GOP House leadership, having successfully engineered regime change at the expense of Liz Cheney. Cheney might have had a more "conservative" voting record and a pedigree, but Elise had the Trumpian star of approval. The singular issue in that race was willingness to play along with the defeated president's lies as he tried in vain to stay in power against the will of the voters. When Cheney determined that a coup attempt was over the line, Stefanik put her chips all in. She endorsed a lawsuit that would overturn the election. She went on Sean Spicer's Newsmax to claim she had some "concerns" about the Dominion voting machines, a claim that is so absurd and defamatory, others have faced legal ramifications for it. Even *after* the Capitol was stormed, she voted to cancel the legal votes of citizens in Pennsylvania, a state she does not represent.

Once she realized how high she got smoking the good shit, she wasn't about to go back to the regs.

By 2020, Musser and all the other members of her original schwaggy feel-good crew had moved on or been dispatched, unwilling or unable to match the boss's fervor for the new MAGA tone. One of the stragglers from the original posse departed after January 6th, telling me they could no longer be a part of her team in good conscience. Others hadn't been given that option. The same person who told me the first Stefanik campaign was the best experience they had ever been a part of was fired summarily on a conference call after suggesting to the boss that she use the reserves of goodwill from the impeachment act to tack away from Trump a bit.

Stefanik had spoken at that staffer's wedding. They thought she had been a friend. But she had determined that the relationship with her new patron was the only one that mattered. She had no interest in tacking back. She wouldn't halfheartedly Say His Name. She would intone it with adoration, and anyone who would not join her in prostration would have to be excommunicated.

It might have seemed callous, but when you are a star, they let you do it.

From Harvard to Congress, Stefanik had put her personal ambition first and she wasn't stopping now. Muslim Bans. Sexual assault apologetics. Attempting to make a former game show host an unelected autocrat by advancing fabricated conspiracies about our elections being fraudulent.

She chose to go along with this because it was her path to power. And all indications are that if Trump runs for president again, she will have her eye on the penultimate rung on the striver's ladder, the vice presidency.

Throughout all this she may tell herself that she's just doing what voters demand and that she had no other choice if she wanted to succeed. But that shit ain't the truth.

Elise Stefanik is in charge. There were many paths available. This is the one she has chosen for her life.

Deep down, I suspect she's happy with it.

13

The Cartel-Cashing, Team-Playing, Tribalist Trolls

Mike Shields fits the mold of an establishment Republican creature, replete with baby face, boxy suit, and beer belly. He grew up as an American kid on an air force base in the United Kingdom and, like Stefanik, harbored a Maggie-crush, fashioning himself as a typical Thatcherite conservative. As you might expect from a right-wing Anglophile political nerd, he even had a favorite Maggie moment, frequently sharing with colleagues the famed video of the PM, adorned in her royal blue pantsuit, smacking down dowdy MP Simon Hughes for concerning himself too much with the pesky wealth gap rather than lifting all economic boats. Like many of his fellow Gen X Republicans, it was this era's trickle-down economics that animated him. Through it all, he developed an unshakable belief that socialists were the enemy and that any enemy of the socialists was an ally.

Shields began his career as the RNC clips boy. He would get up at the crack of dawn to cut out articles for then-chairman Haley Barbour, a story he likes to tell (and tell and tell) to those who work for him, in an attempt to engender a commitment to the mission. From the clips desk, he rose through the ranks of party politics on a trajectory not much different from mine, specializing in research and political organizing rather than research and communications. He made his bones managing the campaign for Republican Dave Reichert, a middle-of-the-road former sheriff who won in somewhat surprising fashion in the liberal Pacific Northwest, positioning himself as the most environmentally friendly Republican in America, a distinction that Major Winchester might say is roughly comparable to being the finest ballerina in all of Galveston, but was good enough to win over suburban Seattleites.

Shields parlayed the Reichert success into a role at the National Republican Congressional Committee—the group that oversees House races—where he was known for being laser-focused on recruiting and identifying more moderate candidates who can win in suburban areas like his former boss had. He spent the ensuing half decade building a brand around D.C. as a savvy operative who knew how to get Republicans elected in purple areas by pushing the party to grow the tent and bring in swing voters.

So, when he plugged into the autopsy process as Reince's newly minted chief of staff, we found a man who was a perfect dispositional fit for all the material that was in process.

And yet, out of all the cookie-cutter Republican strategists in Washington you've likely never heard of, it might have been Mike Shields who was rewarded the most handsomely when a man who was his dispositional opposite wiped his arse with everything we had proposed.

But Mike wasn't alone. He was merely the prom king for an entire class of swampy squishes who thrived in Trump's Washington. How did these RINOs manage to navigate the supposedly populist takeover so successfully? And how did they come to terms with the sacrifices that success required?

• • •

Shields came to the RNC less than three weeks before the autopsy's big reveal and immediately grabbed hold of the digital portion of recommendations as the place he could have the biggest impact, despite having no practical experience in the area. The Romney campaign's beached ORCA had given him the perfect opportunity to argue that everything the party was doing on the technology and data side was wrong and only Mike—and the buddies he would later do business with—could fix it. The overhaul he oversaw ruffled lots of feathers among the old guard of consultants who had spent decades cashing checks through the entrenched system, and they were embittered that he broke up the racket.

The Silicon Valley experts Shields brought in to handle the zeroes and ones recall him as having a particular interest that aligned with the autopsy's mission. He wanted to see how a new digital operation could be leveraged to expand the party beyond its Caucasian base, engage with people who spoke English as a second language, and signal that the party was more welcoming to different races, religions, and sexualities. This commitment to broadening the party defined the early part of his tenure at the committee. One female staffer who considered him a mentor said that he was dedicated to empowering women in a building that had been dominated by old white men and to bringing more melanin to the white-bread party's elected officials. She recalls having a passionate ongoing internal debate with him over how to best achieve this goal, and one of the projects they undertook to that end was a "Rising Stars" initiative, which focused on promoting a more diverse array of candidates.

It turned out that much of this roiling internal debate was academic, because in practice the stars were not aligned with where the party was headed. The two most prominent members of the inaugural class of four—Georgia state representative Byung "BJay" Pak and Texas congressional candidate Will Hurd—had trajectories that were emblematic of how the autopsy's recommendations were received by the Republican electorate.

A black, moderate policy wonk, Hurd was the golden boy of that inaugural class. When the RNC first featured him, he was the nominee for a Texas congressional seat that he would go on to win. He later made a name during a viral Facebook Live of his bipartisan road trip with liberal golden boy Beto O'Rourke, which offered the slightest tinge of hope for those of us who were desperately yearning for some collegial bro-comity in the fallout from Trump's 2016 victory. But that glimmer of wholesome bipartisanship was short-lived. Hurd stayed in Congress for two more terms, trying to balance his desire to have an impact on policy with the torture of having to navigate a president whom he palpably disliked. In 2019, I had a few conversations with Hurd's staff about their boss's loose flirtation with the idea of a Trump primary in 2020. In the end, that was too daunting to take seriously. Instead, Hurd decided to retire from Congress at the ripe old age of forty-two in part because Trump's racist comments "weighed heavily" on him. At the time of his retirement, he was the only black Republican in the House of Representatives.

Pak's experience with the Trumpian buzz saw was even more dramatic. He never reached the same political heights, choosing instead to leave his seat as a state representative to return to a career as a prosecutor, but that didn't allow him to escape Trump's shadow. In 2017 he was nominated by the president to become the U.S. attorney for the northern district of Georgia, where he stayed, making few waves throughout Trump's term. Following the president's embarrassing Georgia loss, Pak found himself in the crosshairs of a lame duck who was upset that "his" attorney was not being aggressive enough in investigating the claims of fraud that Trump's Kraken-team was fabricating in an attempt to spare his ego and upend the world's longest-running democracy.

In the notorious leaked phone call with Georgia secretary of state Brad Raffensperger in which the defeated Trump was demanding that more votes be "found," he also railed against Pak, claiming this "Never Trumper" U.S. attorney was standing in the way of their election subversion efforts. Pak caught wind of the convo and, expecting that his firing was imminent, resigned before Trump had the chance to sack him. He emailed his fellow U.S. attorneys that morning, asking them to hold the line in the face of "unprecedented challenges" coming from the man who had appointed him.

The future faces Shields wanted to elevate ran headlong into a party that was no longer interested in seeing them.

In 2015, he left the committee to run a super PAC that focused on electing Republican House candidates, passing the chief of staff job to his then girlfriend and now wife, Katie Walsh. Together Shields and Walsh managed to succeed in the same way all the Trump-era cashers did, walking the MAGA/establishment tightrope deftly, without ever fully alienating either side. This did not come without obstacles. Walsh was spotted crying unhappy tears on election night, accused by some of Trump's top loyalists of attempting to boot him from the ticket after the Billy Bush *Access Hollywood* tape, quoted by Michael Wolff comparing talking to the president to "trying to figure out what a child wants," and targeted by Trump himself as a suspected leaker. Yet she and Shields managed to survive the swamp purge, utilizing leverage and relationships and powered by pride in the work that had gotten them there.

The leverage came from the RNC, which controlled key assets for Trump's fundraising and political future through the data trust and email lists that had been upgraded as part of Shields's autopsy remit and supercharged on the back of the Trump brand during Walsh's tenure at the committee. The amount of cashish that these lists brought in for Trump was so significant that, according to ABC's Jonathan Karl, as late as 2021, Ronna "Romney Romney Romney" McDaniel was using them as ransom to prevent Trump from dropping the party entirely after his defeat.

In addition to the lists and the data, the couple had friends in high places. Trump son-in-law Jared Kushner had a fondness for Walsh, presumably because the White House was filled with so many Peter Principle Disprovers that Kushner felt like a parched man traveling the desert in search of a minimally competent human oasis. He was so enamored with Walsh that during the reporting of a *Washington Post* profile on the couple, he emailed the reporter out of the blue offering that "Katie was one of the unsung heroes of the 2016 campaign."

But the key relationship was one that the couple developed with Trump digital director Brad Parscale, one of the very people whom Walsh had been blaming for Trump's expected loss in that call to a reporter I had overheard on election day 2016. In spite of that private slander—or possibly due to Parscale's ignorance of it—Shields and Walsh became valued confidants for Parscale, offering experienced guidance, a familiarity with the D.C. ecosystem, and access to the RNC's resources to a guy Trump had plucked from a podunk digital marketing company in San Antonio that had been building basic websites for the family real estate company.

So, after Trump won, Shields and Walsh teamed up with Parscale to create a three-headed monster that had influence over the purse strings at the Trump super PAC (Parscale), RNC (Walsh, where she returned following a brief and tumultuous stint in the White House), and congressional campaigns (Shields). Thus began what a former friend of theirs described to me as Walsh and

Shields's "Claire and Frank Underwood" era: unapologetically amassing power and wealth on the back of a candidate whom they had previously abhorred and, if some in Trump's orbit are to be believed, had actively tried to sabotage.

The couple's 2017 wedding in Kiawah Island, South Carolina, marked the official uniting of the tribes. Parscale, whom the betrothed had met barely more than a year prior, attended alongside Priebus and much of the RNC's high command. One of the more perverse parts of D.C. culture is that many inhabitants turn their weddings into these quasi-networking events, either out of ambition or a lack of real-life friends or both. I was once invited to a top political adman's wedding on a whim at a work happy hour. And the invite was serious! I barely knew them! When the pictures from this soiree showed up on Facebook a few months later, I noticed that I recognized 90 percent of the people in attendance. Somehow this couple had lived four decades and only made work friends. No wonder it was so hard for these hacks to drop the party over Trump. Republican politics was their identity, career, and social circle all wrapped up in one.

For Shields and Walsh, the Parscale friendship was fruitful and together they brought in millions in consulting fees over the next four years. As I called around to their friends and former friends trying to understand why they did it, the answer kept coming back to the quid. A fellow consultant who knows the racket explained the motivation rather simply.

"Shields had never been in a job that made more than two hundred and fifty thousand dollars a year in his life," he told me without irony. "This was his opportunity."

Only a quarter-million bones? Where is Friar Tuck when you need him, this might require alms for the poor!

While such an assertion may seem farcical on its face, this

comment betrayed a real insight into the mindset of the D.C. consultant class. Among the elite members of this cadre, 250 g's is the minimum ante, and so when a person at that income level socializes in this rarefied company, they look around and start to realize how much they are leaving on the table.

In August 2020, the couple demonstrated the lengths they would go to protect their cartel in the face of what they perceived to be a threat. Trump's 2016 deputy campaign manager, the felonious Rick Gates, was doing a book tour following a brief stint in jail for lying to the feds, during which he fingered Walsh as a ringleader of an effort to remove Trump from the ticket in 2016 following the pussy tape.

One would think this would have been water off the duck's back for someone like Walsh, given how deeply she had immersed herself within the Trump orbit and how unreliable a narrator Gates was.

But nope.

She treated this accusation as an existential threat and took an action I cannot recall having ever seen a political staffer who was not under criminal investigation take in any circumstance prior. She retained a lawyer to push back on the supposed slander and in the press threatened to sue Gates.

The lady doth protest!

Her lawyer's flamin' hot threat went as follows:

"The statements with respect to some effort to dislodge the president from the ballot with respect to Ms. Walsh are demonstrably false and people who repeat those false statements run the risk of significant damages," [James] Wareham said. "The effort to destroy her business will no longer be countenanced. Action will be taken."

There it is. Right there in the legalese. Accusations that she had not been fully loyal to supreme leader Trump might "destroy her business" and thus could not be countenanced.

The Trump suck-up charade had become big bizness, so they couldn't give an inch.

This rigidity in defense of the bounty was on display in the middle of 2017, when I appeared across from Shields on CNN the day after the Priebus firing-by-tweet. You remember? The one Trump hadn't warned him about even though they were on the phone together three minutes earlier? That one.

During this hit, Shields was defending the petulant president's disgraceful treatment of the man who had made him RNC chief of staff. I took the contrary view, lampooning the notion that we should want a man-child president who is a messy bitch who lives for drama and fires people over Twitter for the lulz.

The segment progressed into a broader disagreement over whether good people would want to work for someone who gives his staff this kind of boar-on-the-floor treatment.

I argued that the presidential tantrums were not attracting the best and the brightest. Shields objected. He said that there are "plenty of people" who are looking to *serve* in the Trump administration.

I found this argument absurd and was certain that I had the upper hand, because I knew that Shields also knew it was absurd. So I began interjecting giddily multiple times, asking Mike directly: If it were true that any loyal patriot would want to work for Trump, why was it that *he* hadn't done so? If Trump was so appealing and there was such value in public service, why was Shields on basic cable with me and not on the tarmac with Reince?

I gave it a few tries, but he never did quite answer. He ducked and danced around my retorts; Mike's nothing if not a deft debater.

After the Trump term in office was complete, I took one more run at him. It was an obliging, off-the-record, chat. The standard justifications of the team players were all there. The ingrained distaste for the perceived socialist Democratic menace. A lifetime of service to the side. More specifically, a real, deep-seated fulfillment over what he felt he had accomplished in the course of that service. Shields had used the autopsy to completely rebuild the data infrastructure for a party that he loved but had been on a losing streak. He did so in the face of ridicule and slander from people whose bottom line was hurt by his overhaul. Despite the fact that the president who benefited from that work was not his cup of tea, it was still a successful ORCA of his own making. Rather than suffer through watching it flail about on the shore, Shields got to see his baby sky through the air over the rock-lined jetty to freedom and victory!

And just as it did for Jesse in the movies, this gave him some mixed emotions.

On the one hand, he was downright chuffed at the achievement. On the other, he was worried whether this was safe, given the wanker at the wheel.

Being conflicted about seeing something you built succeed but in service to evil ends is natural. I experienced this very sensation during the Pruitt confirmation. The question becomes, what does one do to reconcile those mixed feelings? Block out worries and serve the evil? Walk away? Try to channel it for good in your own little corner of the world? Throw your hands up in the air and declare that nothing you do matters anyway?

In this case the most apt answer to that question might just have come from Thatcher herself.

"Pennies don't fall from heaven, they have to be earned here on earth."

For D.C. political strategists at the highest levels of the game, that was as good a rationale for navigating that cognitive dissonance as any.

• • •

The autopsy's other entrenched establishment figure blazed a slightly more tortured trail. An amiable southerner with a pedigree, Henry Barbour was the first call Priebus made when he was launching the party review, thanks to his broad appeal within the committee, surname, and reputation for not rocking the boat. It was Barbour who brought Sally Bradshaw and Ari Fleischer aboard in order to round out the team that would end up recommending a kinder, more welcoming GOP.

His arc in the intervening years is a stand-in for almost every compartmentalizing establishment political operative I worked with who was genuinely affected by their internal conflicts over Trump. They saw the president for who he was but sublimated that to service to the team, because they felt hamstrung by ideology, money, career, and, uniquely in Barbour's case, the golden handcuffs wrapped inside his DNA. The story of these functionaries in the consultant class goes something like this:

They hated Trump during the 2016 primaries and spoke out against him from time to time. They probably supported Rubio, while the squishier among them fancied Jeb and the more ideologically driven backed Cruz. They all grumbled about Trump as he rose during the primary and some even threatened to oppose him if he won the nomination—at least while they thought that outcome remained unlikely. When the improbable began to become inevitable, they were chastened and to a man they *publicly* backed Trump, despite their reservations, with a rationale that went something like, "If Crooked Hillary became president, that would be catastrophic because humina humina humina I'm required to say this for my career to survive."

In the privacy of the voting booth, a handful of them voted for

Trump. "I didn't *actually* think he was going to win, or I wouldn't have," one confessed to me in a moment of weakness, hoping my good standing as a Never Trumper bestowed the pastoral power to grant absolution. Most secretly voted against him, checking the box for Evan McMullin or writing in Zombie Ronald Reagan, a fact they shared with their spouse and liberals who they hoped would still like them. Getting all the way to Hillary was a bridge too far.

After Trump became president-elect, many took a step back from their public presence as a political commentator, even though they had been a frequent dial-a-quote for reporters over the years. Their Twitter feeds morphed into a mash-up of "Democrats bad, non-Trump Republicans good" and sports takes. In a given quarter, you might not even realize the GOP's standard-bearer exists, reading their feeds, despite the fact that they were professionally in service to his party.

When it came to actually working *for* Trump, it wasn't a fit for them, at least at first, but they excused their friends who had fewer career options and were considering biting the bullet. They determined that it was better not to rock the boat and have "good people" in there. Right? Having friends on the inside also helped in their consulting gigs, by the by. In Henry's case in particular, he told me that he encouraged his friend Reince to take the job as chief of staff because it was better for it to be him than the alternatives he considered more "crazy."

When the mood struck, these Bravehearts would share their worries or a little gossip with reporters while nervously making certain that they were off the record or on "deep background." With that invisibility cloak assured, they became part of Washington, D.C.'s most popular Republican club—the "privately concerned."

While the publicly concerned Republicans were spare, the privately concerned were legion. Anytime you picked up a newspaper, you might hear their vantage point. The privately concerned didn't like the president's tweets or the racism or the chaotic leadership style. They hoped he might pivot back to "the issues that got him elected," a groundless fantasy that had the side benefit of ensuring that the reporter they were talking to knew that they weren't one of the baddies, just a loyal Republican making do in a tough situation.

Barbour was a charter member of the privately concerned. In 2017, I bumped into him at a tailgate in Oxford, Mississippi, ahead of a showdown between his beloved Ole Miss Rebels and my LSU Tigers. Before I even had a chance to snag a chicken on a stick from his tent, he was railing about how terrible everything was with the party. How Trump's pestilence was seeping into the grassroots. He was horrified by Roy Moore's primary win in neighboring Alabama and wanted me to know that he was doing everything in his power to ensure his home state wouldn't put up a replica.

This kind of conversation was something I had a lot of familiarity with. People wanted to clear their conscience, tell me they were on the level, highlight the project where they were doing "the right thing." It's human nature. But anytime I tried to press them to go further, to walk fully into the light, they rebuffed me. The privately concerned had obligations, of course. Bills to pay. Employees to think about. They had their ideological priors and fears of the left to balance. Barbour was no different.

During the Trump years, Barbour expanded his footprint in the party, accepting roles on the board of organizations that manage voter data and online fundraising. He also maintained his role managing a consulting firm that advises candidates in the South who all run on a pro-Trump platform because they have no other choice if they want to win. He says he is motivated by "electing good people that could keep this American dream going forward," which implicitly means not Donald Trump, though only to the small number of insiders who know the frequency.

You might think these team players would at least understand that they must take some licks as part of this delicate dance, but nah, trying to neg them over their jig is a sign you don't "get it."

One instance in October 2020 is representative. I fired off a tweeter heater blasting one group of similar team players—those who chose to work for a new pro-Trump super PAC funded by the late GOP megadonor Sheldon Adelson. "This $75 million is going to fund beach houses for a lot of media consultants who tell their friends in private they don't really like Trump that much," I wrote.

The tweet linked to a story by *Politico* about a new super PAC called "Preserve America," which was some elite-level dog-whistle branding. Just enough to evoke a little anemoia without actually having to drop any slurs. Even though I didn't mention anyone by name in the tweet, a former boss that I had been quite close to texted me bitterly. His firm was one of those that was doing their part to Preserve 'Murica, even though he and his partners had frequently vented to me about their revulsion toward Trump. This guy was pissed about being accused of rapacity and argued it was the consultants at the Lincoln Project and the Bloomberg campaign who were the real Cartel Cashers.

In a narrow sense, he was making a point I agreed with. I had savagely attacked the Bloomberg campaign in *The Bulwark* toward the end of the Democratic primary when they continued dropping massive consultant-enriching ad buys well after it was clear he was merely a spoiler for the other, more plausible center-left candidates like Biden. Similarly, some of the Lincoln Project types like Steve Schmidt had raked in ungodly sums both at their PAC and working for Starbucks founder Howard Schultz's independent presidential bid. Had Schultz pulled the trigger on a campaign, his presence would have only served the purpose of dividing the anti-Trump vote and creating generational wealth for its consultants. It was in direct conflict to everything the Lincoln Project would

come to espouse. Luckily, that campaign exploded on the launching pad, but it didn't seem to prevent the consultants from achieving the true purpose of the effort. Schultz paid them all anyway.

So my former bosses' whataboutist pushback is correct in the
micro: there is no shortage of people out there looking to make
a dollar and a cent in the political business. But the moral quandary comes into play when that work is in service of something
that they know is dangerous and harmful and they do it anyway.
The very ex-boss who was mad at me over the tweet had, in the past,
specifically expressed how enraging it was that Trump's language
and actions were having an impact on his kids. Yet, during our
text fight his message was that I "might want to ask first and tweet
second," stating it was *my tweet* that was "part of the problem in
our world."

You see, from the cashers' vantage point, inside the warm,
marshy cocoon, the *problem in our world* was the fact that there were
people pointing out the gross hypocrisy that was rampant in the
Republican consultant class. The problem was *not* that so many
hypocrites were using Trump to land massive paydays. That was
just business. I had broken this comfortable code that all the team
players lived by. Loathing Trump privately was fine. Trashing him
"on background" was even encouraged. But naming and shaming
former colleagues for making bank off him? That was the game's
real crime.

I wish it was just one of those hotheaded disputes in the middle
of a campaign that we could all have a laugh about after. But the
dispiriting truth is when I went back to find the text exchange for
this book, I realized that was the last time we had spoken. These
guys had chosen their team, and I was no longer on it.

If you find yourself rather annoyed that these wealthy men and
women (mostly men) were able to avoid reputational damage and

maintain their high-paying, high-influence gigs while assuaging their guilt with private agita and an occasional righteous deed, I can offer at least a glimmer of schadenfreude.

To a person, their professional life is making them miserable.

Miserable in their new fishing boat. But miserable, nonetheless.

"It hasn't been nearly as fun, it was really fun back when I came up in '05," Barbour admitted.

Over the years, I talked to others like him for *Rolling Stone*, where I gave them their invisibility cloak so they would be candid. I will uphold that anonymity agreement here. But let there be no doubt that their ennui was universal. One admitted to not being able to discuss his job with his wife any longer. Another lamented being called "racist" and "evil." Many of them were exasperated over the fact that Trump encompasses everything they talk about, that they can't just do their job without him hanging over them. A few were deeply conflicted about work that used to make them proud and now made them feel somewhat ashamed, while others had embraced the heel turn, comforting themselves with the view that the left was a unique evil, that they were abortionists, out to get the Christian, white man.

But no matter where they fell on that spectrum, they all decided to stick it out with Trump and keep on keeping on. The work might have been a chore but they were still up in the luxury boxes with the pinot flowing, and the concussions down on the field weren't gruesome enough to do anything about.

• • •

After the insurrection, there was a glimmer of hope that finally there had been some roughing that was just unnecessary enough to stir them from their sybaritic social-professional condition. For

a moment the privately concerneds' true beliefs were publicly revealed. They felt free to say out loud what they had only been whispering in friendly confines.

The most stark reveal came from one of Republican Washington's most unabashed cartel-cashing, team-playing, tribalist trolls:
Josh Holmes. Holmes, who was the top political strategist to Mitch
McConnell, is your classic Republican in every respect, a charter
member of the D.C. establishment, who carried the esteem of influential reporters, staffers, and politicians alike. Five foot seven in
a Rubio heel, Holmes would win the superlative for most stereotyp-
ical Republican Brooks Brothers fit. He has thrived in Washington
as the perfect person for a corporate consulting gig that requires
a token "good Republican" who can put in a call when you need it.
According to mutual friends, a handful of trade groups and corporate players keep his firm, Cavalry, on retainer just for that purpose.

But maintaining "good Republican" status during the Trump
years was tougher than in the before times. Fortune 50 companies
were reluctant to bring on anyone who would bring the citronella
tiki torch stank with them. As the Trump years snail-trailed on,
rather than go full corporate, Holmes leaned into the MAGA Sven-
gali side of his duality, while maintaining a suite of private-sector
clients who got the joke. He embraced the mantle of chief tribalist
troll, gleefully pwning Democrats on Twitter and on Fox and relish-
ing Trump's skilled gamesmanship despite his private reservations
about the man. In 2020, he launched a podcast with a title mocking
Ruth Bader Ginsberg's death, cohosting alongside minor Twitter
celebrity named Comfortably Smug.

During the 2016 campaign, I'd been texting pals with Smug,
given his status as a prominent online Jeb Bush stan turned Hillary Clinton voter. But we parted ways when he eventually landed
on Team Trump to maximize the retweets, a currency he valued
greater than Ethereum. Smug was known, and in establishment

GOP consultant circles revered, for his skill at merciless bad-faith trolling of Democratic politicians and blue-check liberals. For Holmes, balancing his position as the podcast sidekick to a full-time troll while maintaining his obligations as a Serious Consultant and Good Republican created obvious tensions.

I'd hear from journalists and others about how "they really used to respect Josh" and "don't understand what got into him." Even though to anyone with eyes it was obvious. Holmes, like his sponsor Cocaine Mitch, had determined that it was his job to win for his team, no matter what, and anything in service to that was a de facto good. During the Trump era, balancing serving one's team while maintaining some level of respectability meant assuming a trolling posture. This allowed a person to save face by avoiding actively defending Trump's unapologetic cruelty and mythomania in favor of making fun of anyone who opposed it.

In the lead-up to January 6th, it seemed that Holmes might try to find a way out of this bind for himself and his fellow concerned cashers. Trump's post-election behavior had seemed to provide an opening. They might be able to maintain their rep as a hard-nosed attack dog, while ridding themselves of the baggage they were loath to reveal true feelings about. Trump's undermining of the election result was a problem—not in the earnest, democracy-loving sense, but because it was tamping down enthusiasm among Republican voters who had become convinced of the fabricated, cockamamie nonsense about the voting machines being rigged.

In this instance, it was the defeated Trump who was harming the team, and not only the team writ large but Holmes's meal ticket in particular, Mitch McConnell, who would go on to lose his position as majority leader as a result of the party's epic Peach State butt fumble. The morning after the Georgia run-off election that sealed McConnell's fate, which also happened to be the day of the January 6th insurrection, *National Journal* reporter Josh Kraushaar reported that the "mood" among McConnell-aligned Republicans was to declare war on Trump and marginalize him as a figure within the party. The sourcing sounded very Holmesesque and the D.C. political class was abuzz with the old Lucy and the football routine: might *this* be the moment that the "good Republicans" finally turn on Trump?

As the mob formed on the Mall that morning, Holmes fired off a tweet throwing a little cold water on the notion of a coming McConnell/Trump internecine war: "A lot of emotions. People are angry. Nobody is declaring war on anything. We'll get through this."

But as the day went on and the horrors unfolded, his tune began to change. He called Rudy Giuliani a "piece of shit" for continuing to push the insurrection. He defended RNC spokesperson Michael Ahrens, who was getting criticized on the right for calling the attack "domestic terrorism," tweeting that Ahrens was "saying the right thing." By January 10, the emotions had boiled over. Like many Republicans who would later eat their words, Holmes tweeted, "if you're not in a white-hot rage over what happened by now you're not paying attention."

White. Hot. Rage.

For a moment, this was not about gamesmanship. Holmes was just a person emoting online like the rest of us. Saying the very things that he and his ilk had been saying, on background, for a half decade. For a moment, Washington was abuzz with the possibility that maybe the dam was breaking, that the combination of a deadly riot and political defeat would once and for all bring the privately concerned out from the shadows.

But that was always misguided wishcasting. Believing these guys would walk away over a pesky insurrection misdiagnoses why they did what they did in the first place.

Once the dust settled, and it was clear that the voters they required for power didn't share their rage, that the team still needed Trump or they risked losing his supporters, it was inevitable that they would buckle. Trump having the ability to trick a mob of rubes into storming the Capitol wasn't a reason to *stop* enabling him, it was more evidence that his mob must be obeyed.

Holmes and McConnell and all the others who thought otherwise were only fooling themselves. Somehow, despite everything they had been through, they still harbored the delusion that they were in control of the croc. There was a fleeting moment that for some lasted an hour, some a day, others a week, and for a steely few a bit longer, during which they blocked out their rationalizations and imagined how they might get out of their moral bind in a way that was clean and convenient.

But eventually the passions of the day were going to dissipate, which anyone who was paying attention could have predicted. On the night of January 6th, I told the *Bulwark* livestream audience that even though everyone's emotions were raw, the reality was that nothing had changed, and these guys were all going to be back on board with Trump by Valentine's Day.

As it turned out, it didn't even take that long.

They were still team players and tribalist trolls. They still loathed the left. They still thought they were the key men who needed to have their hands at the tiller. They still needed to be in the mix. They still needed to get paid. And they still needed Donald Trump's mob, or else they'd risk losing it all.

It was obvious that everyone would come crawling back. And that's what they all have done.

• • •

Holmes passed on the opportunity to explain for this book why his white-hot rage subsided. We used to be friendly in the anodyne, impersonal D.C. networking sort of way, where you give someone a familiar bro-hug when you see them despite not knowing their kid(s?)' names. But that superficial bond came to an end when I sent a tweet questioning the sincerity of his "white hot rage," given that his firm made $12.9 million from the pro-Trump super PAC. (If you are noticing a trend, my D.C. "friendships" do seem to have been coming to an end when I tweet about their personal finances. Maybe there is something to be learned there.)

I posted a screenshot of the filing of his $13 milly haul and wrote, "sorry but if you cash the election stealing, Qanon tweeting, Muslim banning candidates checks you don't get to pretend like you were the normal one."

Holmes didn't like that none too much.

He messaged, letting me know that he had thought I was someone who "got it" and now he would be coming for me. He blocked me on Twitter, and he hasn't spoken to me since.

It seems from Holmes's POV that it was cool to be ruthless when you argue about politics, but uncool to bring up how much money his firm raked in to help reelect Donald Trump. (Oh, wait, I have just mentioned it again, oops.)

It turned out that it was Holmes's initial instinct from that January 6th morning, while he still had his senses about him, that would win the day.

There would be no internecine war. The cannons would once again be aimed at the other side.

The enablers' moral sacrifices had been compounding over the years and they were dug in much too deep to stop over a farcical putsch. They were akin to the characters in that fifth *Squid Game*, getting squeamish about being responsible for the death of those they had teamed up with, but too close to the piggybank payoff to give up.

When I asked Mike Shields about this, wanting to know if Trump had ever acted in such a vile manner that bailing on the cartel was something he considered, his answer was guarded but revealing.

He said he didn't trust me enough to answer honestly. Then he let out a big, uncomfortable laugh. He followed up his laugh by saying, I guess that tells you all you need to know.

Indeed it does.

Henry Barbour showed a little more leg. Like Holmes, he spoke out after January 6th, but with a bit more staying power. At the RNC winter meeting two days after the insurrection, Barbour addressed the assembled masses and stated clearly that Republicans had lost, and they needed to act as such. Acknowledging that an electoral defeat that happened did in fact happen might not exactly seem like a heroic act in a vacuum, but in *that* ballroom, it was downright countercultural.

Many RNC members may have agreed with Barbour in private, but few dared speak it aloud lest they risk the wrath of the Trumpy Stasi in their midst. Others had gone full conspiracy, and Barbour's dissent was a notable contrast to Priebus and Stefanik, who were continuing to publicly flirt with the notion that there may have been some electoral funny business. In February, Barbour maintained that posture, giving an interview to the immaculately named southern political blog YallPolitics in which he blamed Trump for the loss in 2020 and argued that in the future the GOP needed to "embrace what Trump did well and reject what he did wrong." Later he became one of just a handful of RNC members to publicly state that they voted against the resolution that would censure Liz Cheney for investigating January 6th, which the party monstrously described as "legitimate political discourse."

Barbour was still trying to do his part to nudge things forward.

To reanimate some of the autopsy's recommendations that had been thrown by the wayside.

In the spring following the insurrection, I called him to reflect on everything that had come to pass. I wanted to know what he saw as the direction for him and his privately concerned pals, with Trump out of the White House but still holding on to his position as the de facto party leader.

During that call, Henry reiterated how pissed he was about January 6th. And it wasn't just lip service. His anger and frustration were palpable through the phone. He left no doubt that if given the chance, he would wave a magic wand and make things go back to the way they had been before all the madness.

But at the end of the call, when it came down to the question of whether he would oppose Trump next time and walk away from everything, his voice caught. He hoped that it wouldn't come to that but hedged on what he would do if it did. While I don't have a crystal ball, past performance is the best predictor of future results.

For the company men there may have been days of rage, but the enraged were all still on the team in the end.

14

The Junior Messiah and the OG Demagogue

In November 2016, Alyssa Farah participated in a family tradition of sorts. She was headed to the polls with her father, Joe, to mark the latest chapter in our great democratic experiment.

This was not your standard electoral outing, in a few respects. For starters, Alyssa was the spokesperson for the Freedom Caucus—a collection of rebellious Republican rabble-rousers in the House of Representatives, and Joe was the longtime editor-in-chief of a far-right conspiracy website called WorldNetDaily.

But that's not what made this day unusual for Alyssa. Being immersed in reactionary right-wing politics was her everyday existence. This particular electoral assignation was different because (a) for the first time, she was not being fully forthright with her father regarding whom she was planning to vote for (another great American tradition), and (b) for the first time, her father was visibly excited for a candidate.

For her entire life, Joe had been the contrarian, the disgruntled anti-establishmentarian, a thorn in the side of the Republican candidates who weren't sufficiently responsive to the demands of the kookiest corner of the grassroots, where he was a guerrilla commander. But during the 2016 Republican primary, to Alyssa's private horror, it was her father's dream candidate who emerged victorious against the lily-livered ruling class he had spent years battling.

Joe was the human manifestation of Trump's political id. He had been a direct source for the racist conspiracy that launched Trump's career. Much of what came to define "Trumpism" bubbled up not from the candidate's big, beautiful brain, but from the seedy dregs of the conservative online ecosystem the senior Farah had midwifed.

WorldNetDaily, founded in 1997, was one of the original online homes for conservative digital cranks and wingnut populists—all the "deplorables" and "hobbits" that Breitbart would center a decade later. Since it predated the social web, WND existed in a silo adjacent to, but not entirely separate from, the types of conservative media sites that most D.C. types frequented. Over the years, Joe would wax and wane in his mainstream acceptability, popping up on *Hannity* or *Cavuto* from time to time. But to those of us working for establishment Republicans, WND felt as far away from our wheelhouse as the *National Enquirer*, which, by the by, ended up being another outsider rag Trump used to his advantage.

While we campaign hacks were feeding voters a sporadic slab of steak on *Fox & Friends*, Farah was providing daily vampire facials, injecting the platelet-rich blood straight into his readers' foreheads. In the 1990s it was Farah's WorldNetDaily that was a cornerstone to the right-wing conspiracy-mongering that conjured insane fantasies like the "Clinton Kill List," which purported to implicate the first couple in the "murder" of Vince Foster, a longtime family friend who tragically committed suicide. Some of WND's other choice cuts include the claim that Muslims planned to conquer America by 2020 (*hurdle cleared, phew!*), a secret plan by U.S. elites to create a North American Union (*which underlies the NAFTA superhighway questions we'd get at McCain events*), and the belief that dinosaurs didn't exist, natch.

The "news" magnate didn't really hit the jackpot until he landed on his most significant contribution to the American body politic: birtherism. Were it not for one Joe Farah, the future birther-in-chief might never have discovered the issue that engendered a romance between rank-and-file evangelical Christians and a potty-mouthed, thrice-married adulterer who overcompensated for his tiny hands and aspic belly by periodically assaulting buxom blondes.

In 2011, when most Republican elected officials were implying Barack Hussein Obama might be ineligible to be president while also pretending that the issue only existed in the minds of the media members who wanted to embarrass them, Trump saw an opportunity to insert himself by saying the quiet part aloud. He found his Republican footing as the front man in the hunt for the supposed "long-form birth certificate" that right-wing bigots and opportunistic bungholes had claimed would prove that the first black president wasn't actually from America, rendering his entire presidency fraudulent. This "theory," if you want to call it that, was perfect for Trump. It required some performative flair to make the sale. It resonated with "regular joes" while being seen as ridiculous by elites. It was racist enough that he could do the Archie Bunker shtick but had just enough subtext that allowed him to stop short of going full n-word. Most critically, birtherism allowed Trump to separate himself from all the other patsy pols who were just too weak to fabricate a xenophobic conspiracy against a political rival.

As the media momentum grew from this gambit, Trump continued plumbing the depths of the theory, eventually tracking down the experts: Farah and his colleague, star WorldNetDaily columnist Jerome Corsi, who authored *Where's the Birth Certificate?*

The Case That Barack Obama Is Not Eligible to Be President. (The book came out right after Obama produced his birth certificate, but was still a bestseller, if you want the dictionary definition of "motivated reasoning.") When the future president first called Farah, he proposed dispatching "private investigators" to Hawaii or even Kenya to "get to the bottom of it." In an interview with the *New York Times* about his conversations with Trump, Farah said, "[Trump] was looking for affirmation that he was on the right track. He was looking for a smoking gun kind of sound bite that would resonate with people."

Farah, seeming to not understand that Trump's fortune was built on a throne of lies and that his entire business was a public relations house of cards, found himself "impressed" that Trump was willing to put in the time to prove the cockamamie theory his site had given rise to. "This was a busy guy, this was a multibillionaire [*Editor's note: LOL*], and I was surprised that he was willing to spend that kind of time on it," he said.

After Farah provided guidance on how to go about the supposed "research," Trump was off to the races. He didn't need to consult Joe personally as much in future years because his best crackpot ideas began to come directly to him via Twitter mention instead. But despite not being in constant contact, there was still a direct line from Farah to the unhinged MAGA web that powered Trump's rise. It's this influence on the bloodstream of the Republican electorate that made WND more poisonous than any list of its most outrageous stories can capture.

While the site claimed to be "conservative," the material they were feeding people was anything but. WND perpetuated the notion that all the country's democratic institutions were corrupted by sinister, unseen forces. That readers' countrymen and women were a hated enemy. That foreigners were invading the country and ruining all the things their readers held dear. That the end times might be nigh. That tyranny is at the doorstep. That their political foes wanted to stamp out God-fearing real Americans' way of life. And that all of this destruction was backed financially by hostile, rootless cosmopolitan sources.

To anyone who followed the ravings of the MAGA mob: doesn't that all sound kinda familiar? The QAnon movement is just World-NetDaily with a resurrected JFK Jr. shine job and a pedophile-ring cherry on top.

So, of course, Joe was absolutely giddy when he went to the polls in 2016. This was never supposed to happen. His people were the antagonists, the apocalyptics, the outsiders. Yet here he was on the cusp of having a president who would espouse the pathologically deranged worldview that he had been contaminating the political water table with for decades. A lifetime of work was about to be validated in the most unexpected of ways. The hobbits were about to be in charge. Never before in our politics had a stray mutt caught a more improbable car.

No wonder his daughter didn't want to tell him she wasn't sitting shotgun.

• • •

"I got in the booth; I was so sick of him. I just didn't feel right about it," Alyssa told me as we sat in the parlor of the Georgetown brownstone she shares with her fiancé. "I didn't make my decision until I was doing it. I wrote in Paul Ryan and Mike Pence. I didn't tell anyone except my boyfriend."

In the intervening years, she never did tell her father about that private betrayal of his dream candidate. This Ryan-voting-reveal comes long after the fact. After she went on to become Mike Pence's spokesperson. After she left there to *serve* as a communications aide in the Department of Defense. After she decided, against her best instincts, to become the communications director for the man she had once been sickened by. After she bailed on him over the Big Lie. After she held a clear anti-insurrection line when none of her former colleagues would. After she agreed to cooperate with the January 6th commission, which would investigate many of them.

Unlike most of the others I spoke to for this book, Alyssa and I had not been D.C. friends in the pre-Trump era. I was a campaign guy, and she a Hill rat. We had plenty of mutuals; it's a small town, after all. But to my recollection we had never actually met.

I watched her in the aftermath of January 6th with interest, wondering why she and Stephanie Grisham seemed to be the only Trump insiders to say without caveat that things had gone too far. To be honest, her actions were so aberrant that at first, I didn't really believe it was sincere. I figured there had to be some ulterior motive under the hood. How many times had we been burned by conniving Trumpers who returned to his warm embrace as soon as it was convenient? Remember the cover story where Glenn Beck told us how he was "sorry about all that"? Turns out he was sorry-not-sorry.

I fired off a nasty gotcha tweet during what I presumed was her cynical media rehab tour.

"In this same article @Alyssafarah does not rule out Trump 2024 and says she respects the President," I snarked. She replied matter-of-factly, "I ruled out Trump 2024, if you read." (As usual in these petty Twitter fracases, the distinction was semantic. When asked if she would support Trump 2024, in the article she said, "not at this time. It's a long time away but not at this time.")

My skepticism abated a bit when I saw that she agreed to an interview with Mehdi Hasan, a rabid leftist and one of the tougher interrogators on cable news. On his show, she went through a gauntlet of hostile questions about the broader GOP's complicity in the insurrection, her apologia for Elise Stefanik's active attempts to support Trump's election overthrow, how she could work for someone who made racist statements, and, lastly, once more on the question of Trump 2024. Farah replied that she would oppose him. Months later over email, she became even more emphatic, telling me that she is "committed to using every platform I have going forward to make sure that man is never in the White House again. It took me too long—I admit that—but it's my #1 priority."

As the only prominent Trump staffer to stick with him through the 2020 election and then not waver from walking away from him after the insurrection, Farah is maybe the singular example of someone who broke free from the various Trump Enablement Complexes, making her mindset essential to understanding what might make others do the same.

Despite our lack of relationship and the minor Twitter tussle, I reached out. She agreed to meet with me the next time I was in D.C. . . . if we could find a place "where there won't be wandering eyes." Departing the Trump grip was one thing. Being spotted consorting with the Never Trump enemy was still a bridge too far. Clean breaks are hard.

A few months later, despite my mean tweets, she brought me into her home, away from prying eyes.

As I entered her brownstone, she informed me that wine has calories and her wedding day was approaching, so she was instead pouring a special low-cal concoction—vodka with a splash of pomegranate White Claw on the rocks. I gladly obliged, and Claws in hand, we began a multi-hour tour into her life's choices while a summer rain pattered on the cobblestones outside.

Over the course of the next several hours—many more than I had figured on—I found us to be more connected than I had anticipated. She wasn't a person who perfectly matched my cynical imagination. Sure, she was trying to spin herself a favorable post-Trump narrative. But she also was raw and beleaguered and seemed to be engaged in a genuine reflection. We chuckled a bit about our respective Lebanese families. We commiserated over erstwhile colleagues and friends we had lost over our supposed betrayal of the team. But the comfy vibe check did have some limits. For starters, I would never live in the prepster paradise of Georgetown, seeing as I do not own any sweater vests, and when Alyssa's fiancé interrupted us mid-interview he was wearing an ensemble so waspy that it blinded me for a period of a few seconds, rendering me incapable of writing down the particulars of the fit. While I'm not 100 percent sure that the collar was popped on his boating shirt, for purposes of this story we should just go with that. The more relevant difference wasn't sartorial in nature but ideological. While I came up through the establishment RINO ranks, she was schooled as a TruCon, attending Patrick Henry College, an extremely conservative liberal arts school in Virginia, where she got wrapped up in Young Americans for Freedom, a counterpart to the College Republicans that is oriented less toward elections and more toward conservative dogma and indoctrination of the nation's youth. She became "one of the women who was radicalized by Sarah Palin," she says laughing, not because she was making a joke but more out of embarrassment.

"Interning in D.C. at YAF, I wanted to dress like her. I thought, I'm gonna be the next Palin." Through YAF she got a job working for Laura Ingraham on her radio show and she did not leave that experience with the best taste in her mouth. "[Ingraham] was actually the beginning of my eyes being opened. She was the first person I realized the shtick on TV was not who people are. A lot of it is more or less acting." (While the general comment about the performative nature of the medium is well taken, some of the subsequent stories she relayed about Ingraham throwing cell phones at employees, calling Meghan McCain an "overweight plus-sized

Barbie," and telling Alyssa she was "pretty but not smart" made it sound, to me, like Ingraham's on-air persona is not that far from reality.) Her real eye-opener was learning that the bullshit about adherence to the Constitution and "principles" that underscore the YAF program was easily shuffled to the side by the purportedly principled media moguls in Conservative Inc. when ratings and lib triggering required it.

While Ingraham may have grated on Alyssa on a personal level, she maintained her general conservative sensibility and found other players in that vein whose style of stratagem appealed more, namely Andrew Breitbart. Breitbart delivered another early moment of clarity when the man leading the #War against the left took a detour to confront her own father about his tactics.

At a 2010 Tea Party event, Breitbart and Joe Farah got into a heated argument in front of Dave Weigel, a blogger at the time who is now a campaign journalist for the *Washington Post*. Breitbart was lambasting Farah for wasting time on the birther issue. Farah shot back that Breitbart was "not a journalist," further enraging the firebrand. (Sidebar: I concur on both counts. This argument may have been a "the worst person you know just made a good point" meme two-fer.)

This exchange made an impression on Farah's coming-of-age daughter. "It was the first time I had to think through what you are pushing and why it matters. . . . I found myself silently agreeing with Andrew." Andrew's reliance on the tactical considerations in pushing back so aggressively on birtherism allowed her to disagree with her father as a strategic matter, without having to engage in a fundamental reassessment about what it said about the broader movement. Like many of us, Alyssa had convinced herself that the element WND was cultivating was just the crazy uncle locked away in the basement, that it didn't require any examination or reflection on the politicians who were courting their support.

She credits her mother with helping her have a broader "perspective" about the impact of things like birtherism. "I look back on that and kind of cringe. I'm extremely aware of gaps in my knowledge of racism that have exponentially developed [since then]. It's totally on me."

After Ingraham, Alyssa went to work in the press office of North Carolina representative Mark Meadows on Capitol Hill, and she loved it. She got along famously with the boss. She was "very comfortable with the notion that our goal in the Freedom Caucus was to push leadership further to the right, to push for more conservative policies."

She saw the 2014–15 Freedom Caucus experience as her platonic ideal. As she recalls it, these rebels were principled fighters for spending cuts and other True Conservative policies. But in practice, their behavior was more nihilistic and reactionary than prudently conservative. Farah spearheaded the media strategy around her boss Mark Meadows's attempt to remove John Boehner as Speaker for perceived sins against the supposed spendthrifts, but when Trump came around, the entire caucus of deficit hawks transmogrified into profligate parrots.

Despite her right-wing street cred, at the time, she was harassed by the Breitbart crowd that wanted the Freedom Caucus to be tougher on the border and address that oh-so-urgent threat of sharia law's emergence in America. She remembers, specifically, Breitbart writer Julia Hahn trying to pressure the caucus's members to "raise their hand if they want to deport all Muslims."

In 2015 she got an early sign of the rift to come as Trump began to rise as a candidate. Meadows was leaning toward endorsing him, citing the energy for Trump among the grassroots in the district. But Alyssa "really, really pushed him on Cruz," though she told me that her only personal contribution to a 2016 primary candidate was purchasing a tank top emblazoned with a throwback picture of a sideburned Young Jeb that I had designed (it turns out our sartorial sense has at least some overlap that I hadn't noticed on the surface!).

In the end, Meadows relented, and Alyssa rushed to book him on Fox to make the endorsement while there was ostensibly still time to stop the Trump train. Cruz would go on to win the Iowa caucuses three days later, the high-water mark for his campaign. In a preview of what was to come, Trump said Cruz won due to "fraud" and called for a redo.

But once the loco locomotive started rolling down hill, Meadows was eager to get on board. Alyssa remained skeptical. During debates "I would live-tweet attacking him," she said. However, this cannot be confirmed. All those tweets have since been deleted, as was the custom of the anti-Trump turned privately concerned Republican set.

During the Republican convention, while I was ripshit in Richmond, Alyssa was staffing her boss in Cleveland. "I was in the NRCC suite and sitting with a reporter—four minutes in I said I can't, let's just step out. It was the most depressing convention. It wasn't like Romney-Ryan, which was so exciting. The Khizr Khan thing wrecked me. I thought it was so cruel."

She noticed that Trump's exceedingly personal belittling of Khan and his wife, Gold Star parents who had spoken out against him at the Democratic National Convention, was reflected in those who showed up in Cleveland to cheer him on. In the middle of his acceptance speech she went to the restroom, where she encountered a very drunk woman who said, apropos of nothing, "'I fucking hate Hillary I want to put a bullet between her eyes.' I said to the woman, 'No you don't. You just don't want her to be president. We shouldn't want violence.' I remember walking out stunned."

Sometime after the convention, she got a call from Jason Miller, the Trump communications director who had jumped ship from the Cruz campaign when it was clear Trump was going to win. (This type of abandonment was in the Miller DNA. He later gained notoriety for refusing to pay child support to one of the women he had an affair with during the campaign.)

Miller's paunchy, chinless guile didn't persuade her. Despite the fact he was offering a salary significantly higher than what she was making on the Hill, and that she was living in a shitty apartment in D.C., she just couldn't get there when it came to working for Trump. "I thought about it maybe for like a day" before politely declining, she said.

The polite, conscientious objection continued, but it became harder and harder to fight the Trumpian exigencies as the campaign wore on. Her boss's wife, Debbie Meadows, organized a "women for Trump" bus tour back in the district and asked Alyssa to staff it. She told me that she had to let Mrs. Meadows down softly when it came to accompanying her on the tour, but agreed to provide some "back office" support in D.C.

A few months later, she was with her mom and sister on a girls' trip, sitting in the backseat of the car transcribing the text of an op-ed that Freedom Caucus member Jim Jordan was dictating to her over the phone. After they got off the call, Farah was given a heads-up about an impending story that would reveal Trump had bragged to Billy Bush about how hot his sexual assault victims were. It fell on Farah to relay the details back to Jordan before he got to his next event. Jordan couldn't get to a quiet place, so Alyssa had to repeat several times, at increasing volume, "He said 'grab them by the pussy,' sir," while her mom and sis listened in. "That one freaked me out," she told me. "My mom is a journalist, and for her, there's like nothing new under the sun. Well, this time she thought there must be something new under the sun."

While a brazen admission of serial groping may have cracked her mother's steely reserve, the Freedom Caucus band played on as if nothing had changed. As the election drew nearer and Congress did even less than usual, Alyssa did what was required of flacks in her shoes, actively pushing anti–Hillary Clinton material but largely ignoring Trump. She rationalized it as many others did.

- She found Clinton "unacceptable," too. (*Demonizer*)
- The Freedom Caucus was planning a Jordan-for-Speaker coup, bringing her that much closer to the top, so they had to demonstrate that Republicans needed a real anti-Clinton "fighter," unlike that cuck Paul Ryan. (*Striving*)
- Plus, she didn't think Trump was going to win anyway, so no big deal. (*LOL Nothing Matters*)

Oopsie. Doopsie.

On election night, she claims to have put herself to sleep before she knew who won. (This seems, to me, like a false memory, seeing as the winner was pretty clear by the 10 p.m. hour.) Nevertheless, she awoke to find that the man she had judged as cruel, racist, bizarre, weird, unconservative, mean-spirited, and offensive was president-elect of the United States.

Her father's website had been anthropomorphized into the leader of the free world. And she needed to figure out what to do next.

• • •

On the surface, it may have seemed like Joe was the Farah with a better chance of working for the incoming administration. He was no more porangi than half the other jabronis walking around the West Wing and Alyssa had all those mean tweets that could be used against her by more loyal rivals angling for jobs. Still, she also had an obvious appeal to the White House.

Trump liked to hire people who "looked the part," and if there ever were someone who fit that bill, it would be Alyssa, whose striking features could transition her easily into a role as the dogged flack in a big-screen send-up of the Trump era. Plus, her résumé and surname brought conservative credentials and anti-establishment aura. Given all that, and the shallow bench of high-level operatives available to Trump, it was inevitable that the White House would come calling, eventually. Eventually came quicker than she expected.

"Meadows encouraged me to reach out to [Trump aide] Hope Hicks. I did. She asked me to come in. We talked for a half hour. Sarah Sanders joined us. At the end of it, she was like, will you come work here?"

Now, when she related this story, the thought of being in that room generated involuntary shivers. Talking to Scott Pruitt on the phone was something I got my head around. Sitting across from Hicks and Sanders in the West Wing? No. Never ever. Ick.

Alyssa didn't share my disrelish. She insisted she respected them, despite having disagreements, the same way she had disagreements with Boehner or Obama's team, a comparison I find rather wanting (I mean . . . John Boehner's flacks never smeared sexual assault victims of the boss for kicks). But her respect didn't translate into actually going to *work* with them. "It wasn't a job that I wanted, and I wasn't sure that I wanted to go into that team. A week after that, Pence's team reached out. And I interviewed with them, and it just clicked."

For me the "Pence is normal/stable compared to Trump" case never really landed. Vice presidents have no *actual* duties besides being truckling toadies to their boss and no vice president in history truckled harder than toady Pence. During the 2016 campaign, I remember getting an exasperated call from my father on this score. He had been forwarded a *Wall Street Journal* article in which

I trashed Pence. He knew I was a Never Trumper but hadn't followed all my various apostasies against the party closely, so this broadside in his personal paper of record caught him off guard.

He understood why I loathed Trump but just didn't understand why I had to be so mean to Pence, too. It felt to him like I was acting a bit rash, drifting away from my principles, or his conception of my identity. These sorts of realizations and crack-ups were happening often around this time. Separating oneself from an identity creates disharmony when people in your life are forced to change how they see you. It's another reason pulling away became so hard for those ingrained in the GOP political class; there was an associated loss that was hard to reckon with.

But I had been down the identity-changing road before and was prepared to just rip the Band-Aid right off. Whereas Alyssa and my father might have regarded Pence as a regular old Republican navigating a kooky boss, from my vantage point Pence and the boss were one and the same. Finkle is Einhorn, Einhorn is Finkle.

Where I saw pathetic, servile, loafer-licking complicity, Alyssa saw a narrow reed of independence. How to explain this was something she had obviously spent a long time ruminating on. When I pressed her, she launched into a three-minute soliloquy that I think is important to share in its entirety.

I hope you will internalize and consider this, but you don't have to accept it. My position is this. It's something I had to really think about. At that point, he's eight months into his presidency. He's there the next four years. Governing is happening under him whether we want it to be or not. Call it good, call it bad. That is the commander-in-chief and the leader of the free world. I had good friends who I totally respect who chose to be conscientious objectors. I was close to that but thought, I shouldn't say I was close to that. I respect that. I don't respect the notion that everyone who objected just shouldn't have gone in or you would have had an administration that was staffed by like thousands of Steve Bannons. And I mean that. There are jobs and structures within government that have to be done, and they have to be done by professionals, by experienced people. I should also say I've never in my life agreed with any politician more than like eighty-five percent. Are there red lines is sort of a hypothetical. The Muslim ban: superoffensive. I'm Syrian and Lebanese. One of my best friends, who I worked with in Pence's office, is Muslim American, like me. It's offensive and it's bad policy. What I liked in Pence world is when bad policies happened, we acknowledged it. We did it respectfully and with respect for the chain of command and did our best behind the scenes. Almost every egregious policy—and I don't say this to like pat him on the back—it's Mike Pence behind the scenes finally getting it to come to a . . .

I have to cop to interrupting here, because that was all the Pence apologetics I could stomach. But for 180 seconds Alyssa perfectly encapsulated the Junior Messiah mindset that so many Republican staffers adopted in the Trump era. Someone had to take these jobs and nudge things in the right direction. Didn't they?

I'd heard from a few other Junior Messiahs in my day, so I was prepared to push back on this argument with my patented "Corey Lewandowski Theorem™" (CLT). The CLT posits a counterfactual in which the JM is replaced in their job by the goon who ran Trump's campaign.

Lewandowski, if you are unfamiliar, is a miasmic cretin who once drunkenly harassed a married woman at an addiction-awareness fundraiser in a Benihana with a PUA routine that included boasting about stabbing multiple people to death. He's a shriveled skin-flute-looking man with no appreciable skills outside of recognizing the popularity of unrestrained Trumpism and thus represented to me the bottom-basement replacement-level appointee.

If the JM could not say for certain that there would be any material impact on the welfare of the American public if they had been replaced by that steam-tray hot dog, then they were not, in fact, a messiah, but just another person rationalizing their promotion.

The CLT pushback, well, it caught Alyssa off guard. (Maybe I came in a little hot.)

She became visibly annoyed at the notion that it would even be a question that she might fail the CLT. And after a moment to gather her thoughts, she cited a number of proof points that aren't the "most sexy things in the world" to show that the Pence staff did make a difference. She then began to address the question of who might have replaced her on staff, before going off the record. Without betraying the particulars of her off-the-record comments, I will say that no matter how one feels about any individual candidate for a Trump administration job, it is obvious that whoever replaced her would have been terrible! It's just math. Most people who worked for Trump were terrible! The question was whether having a terrible person writing press releases would have made any real difference when the boss they were flacking for was out there suckling on Trump's toes. I would often get pushback from JMs on this point. Their position relies on avoiding the risk that a morally disreputable white nationalist would take their job working for a terrible white nationalist sympathizer, so they must continue working for the terrible white nationalist sympathizer to prevent any more terrible white nationalists from having a deleterious effect on the principal.

This logic is circular. It justifies anything! Alyssa was a flack; she wasn't securing loose nukes!

But she holds on for dear life to the belief that she was indispensable. Without it, everything else crumbles.

• • •

After the VP's office, Alyssa went on to work for the Department of Defense, moving into a role that she says constituted her dream job. "It was the first time I had worked in a nonpolitical environment. I'm a little embarrassed to admit it took me till I was twenty-nine to realize there are issues more important than partisan policy lines. It definitely made me look at it differently. And the magnitude of the issues. It kind of trivialized what was annoying at the White House."

But like all satisfying dreams, this one ended too abruptly.

Less than a year into her job at the Department of Defense, she was invited to the White House for an early-pandemic event honoring her former beloved boss Mark Meadows, the incoming chief of staff. While everyone at DOD was wearing masks and isolating from the colleagues, the vibe at this party was laissez-faire. As it turned out, the White House was one step short of one of those COVID chickenpox parties that *The Federalist* was pushing for where the infected take on the rainbow challenge.

It was at this superspreader soiree that a maskless Meadows tempted her with the forbidden fruit. "He asks me to come to the White House. He says he's gonna shake up the comms team and 'I want you to be press secretary.'"

Being the spokesperson for the president was not a job she was interested in. But getting closer to the action was. She countered that she might consider a totally behind-the-scenes role, "to try to like professionalize the comms shop, so reporter inquiries are actually being responded to. Let me do the basic functions and hire a spokesperson."

Meadows was prepared for that answer and already had his backup options in mind. It would be either the eventual choice

Kayleigh McEnany or Jenna Ellis, a lunatic who would go on to gain notoriety as the front woman for the Kraken-head legal team that tried to overturn the election and maintain Trump as an unelected autocrat.

Once again, the Junior Messiah's instincts were reinforced by the prospect of the crazier and stupider alternatives presented to her. She asked Meadows for some time and decamped to her fiancé's lake house in New Hampshire. There the secretary of defense, Mark Esper, and her soon-to-be husband both tried to talk her out of taking the job. They appealed to her love of her existing gig and the stability there.

While she listened to their entreaties, she was drawn to the allure of working with her former boss at the White House. Getting the gang back together. Being in the mix. And telling herself she could make a difference in the midst of a generational crisis.

As she weighed this decision, she and her fiancé went on a hike during which she had a full-blown panic attack. A kind she had never had in her life. She had trouble breathing and thought it might be a medical problem, but it wasn't. It was her body trying to tell the brain what it already knew but had locked away in a deep dark corner: taking this job is a really bad idea. But Alyssa didn't get the message.

I push her on all this. On how she had to have known becoming Donald Trump's communications director was a disaster in the making. She slouches over, defeated. Her voice softens and she says, "Like everything, I was naively convinced if I did things the way I thought right, then I would be fine and, you know . . ." She trails off.

For the next hour, we parry back and forth and back again. With me asking why she didn't speak up sooner if it was so bad. With her describing how all the horrors that she saw on the inside only strengthened her resolve to stay.

She told me how she almost stopped the bleach-injecting press conference. Almost.

How she broke a bureaucratic logjam that was preventing PPE from being released to HHS from DOD. And how she even talked the big guy into sending a tweet that likely saved the *Stars and Stripes* military newspaper from getting shuttered. (How is that a real sentence?)

Time and again, she fell back on how much she was needed and dismissed the power of any one person's protest resignation as a fantasy of people in the D.C. bubble. "If I had resigned in protest, it would be a news cycle, I would do some CNN hits, it would functionally change nothing." She bristled at any arguments to the contrary.

Days after we had finished talking, she was still wrapped around this axle. She was stewing over the fact that I had been unpersuaded by her conviction that she was needed. I received an email recapping her frustrations:

> Separating me from the discussion—I'd once again raise the notion that the wheels of governing at every level couldn't and shouldn't have just come to a screeching halt everytime the President made a bad decision. [A]nd if you're approaching this under the assumption that no people of good faith served in any level of the WH or Admin (other than those who resigned and switched their careers to speaking out)—you are missing a lot about the moment.

Some of that is hard to argue with! The question of how legitimate public servants should handle the election of a madman is not a cut-and-dried moral matter. I told her as much while reiterating that I still land on the opposite side. But she was determined to win me over. A few days later I received another missive, in which she listed some examples of ways people who decided to stay on the inside made a difference. From her personal experience:

> Directly talked potus out of firing Esper—twice
>
> Directly talked him out of firing deputy NSA Matt Pottinger
>
> Advocated against invoking the insurrection act—a week before the Barr mtg that's been reported
>
> Convinced him to not use racist birther attack on Kamala Harris when Stephen and Jenna pushed
>
> Regularly encouraged him not to fire fauci
>
> Pushed him to not replace doctor birx with scott atlas on the covid task force

I want to stop here for a brief pause, even though this is not the end of her email.

Look at this list. All I can think about when I read it is, *Dear God a maniac was in power and he must be stopped.* The president wanted to put an unhinged quack in charge of responding to a pandemic killing hundreds of thousands of people! Declare martial law to stay in power against the will of the voters! Fabricate a racist lie against his opponent . . . again!

Anyone who can make this list knew full well that this was a psychopathic monster. That every day he was treated as a marginally normal president, it became that much easier for voters on the fence to convince themselves he should be kept in charge. *Why wasn't everyone who saw this doing everything in their power to stop him from being president one more day?! He was very nearly reelected. Ahhhhhh.*

But I digress.

With a month left in her job, Alyssa had decided privately that she wanted Joe Biden to win, though she wasn't going to say anything about it. She slogged her way through election night. As an unhappy Trump vented in his residence, she drank with people in her office and avoided his wrath. Later she went to the Map Room, where Trump was "freaking out at people." According to her account, by 11 p.m. the White House communications director had seen enough.

Before all the "late-night dump" craziness of election night came to pass, she went home and got into bed, just as she had four years earlier.

In the following weeks, while some in the White House plotted their "Stop the Steal" spin, Farah went through the motions of her day job while keeping an eye on the next opportunity. She advised her staff to go through the same process, since she was not at all persuaded by the notion that her boss might yet stay in office. This assuredness put her on a bit of an island. As the crazy proceeded, she became increasingly flabbergasted by how pervasive the conspiracy-mongering was internally. Even people she had once respected, like Meadows, were buying into the notion that the election could really be overturned.

So, she began more aggressively plotting her exit, having dinners with reporters and friends, figuring out how to wash the Trump stench off her résumé. It was at one of those dinners, at an Indian restaurant across the street from the White House, that her years in Trump's employ unraveled at long last. She had maybe one too many drinks (understandable), vented too loudly about her coup-plotting colleagues, and things spiraled. Word of her "betrayal" got around the White House.

She moved up the timeline of her departure, and the next day the *Washington Post* reported that she was out.

If we were not living in the upside down, a story like this would not merit recounting. Having some rowdy networking drinks and then resigning a few weeks after a losing election is not exactly breaking news. It's SOP and exactly what I did after every campaign I lost. But she was not in normal times.

Farah's resignation was seen as a finger in the eye to Trump's preposterous attempts at election thievery, a signal from the inside that it was time to close up shop. In the headline of the *Post* story they wrote that this was a "tacit nod to Trump's loss." (Duh.) Alyssa told me, laughing, that in another example of her naivete, she thought that once she spoke out, a lot of people would follow. But it turned out that after her, the line at Sane Station was short.

By January 6th, Farah was staying at her fiancé's family's home in Florida. She was out of the game but not completely off the grid. That morning she had been texting Jared Kushner with some advice on COVID messaging. As the morning went on, she began to mentally distance herself from the proceedings on the Mall.

She was baking with her future mother-in-law, enjoying a pleasant Florida respite and not really paying mind to the television that was on in the background. Eventually the madness caught her attention. She realized the life-and-death stakes and tried one last time to save all of us from the mad king.

She called the president on White House Signal repeatedly, to no avail. She texted Meadows, begging him to do something, anything, to help make it stop. But as we all now know, they were not interested in stopping the mob. They wanted the mob to succeed.

As the madness unfolded, Alyssa wasn't just concerned about the actions of her former White House coworkers. She also became deeply worried for the safety of her best friend, who was in the Capitol, her former colleagues staffing Vice President Pence, whom the protesters had come to hang, and for one other person she thought might be in danger—her dad.

Despite suffering a stroke in 2019, Joe Farah was still writing for WorldNetDaily in the aftermath of the 2020 election. He was fully on board with the MyPillow Putsch, telling his readers that the election had been stolen from Trump and they should once again go to battle for their freedoms. As their leader, Joseph Farah did exactly that. He trekked to the Mall, where he stood shoulder

to shoulder with his people, watching the beast he had unleashed
storm the Capitol steps in an attempt to delegitimize yet another
Democratic president.

This snapshot of the Farahs on January 6th was a synecdoche
for the entire Republican Party's decay. There they were—the
conspiracy-monger standing amid a treasonous paroxysm of lunacy he had incited, and the daughter who knew better but who
kept thinking she could manage and contain the crazy, desperately
grabbing for any ally or lever to help her do so, right up until the
moment in which the party and the Capitol were swallowed whole.

• • •

Alyssa Farah is not really that different from hundreds of other
ambitious creatures at the highest levels of Republican politics.

People like Reince Priebus, who in the months after the insurrection continued advocating for the absurd "audit" of the
Wisconsin election results. Or Sean Spicer, who hosted a show on
the network that was the television home for insurrection mania.
Or Elise Stefanik, who voted to cancel legal ballots cast by American citizens so that a man she had once been disgusted by could
become an unelected autocrat. Or my old colleagues at America
Rising, who toiled away at their Joe Biden research and compartmentalized the reality of who it was they were really helping. Or
the myriad consultants like Josh Holmes, Mike Shields, and Katie
Walsh, who got rich helping someone they knew was maniacal. Or
Lindsey Graham, who took the very same actions Farah had on January 6th, only to backtrack the moment after he was shouted down
by an airport throng and realized he needed to become anti-anti-
insurrection to stay in the mix. Or the National Republican Senate
Committee staffer who told me that they justified going along with
the coup up until January 5th because they were oh-so-terrified of

what would happen to the country if they lost the Georgia run-off, giving the Democrats a 50-50 Senate, with moderate Joe Manchin of West Virginia as the critical vote. Or all the other enablers who are breathing a sigh of relief that I didn't mention them in this book, but who sometimes roll around in bed at night knowing their wives or kids or friends look at them with a little less respect than they once had because they look at themselves that way.

The only real difference between all of them and Alyssa is that they were still in the game, clinging to the rationalizations that got them this far. But for Alyssa, when the Capitol was besieged, something changed. The story she had been telling herself had become inoperative. She no longer had a role in government that required rationalization to function. She had no ability to save anyone. Her internal ambition was overwhelmed by her conscience and a different part of the id: the desire within us to be seen by those we care about as righteous and good. The desire to not make the same mistakes with our children that our parents made with us.

At the end of our interview, I asked Alyssa why she agreed to go along with this book at all, given that anyone who had even a passing familiarity with me or access to a Google machine would know that I was not planning to write a puff piece on Donald Trump's communications director.

She got choked up and wiped her eyes. After a few breaths, she offered this: "I've been thinking a lot ever since my dad had his stroke about mortality and legacy, and marrying into a family where I'm so proud of who they are and grappling with who my dad could have been and what he's not. I don't care about money or different things, but I want my kids and grandkids to look back and be like, she was someone who did the right thing. I don't need anyone to pat me on the back or anything. I want history to remember me the right way."

Honestly, same.

15

The Demonizer and the Never Trumper

I still couldn't wrap my mind around Caroline.

There was a map in my brain diagramming all the rationalizations and self-deceptions and justifications of my peers, but I couldn't precisely locate her on it. How did a friend of mine end up on the National Mall sitting next to the most contemptible Trumpian gutter trash? Enlivened by a speech that was equal parts ridiculous and dangerous?

I had to go to Santa Monica to find out.

The night featured much dithering, reminiscing, and anxious slamming of tequila before I came to terms with the fact that her truth was not going to materialize as an apparition on the pier. To get anywhere near an answer, I was going to have to work for it. So, after what felt like a fortnight of humina humina humina, I reached from the banquette across the small table filled with empty glasses and an assortment of half-eaten Mediterranean dips, set down my iPhone, turned on the voice memo recorder, and turned back the clock to the start of our relationship.

How in the hell did we get here?

• • •

During the Huntsman presidential campaign in 2012 I would write a daily email that went out to reporters, donors, and other "stakeholders" (political campaigns love to talk about "stakeholders," a catch-all term for people we might need sometime and/or people who want to feel involved without having anything productive to offer).

My email was called the Morning Hunt. Each newsletter included an H-Jam, a hipster music nerd song of the day. Early in the campaign I was told that one of the gals in the finance department was crushing on the tunes. So I went back to their bullpen, we geeked out a bit, she suggested Ghostland Observatory's "Paparazzi Lighting" for the next day's Hunt (I went with Ghostland's rendition of "The Band Marches On" instead, editor's prerogative), and the seeds of a friendship that wouldn't truly blossom for a few years were planted.

A few weeks later, Caroline was laid off, and the favored few who remained employed were dispatched to New Hampshire, the site of our campaign's Waterloo. Some of the staffers were embittered by this turn of events. Huntsman was the scion of a billionaire; money was no object. He had made us move to Orlando, of all places, in the middle of summer. Most were locked into six- or twelve-month leases and had only been there for one or two. Before they could even sneak away to go Drinking Around the World at Epcot, they got the ax. It was hard to blame them for being pissed.

But not Caroline. Despite her unceremonious dismissal, she

was unfazed. She stayed irrationally loyal to our hopeless campaign. She got permission from her then-paying employer to leave at 2 p.m. every Friday afternoon to take the flight from Reagan National to Manchester to volunteer for the guy who had fired her. Almost every weekend she would hop on that plane to help with anything that was needed and party with the team.

During those jaunts north, she became buddies with the Huntsman daughters (Liddy, the youngest and rowdiest, in particular), and when they were all together, they would paint the town red, to the extent that is possible in a place so dreary. And, oh how dreary it was. I'm not certain the sun peeked out more than thrice during our months in Manchester. Some called our new home Manchvegas, ironically, but I preferred the more on-the-nose Manchganistan. Among the locals I can testify there was not a single sexable creature of any gender or orientation. So when you went anywhere with the glamorous Huntsman daughters, you might have thought One Direction just walked into the bar or that *The Simple Life* was taping a rusted-out New England reunion.

Young, pretty, and not afraid of the spotlight, the Huntsman girls had become a fixture of the campaign. While they were mostly well-intentioned, their growing profile had become a headache for the comms department, outshining their milquetoast diplomat father, who was less suited for the Game's increasingly pithy political combat.

This meant that those of us charged with trying to puff up dad's brand would often have to try to clip their wings and channel their efforts for good in order to avoid this unflattering comparison. The clipping was received, at times, with hostility on the home front, which created tension in the ranks and resulted in my looking for creative ways to deliver the message. Once, after Huntsman's guest appearance on *Saturday Night Live*'s "Weekend Update," I even approached Seth Meyers and Paul Rudd to ask if they might pass along to the girls that their media tour was cockblocking Dad a bit. Seth claimed he did me that solid at the after-party, and though I'm not sure what exactly he ended up saying, it did seem to buy me a week of peace.

As a result of this tension, I didn't get to see firsthand all the escapades that Caroline embarked on with the Huntsman girls which campaign aides would whisper about on Monday mornings. That made me wonder if I had misunderstood my friend all along. This was the underpinning of my initial theory of the case.

Maybe she was just a political groupie with some spare cash and there was a straight line from dancing on a bar on New Year's Eve in Manchganistan with the glitzy Huntsman gals to drinking in the Tonga Room with a Trump son eight years later and there wasn't much more to it than that?

I pressed her on that thesis, and she rejected it, drawing a line that went even further back.

• • •

Caroline first fell in love with politics as a twenty-year-old at Auburn University when a friend loaned her John McCain's book *Faith of My Fathers*. For Christmas that year she asked her parents for a flight to New Hampshire and ended up spending her winter break knocking on doors, waving signs, and sleeping on an "old lady's couch" in the First in the Nation primary state. After that trip, she was hooked. On McCain. On politics. On the Game.

While I was filling my newly emptied closet with fresh gay fits and feeling a mix of bitterness and jealousy toward my friends who remained with the campaign that I had departed the summer before, Caroline was putting up Craigslist ads and driving fellow Mc-Cainiacs to primaries across the South. Skipping class to scamper off to South Carolina, then Florida. This behavior made no sense to her sorority sisters who had more conventional collegiate interests, but she gave them the Heisman hand because she had come to worship John McCain. When he won the primary she took off the summer and fall semesters to intern in his Crystal City, Virginia, headquarters.

It was there that the first sign of our parting sprouted, as she recalled the big inflection point of that internship, the reveal of McCain's vice presidential nominee, Sarah from Alaska. My horror at the Palinized GOP apparently wasn't shared by Caroline, who fell in love with the Maverick sidekick. Like Farah, Caroline confessed to being "obsessed with Sarah Palin," which in retrospect was clearly an early litmus test for people's behavior in the years to come.

You liked Palin even *after* the campaign in 2008, I asked, bewildered.

"Yeah, after the campaign," she said.

"None of the crazy Palin shit bothered you?"

"Not at all. Because I wasn't a political operative or anything. I fell in love with people in politics. . . . I didn't know where I stood ideologically on things. I was learning it as I went and latched onto people I enjoyed or didn't enjoy."

This didn't track with me. Caroline and I had long bonded over our distaste for the more extreme GOP candidates, which was based, I had assumed, in our shared squishiness.

Over the years we both were teased by our friend group for our record of backing losing RINO candidates. I didn't work on a single successful campaign between my 2002 internship with Bill Owens and the consulting gigs for Nikki Haley, Scott Walker, and other winning midterm candidates in 2014. Caroline had the same experience. She fundraised for Olympia Snowe (the Maine Moderate), Jon Bruning in Nebraska (a Senate candidate who lost to Trumpy Tea Party senator Deb Fischer and went on to support moderate

Democrat Steve Bullock's presidential campaign in 2020), and David Dewhurst in Texas (the centrist who lost the primary that gave us Lyin' Ted Cruz).

Up until 2014 she had never sipped from the sweet chalice of victory.

"It was like the big joke, I had worked for every moderate who lost."

Despite describing herself as not having a fully formed ideological framework in explaining her fondness for Palin, there were clear signposts that were mixed but largely pointed her to the middle, at least on cultural matters.

When I told her that Huntsman was the candidate whom I agreed with most on issues, she said "same." She did go to the hardline Mises Institute of economics at Auburn. (Ludwig von Mises was the Austrian economist beloved by free-market conservatives and libertarians.) But she said she has "always been pretty liberal on social issues. I am pro-life, but I would hold my best friend's hand if she needed to go get an abortion. So, I don't know what that makes me, but I'm anti-judgmental on it."

She was generally attracted to candidates who valued bipartisanship and service. "I read Huntsman's bio and fell in love and was obsessed. It was the same as McCain. Country first. I actually loved that he [Huntsman] went to serve as ambassador under Obama. When you are asked to serve, you do. My age group, I don't really know anyone who was against gay marriage. I liked him for that. I always had been for gay marriage."

So how does any of that mesh with becoming *obsessed* with Sarah Palin, of all people? I pressed, relaying that Palin turned me off in kinda the same way Minnesota's Michele Bachmann did.

"So, I totally couldn't stand Bachmann," she said. "But Palin I loved. I think I just fall in love with politicians, the people, versus more than the weeds of their political identities."

For her the connection was more akin to rabid team fandom. She was Drew Barrymore in *Fever Pitch*, Dan Aykroyd in *Celtic Pride*. Her deification of McCain was such that years later she took a trip to Vietnam, solely to see the so-called Hanoi Hilton prison, where McCain was captive.

"It's actually a horrible place. It has all this propaganda. It shows McCain like playing basketball, basically makes it seem like he had the greatest time. It's really upsetting when you go there."

She was providing a connection. From the flights to Manchester for the beloved candidate who fired her, to Vietnam to see where her hero had been tortured, all the way to the packed hangar rallies with Trump Force One.

In one sense, it tracks, I guess. But of all the people to fall for next . . . Donald Trump?

• • •

It didn't happen immediately.

In 2014 she had moved to South Carolina to run fundraising for Lindsey Graham's reelection campaign. The South Carolina RINO had a tough primary from five far-right freaks plus future GOP congresswoman and anti-anti-insurrectionist Nancy Mace. Caroline was brought in to create and manage a financial death star. The effort was a tremendous success. Lindsey O. Graham-nesty bulldozed the populists and teabaggers, winning in a landslide, a result that filled Caroline with pride. Success, at long last! I had naively hoped Graham's victory over the populist right was a harbinger of things to come in the upcoming presidential primary.

In 2016, when Graham decided on a moonshot bid for the presidency, she decided to eschew the offers from bigger campaigns and stick with him. It was his influence that led her to dislike Trump initially. Graham had a deep, personal well of hatred for Mango Mussolini that I can be certain was not performative because I heard the full sermon firsthand. After Graham dropped out of the presidential race, he endorsed Jeb and became my boss's campaign trail sidekick. For a brief while, the nation's preeminent Little Mix got his fix from us, using Jeb as his temporary pilot fish. So, I spent much of January 2016 traveling with the two of them along the eastern seaboard, with campaign events in New Hampshire and South Carolina and pit stops in New York for media appearances and fundraising. We generally loved having Lindsey on the trail, as he had a knack for keeping our spirits high despite the depressing poll numbers, regaling us with hilarious stories from campaigns past. Say what you want about Graham's pathetic future as Trump's personal ball cupper: the man can spin a yarn. His tale of the time he ran afoul of an activist group representing the Little People of America had me in tears.

When he wasn't giving us his latest tight five, he mostly wanted to rant about Trump. One night stands out in my memory. After a marathon day of media hits capped with an extremely unpleasant taping of Anthony Scaramucci's low-rated Fox Business show, Jeb, Lindsey, and I retired to a nondescript hotel bar in midtown Manhattan. The three of us sat at a little low-top table away from the crowd. Jeb and I were drinking scotch. (I'm a bourbon man but liked to be sporting when with the boss.) Lindsey had Chardonnay. The night went long with both of them doing two drinks to my one. As the booze flowed, Lindsey began relentlessly pummeling Jeb about the need to hit Trump even harder than he had been. He is a racist! He's un-American!! He would ruin the country!!! He went round and round about birtherism and the Central Park Five (Trump had taken out ads calling for the death penalty for five black men wrongfully accused of a 1989 rape). As the night went on he got increasingly hot and bothered. He was equal parts convinced that Trump couldn't win and horrified at the prospect that someone as bigoted as Trump was might actually get it done.

Jeb kept making furtive eye contact with me, desperate for someone to move the conversation to the NFL playoffs or the next day's schedule or freaking anything besides Trump. It's not like he didn't know any of this; he had been trying to punch back at Trump for months, to little effect. But Lindsey was a dog on a bone. We couldn't get him to talk about anything else.

Eventually, Lindsey dipped out to the bar or bathroom and Jeb found the opportunity to sneak to bed, telling me I had to stick around and keep him company. When Lindsey returned, he didn't miss a beat. He wanted to plot what we could do to stop the racist menace, offering ideas of varying quality. I nodded, agreeing with the thrust of his concern, but not sure we could pull most of it off, given our campaign's past performance on Trump offensives. Nonetheless, Lindsey figured I was his best ally on the matter, and for the next few weeks, I would get calls at random hours from blocked numbers. It would almost always be Lindsey with his latest idea for how to ensnare Trump.

If that was my experience, barely knowing the man, you can imagine the earful Caroline would get as they traveled the country together asking rich people for money while Trump's poll numbers continued to rise. At the start, Lindsey's Trump Derangement resonated with her.

"I didn't know anything about Trump. I didn't take him that seriously when he started running. I remember yelling at one kid at my house who told me he was a Trump supporter, and I threw him out," she said.

"When you hated him what did it have to do with?" I asked.

"I don't remember. It was just because I was told to. It might've been the refugees."

The refugees. Of course.

You see, Caroline's compulsive behavior wasn't limited to just candidates. An issue or topic would move her, and she would glom on to it. Over drinks at her house the conversations would always turn to her latest obsessions. She'd tell me that she got so obsessed over something or other that she would go down hours-long Google rabbit holes and lose entire days researching it.

I searched my text history for the word "obsessed" and found mostly messages from Caroline. Over the years she had mentioned everything from my daughter to the Kurds to in-home massages to "Columbia gays" (being obsessed with her, in that instance).

Toward the end of the Obama presidency, her obsession was with the plight of the Syrian refugees. She saw the pictures splashing across all our screens and couldn't get them out of her mind. Unlike the rest of us, however, she did something about it.

After reading about a train station in Germany that had become a choke point, one weekend, on a whim, she flew to Munich. By herself. I had remembered her going but didn't realize it wasn't some sort of organized trip put on by an NGO or a political organization. She had just decided something needed to be done, so she picked up her shit and went, just like she had as an Auburn undergrad who wanted to help John McCain's campaign.

After landing in Munich, she bought a full month's rent worth of children's backpacks, filled them with food and coloring books and candy, and brought them to the station she had seen on the news. For two days she stood alone outside München Hauptbahnhof, holding a sign that said, "Welcome. America loves you," which she adorned with a U.S. flag and some hearts, handing out the backpacks and embracing the sweet Syrian kids who had been thrust out of their home by a bloodthirsty tyrant.

She didn't know anyone in Germany. She didn't go to the clubs or the museums. She didn't leave the train station for forty-eight hours.

"It was like nothing you'd ever see in your entire life. It didn't stop. A train would come in and it was just children pouring out. From six a.m. until late into the night. They were so happy and appreciative. The journey they took to get there was insane. The worst journey you could ever imagine."

For a few minutes we reminisced about how much that experience moved her. How we had looked through her pictures, and how I had told her at the time how much I wished I could adopt one of the little kids who had lost their family.

While I was daydreaming about what I might do, she just got off her ass and did it.

A few years later, during the Trump administration, she went back to see what had happened in their homeland. This time she had a wingman and a translator. She wanted to help build safe houses for gay and trans Kurds. They flew first to Qatar and then had to book a separate ticket to Erbil, since that was the only way they could get there. She had become "obsessed" with the refugee community but especially the gay safe houses in Kurdistan. They stayed for ten days, meeting more and more people. Anyone who would see them.

Hearing her reflect on the young men they met in the safe houses, thrust out of their towns, rejected by their families, in immense physical danger, I was a ball of emotion and confusion. The friend I knew was in there. My memories weren't playing tricks on me. I hadn't totally just misjudged her.

And yet! The Muslim Ban. Zeroing out refugee admissions. Child separation. Liking heroes that weren't captured. Graham's righteous indignation.

How did all this mesh?

What I found were many of the rationalizations I had identified in my former colleagues. But for her there was something more as well. She had become deeply, personally enamored, you might say *obsessed*, with Donald fucking Trump.

• • •

"When the debates hit, I just became obsessed with him. It was just Trump eviscerating people on this main stage. I started texting with [my friends] Dan and Dave. We would send each other clips all day long."

We had created a big presidential game show. He was excelling at it and she was increasingly tickled by his antics.

As the campaign went on, it became a process of elimination. She could never stand Cruz, dating back to her work with Dewhurst. Jeb was so weakened by the alpha Trump act that she couldn't picture him on the big stage any longer. She grew to dislike the smarmy, beta Rubio.

After Graham dropped out, she got a call from Reince Priebus's finance director at the RNC, asking if she would run fundraising for the GOP convention in Cleveland. Most of the other people with the résumé for such a job were still working for one of the primary candidates, which gave Caroline a lot of leverage. It was an unbelievable networking and career opportunity, so she jumped on it. At the time I teased her via text. "If Jeb is the nominee, I'm going to layer you. If it's someone else, I want all the party invites. If it's Trump you are DTM."

Already hooked in by Trump's magnetism and comedic stylings, when she got to Cleveland she became rather protective of her new obsession. The staff was filled with John Kasich stans (it was in his home state) and conservative Cruz crew partisans. As the primary wore on, with Trump on pace to win, the other staffers angled to give their preferred candidates a chance to challenge and defeat him on the convention floor. This rubbed Caroline the wrong way, especially the attempt to help Cruz, whom she hated and thought would "lose forty-nine states." So, she became a self-described "whistleblower," tattling on traitorous staffers to Trump high command, ingratiating herself with the family and close confidants of the presumptive nominee.

When the convention came around, she was so dug in with her new team that all of the criticisms of the candidate became white noise. She essentially ignored those who mocked or were freaked out by the convention; she didn't want to believe them. As Stephanie Grisham confessed, "a bunker mentality" sets in.

For Caroline the coup de grâce came when she was able to deliver a chilly dish of revenge to an old rival.

One of her jobs on-site in Cleveland was to manage the VIP boxes. After Ted Cruz gave his "vote your conscience speech," strongly implying that it was okay to vote against Trump, he came up to visit GOP megadonor Sheldon Adelson.

It was Caroline who got to deliver the delicious news.

"Sorry, Mr. Cruz, the box is full," she said.

Cruz started "freaking out" and demanded she double-check, but that got him nowhere. Adelson was punishing him. She got to be the enforcer and revel as he squirmed.

"It was the greatest week of my life."

• • •

At this point in the story, I'm four tequila honeysuckles in and am ready to just get to the point. We've laughed. We've cried. And despite her assurances, I'm worried we might get cut short. She's missed eleven phone calls during our session. Out of all the astonishing confessions of the evening, I am perhaps most taken aback by the physical evidence of how entrenched in the Trump ecosystem she was. Every minute she got a text or a call from another Trump donor. When she hands me her phone at one point it has 426 missed calls, 643 unread texts, 230,305 unread emails, and two unwatched Snapchats. Wild.

At this point I have gotten my head around the appeal, even if I find it gross. The humor, the bunker mentality, the pwning of Rafael "Ted" Cruz. Like Spicer, she was gratified watching those she had felt spurned by get their comeuppance.

But how did she cleave off all the bad shit? How could someone who would fly to Munich to give candy to refugee kids not see the same Trump that I see? I asked her about some of the most obvious conflicts.

Muslim Ban.

I always just intensely disagreed with him on it.

Not in a way that was categorically different than other things?

It was one of many issues that were out there that I disagreed with him on.

It didn't make you mad?

I think it did make me mad . . . What was I going to do?

You were very hireable you could've done anything.

I was just working for the convention. It was a 501(c)3 . . . What am I going to do, stand up a month out and just walk out.

What about McCain—I like people who weren't captured.

I didn't like that line at all.

So were you blocking out the things you didn't like or were you listening and decided you liked it?

I drank the Kool-Aid. I don't think there is much he could've said.

We continued to go round and round on everything from birtherism to 9/11 trutherism until she said something that caught me by surprise. I asked her to turn the conversation on its head. If there was no level of depravity that would make her turn on him, what besides the humorous slams made her actually *like* him?

I think my evolution had more to do with anger, because at that point I was so angry at the media at the way they treated Lindsey. Angry at the party. And at this point I had lost so many races and I think it was more loving his scorch-the-earth mode. That's where I was politically.

This notion of anger driving her support for Trump was something that echoed what a lot of elite Republican types were saying. Rich Lowry, the nebbish *National Review* editor, wrote on the eve of Trump's losing reelection bid that supporting Trump was a "middle finger" to the cultural left. This seemed to me to be an unbelievably asinine, if understandable, mindset coming from a fussy, middle-aged, Manhattan-dwelling white conservative who resents his more culturally ascendant neighbors. But from Caroline, a socially liberal millennial, it caught me off guard. I pressed her for more. What's to be angry about?

I just don't feel the need to drive around my Prius drinking a coffee Coolatta with a coexist bumper sticker and checking the box like I've solved climate change. Me moving from plastic to paper straws is not actually moving this needle. The liberal culture of judgment, of do as I say, not as I do. John Kerry flying places in private jets. That's why I was so drawn to Trump. I was at a breaking point. [Politics] was bullshit and we knew everything we were doing was bullshit and Trump called it out. If Trump had maybe run as a Democrat, I think I would've been a Trump supporter. I didn't love him because of his conservative credentials.

I was genuinely dumbstruck by this. As someone who loves a chocolate shake, I also find forcible paper-straw usage to be an utterly moronic inconvenience of modern urban life. But connecting that to support for Donald Trump? Being upset with Joe Biden about private companies switching to deteriorating straws? This anger didn't click with me at all. I mean, seriously. Who cares? What even is a coffee Coolatta? I had to google how to spell it! Are we sure Coolattas are an elite lib thing? Apparently it's what Dunkin' Donuts calls their frozen coffee. This feels like the Armstrong of stretches.

Throughout the conversations with former colleagues, it was on this question that I came to find the starkest divide between the hard-line Never Trumpers and our reluctant peers who came to terms with the man. Most of us in the former group weren't bogged down by this animus. We disagreed with Obama on various things but didn't detest him, whereas my friends who stuck around the GOP had a visceral loathing that I'm not sure I realized was there even when I was part of it. When we were sparring with our Democratic counterparts, some of us were kind of faking it, going along with the kayfabe. While the rest of them were employing faux outrage and gamesmanship as well, it turns out that underneath the performance was a much more deep-seated desire to see the other side punished. To watch them get owned. Their grievances were based in part in ideology, but more often it seemed like simple interpersonal annoyance and privilege.

They live in liberal bubbles and find their neighbors' excesses grating. They are sick of being told what they should and shouldn't say or do. They are embittered that the media is always being unfair to them. They are tired of diversity requirements that mean they lose out on jobs to "people of color." They blanche at the DEI packets being handed out at their kids' schools. They find the left-wing sanctimony in the prestige-TV shows they watch grating as fuck. And apparently they are also over people who drive Priuses while simultaneously drinking coffee Coolattas.

All of that annoyance and envy bottles up until it boils over.

During the heat of the 2020 campaign, I interviewed a dozen top-level Republican operatives to try to understand why they were still grinding it out despite how miserable he was making their lives. These were not the Trump Kool-Aid drinkers, like Caroline. They were more in the vein of Henry Barbour. Rented strangers doing a job. For them there was an obvious, mundane reason for continuing (a paycheck), but the one thing that startled me was how many were also motivated by anger. This rage would come out of nowhere from otherwise gentle people. They would lash out at Never Trumpers like me and the Lincoln Project, calling us "motherfuckers." They told me that the media was a "bullshit leftist institution" and that "the mask is off."

One cut through the clutter with this searing admission: "Woke culture has created no other lane for you but to support him on the one or two things that you like, and then you have to countenance all the rest of the bullshit."

They all wanted to cut the left down a peg. Put a cap on the diversifying cultural elite who were flourishing at what they perceived was their expense. Trump was the vehicle for doing it.

I laid this theory out for Caroline, ensuring I wasn't misrepre-

senting her. "Is there something I'm missing here? I literally cannot name a single trait of Trump's I'd want to pass on to my kid.
What were you seeing positive about him that I wasn't? Or was it
you were just happy the other people were triggered?"

"I would say probably all negative," she replied. "I hadn't
thought through much of what a Trump presidency looked like. I
couldn't stand Clinton and the Democrats."

The morning after Trump won, she left for her yearly postelection holiday, this time to Morocco. When she landed in Marrakesh
there happened to be a United Nations climate change conference
going on. The people there were despondent and terrified. Caroline retold the story with a twinkle in her eye. She was exuberant.
Triumphant. Rubbing it in their faces a little bit.

I can sense your glee. You had no concerns?

"None. In that moment it was really gleeful."

As the Trump presidency comes into focus, Caroline does de-
velop a series of issues that she can tick off, which begin to provide
a more positive and substantive orientation for her support. We
fast-forward through the administration and go down a series of
rabbit holes debating the economy, his border and refugee policy,
the Yazidis, and the kids in cages.

On some issues, she has a legitimate and thoughtful case. On
matters that are inconvenient to the preferred narrative, she seems
as if she has no idea what I'm talking about. When I note this
trend of being totally unfamiliar about things that made a lot of
news, she uses all those unreturned calls as a defense. "I miss a lot
of it." And, well, she does get a lot of texts. But what I also come
to find is a common coping mechanism for Trumpists, encasing
oneself so completely in the right-wing media echo chamber that

inconvenient information barely penetrates. For this reason debating the particulars of the Trump era is getting me nowhere. Litigating the merits of the Abraham Accords seems rather beside the point. (N.B.: On balance, the accords seem pretty good to me.)

The waiter came by. She stuck to tequila. I moved to sangria, my heart sinking and stomach starting to turn. We needed to press forward and get to the insurrection before I lost my resolve. Choosing Trump over Hillary was one thing. Teaming up with a troupe of despicable, smooth-brained asswipes to try to install a MAGA autocracy was quite another.

16

The Big Lie

Five hours in, my nates beginning to ache, I excuse myself to the restroom, scroll through Instagram, and take a deep breath. The prelude is over. When I come back, we must get to the crux of the matter: how she got so mobbed up in the January 6th insurrection.

When I sit down, once again, I feel as though I need to start at the start.

Do you believe Joe Biden won fair and square?

No.

I respond with a deep, audible sigh and she, in turn, with a laugh.

Over the next few minutes, she lists all the reasons she does not, necessarily, think Biden won fair and square: pandemic election rules, Mark Zuckerberg, George Soros, and the puzzle of Biden getting 15 million more votes than Obama. It is on that point that she says something interesting: "But I know it's not fifteen million dead voters."

I could see she was going to try to pull one over on me with the "election integrity" do-si-do. This is a popular maneuver for Republicans who want to go along with Trump's nonsense without seeming crazy in polite company. In their telling, the people talking about voting machine shenanigans and the ghost of Hugo Chavez are loony tunes; there remains a more nuanced way in which those wily coyotes cheated. It's the sophisticate's QAnon. They agree on the final answer, parting ways when showing their work. I was prepared for this gambit; Caroline was not my first rodeo with ClassyQ. We went back and forth, taking each layer of the accusations one at a time. Finally I had the matter stripped down to its barest parts.

So you don't think there was a fabricated election result, you think Joe Biden did actually win with real people and real votes?
[Eight seconds of silence.]

Not sure?

No, I'm sure. I just don't know what I'm going to answer on the record.

!!!!!!
We are more than three hundred minutes and a dozen cocktails combined into our summit. We have discussed everything imaginable about her life, her ideology, her insecurities. It has been candid and uninhibited. And the *only* time that she requests to be off the record is to avoid admitting out loud that Donald Trump had lost the election!

At that point, I realize that throughout the entire evening she has avoided saying it. Going back through the tape, there is one anecdote in which she's describing the path forward she was proposing to a donor when she slips and says the phrase "when you lose an election," before catching herself and saying, "well, 'lose,'" putting a four-fingered scare quote around the word.

So, when she tells me that now she wants to go off the record, I am utterly flabbergasted.

"This is a cult!" I yell a little too loudly across the emptying hotel bar, aggressively twisting my hair as I do at moments of agitation. But she just chuckles and refuses to budge, recognizing that the only thing that would constitute a death sentence in the Trump orbit is acknowledging he lost.

Working with Alex Jones on a putsch was fine, even encouraged. Spilling the beans to a Never Trumper for his book might get her some blowback but is recoverable. Admitting defeat is the no-fly zone.

Ruth Ben-Ghiat, a historian who studies strongmen, wrote, "The authoritarian playbook has no chapter on defeat." Acknowledging weakness pops the bubble of disreality. It can't be accepted or broached.

Caroline, with her Trump family friendships, understands the rules of omertà.

• • •

Her path to the Ellipse that morning was, like everything in Trump world, a goat rodeo wrapped in a clusterfuck. The day after the election, she was dispatched to Nevada to challenge the results with a crack team fronted by two of the most loathsome chiselers in Trump's orbit.

The point man was his utterly unhinged former ambassador

to Germany, Ric Grenell, who had previously been best known for sexist Twitter dickering that cost Mitt Romney's campaign a couple of news cycles. Grenell was described by Susan Rice as "one of the most nasty, dishonest people I've ever encountered," and based on my experiences with him, that description is, if anything, too flattering. On the Nevada Stop the Steal effort Grenell was paired with Matt Schlapp, the pudgy troll who runs the Conservative Political Action Conference (CPAC) and gave one of the most startlingly honest interviews of the Trump era when he admitted to a *Washington Post* reporter that after the "pussy grabbing" tape, he was concerned about the message it would send to his daughters if he continued to be a surrogate for Trump, but that he and his wife, Mercedes, washed away those doubts over a bottle of wine, deciding instead to "double down" due to the greater evil posed by Hillary Clinton. It was a bet that paid off handsomely for them. Mercedes went on to become Farah's predecessor as White House comms director, while Matt cashed in bigly on the outside. The Schlapps weren't about to threaten their cartel by reassessing their unquestioned priors about the demons among them.

It was an interesting pair, given that Grenell was the most prominent openly gay Trumper and Schlapp had been one of the most arduous advocates against gay rights in the Bush White House. A friend who attended the Schlapps' wedding, which had, like the Shieldses', been a swampy affair, recalled the awkwardness of witnessing an asperous sermon on the sanctity of heterosexual marriage while sitting next to a clowder of closeted Republican operatives. But while Schlapp and Grenell may have departed company on heterosexual supremacy, they were bound together in their willingness to maintain MAGA supremacy with bad-faith arguments about election theft. That was the only qualification required to be part of this "litigation" team.

When Caroline landed, she discovered that there was no organization at all, outside of the diligent effort to ensure that Schlapp and Grenell were able to garner media attention and lambaste the "fake news" if the latter challenged their dubious claims. Since Caroline was not a media hound, she was assigned a general role supporting the effort to identify any possible examples of "voter fraud," which was also not exactly an area of expertise for a professional fundraiser. She barely had the chance to get this amateur Carmen San Diego routine started when she contracted the novel coronavirus and became the patient zero that sidelined a significant portion of the Keystone Fraudbusters, derailing much of the upstart undertaking.

One morning during her recuperation, she was lying in bed around 6 or 7 a.m. and got a call from a Trump official telling her she had to get a plane for Lin Wood, ASAP. I'll just let her explain it in her own words from here.

"I'm like, who the fuck is Lin Wood? Apparently, he had to get to some press conference in Georgia. So I call someone I knew who had a plane and said you need to go pick up this guy Lin Wood. I call Lin. He says he has to get in the shower. I am yelling at him, saying the plane is arriving in fifteen minutes. He was so cavalier. Getting from Beaufort [South Carolina] to Georgia. So that was my intro to this world. Then I see the tweet he sends out about wanting to have the VP executed, which makes me reflect on myself. We all thought he was this supersmart attorney at the beginning. I was told he was our saving grace. Everything was moving so fast I couldn't track who's crazy and who is not."

(Narrator: She didn't actually reflect on herself, and everyone was crazy.)

Caroline succeeded in getting Wood to his Georgia press conference with RNC chairwoman Ronna "The Romneyest"

McDaniel, but outside of that, the Silver State search for the real killer was a bust. By November 15, it was clear that Schlapp and Grenell weren't doing any better than their more notorious brethren across the country at Four Seasons Total Landscaping in Philadelphia where Rudy Giuliani gave the hilarious yet terrifying press conference about the fraud he was hallucinating in a strip mall parking lot next to a sex shop and crematorium. As a result of these compounding failures Trump campaign chief Bill Stepien decided to partially give up on the ghost and let much of the staff that had been dispatched to Nevada go, including Caroline.

In any other campaign, for any other candidate, that would have been the end of the road. Caroline would have been planning her quadrennial post-election vacation to whatever foreign country would take a person who had twice contracted COVID and our story would be at its end.

For a few weeks, that is how it looked. She flew to Atlanta for Thanksgiving to see her newborn niece (after the fourteen-day quarantine ended) and in December popped down to Florida to visit her grandmother. She said that she found "Thanksgiving to Christmas to be a strange time" (understatement alert).

She personally didn't understand the notion that the vice president could overturn the election but was persuaded by those in her cloistered Trumpian orbit that there must be some possibility that the lame-duck president could still stay in power.

"I was very confused."

During this time donors would call her with wild promises, saying that they were planning to pitch in insane sums—a quarter million dollars or more—by just punching their bank information into Lin Wood or attorney Sidney Powell's website. "It was all they wanted to talk about," she said.

Despite how crazy this seemed on its face, from her perspective, their insistence lent credence to the possibility that the putsch was plausible. These were traditional Republican types, titans of industry, members of Congress, and successful campaign strategists, not just random gadflies.

One woman in particular caught her attention: Julie Jenkins Fancelli, an heiress to the Publix fortune who lived not far from Caroline's grandmother outside of Orlando. Fancelli was adamant that they get together, and their eventual meeting, which would thrust her into the middle of insurrection mania, took place a few days after Christmas, just down the road from the Huntsman campaign office where we first bonded.

When Caroline arrived, she found that Fancelli was . . . wait for it . . . *obsessed* with Trump and the Stop the Steal movement. Being a channel for these donors' whims was Caroline's job, but she also wanted very badly for their electoral hallucinations to come to pass. For Trump to find some carve-out that would keep the party going and let him stick it to the left one more time.

Caroline told Fancelli she would help her point her ample resources in the most fruitful direction. From her perspective, this was a rational act. She figured she could at least make sure the donor's munificence was being directed somewhere useful, rather than being blindly tossed into random coffers on www.LinWoodIs ChristIncarnate.net. But the Stop the Steal efforts were a mutating virus of grift that expanded into several overlapping scams, which made figuring out how best to spend Fancelli's money a full-time job unto itself. She began to make some calls, and when you are representing someone willing to put 300 g's into a ludicrous swindle, your calls get returned right quick. The next thing she knew, she was a middlewoman between a cast of neo-Nazis and opportunists and genuine lunatics and performative lunatics and she only had a week to navigate it all. A few days later, when Trump announced via tweet that he would be attending the January 6th rally and a professional advance team was assigned to the event, it gave her even more of a sense of responsibility to make sure it would all go off as well as it could.

It is amid all this that Alex Jones and Ali Akbar Alexander, the convicted felon behind much of the Stop the Steal efforts, began to work her over in the hopes that she could use her access to the family to help bring the Trumpian stamp of approval to their traitorous asininity. Jones and Alexander, in private, she insists, come off as reasonable. To be honest, I wasn't surprised to hear that. For starters, they are both skilled performers. Jones has duped the millions of viewers who tune into Infowars, and Alexander's confidence game managed to get him into Kanye West's inner circle for a time.

Plus, they compared favorably to many of the other nutcases that this playacting had attracted. Dipsomaniac Rudy Giuliani's thick-headed sidekick Boris Epstein called her "like eighty times" demanding to speak, even though she had no real control over the agenda. Tea Party founder Amy Kremer and her daughter Kylie tried to bully their way into running the show, threatening to call Mark Meadows anytime they didn't get what they wanted. Caroline said Kylie was "one of the most insane people I've ever worked with"—which is telling, because "most insane" is an unimaginably high bar to clear in Trump world, that I can tell you.

These are not very bright men and women. And things were well past out of hand.

After a lengthy exegesis in which Caroline details the internecine drama surrounding all the various incompetents and kooks and quislings planning this rally, she finally explains how she found herself on the permit for the pre-insurrection speech. It basically comes down to this: The president needed something to get done. Most everyone else seemed like a lunatic and she wanted to be helpful. Permits needed to be signed. A/V companies needed to be locked down.

It didn't occur to her that anything bad could come of it, because she didn't recognize that she had been swept up in the lunacy herself. Knowing what we know now, this reflects the utmost naivete and privilege and something bordering on psychosis. As such, I interject.

What did you think was going to happen that day? The election had been over for months—weren't you like, this is preposterous?

No, but because the people around Trump didn't think it was.

Come on, I remember enough times [during the Huntsman campaign] you would say to me: Tim, why are we doing this—this is stupid? This didn't occur to you during this entire time?

No, but it wasn't really my role. Plus, I was excited, it was another Trump rally. It was my two hundredth Trump rally. . . . I do remember thinking, I'm not even paid to be here, what am I even doing, but Trump rallies were always fun and exciting and I had a lot of friends who were coming in and donors and people that were excited to be there, and these things go really fast when you are there, so I didn't have time for the grand thoughts.

She was living in a world with no repercussions. A world where all the downstream effects of Trump's actions didn't affect her and thus weren't real to her. She was enlivened by the show he put on. Addicted to the drama. Keeping that high was an all-consuming

---

end unto itself. She reveled in the chance to play her part, as one of the stagehands twisting a lug nut, ignoring that the world began to burn around her.

• • •

On the morning of the 6th there was a bitter January chill in the air. She bundled up and went out to the Ellipse before dawn's first light to handle logistics, as she always had.

She had reserved a hotel room for herself downtown and catered a separate Trump hotel town house so that the wealthy donors who descended on the Capitol could gather in luxury to watch their congressional serfs attempt to overturn a democratic election once the speech had concluded. On the menu was Chardonnay and chicken fingers and other light insurrection fare.

Once she got to the Mall, Caroline set up the chairs. Put down the names of the VIPs as she had hundreds of times before. Vernon Jones. Bernie Kerik. Rudy Giuliani. Made sure everything was just so. Then she watched the sun come up over the Mall. "I'll never forget, it was just people as far as the eye could see, and I was like, *holy crap.*"

As Trump's speech wound down, she grabbed a couple of the older lady donor types who she thought would struggle to navigate such a large crowd and might benefit from getting someplace warm. They ducked out before the speeches and the incitement was through, parting ways with Jones and the others, who went to their "command center" in the Willard Hotel.

They walked over to the Trump hotel, Caroline took a hot shower and came downstairs to the main gathering area with a bathrobe over her dress and bundled up on the couch. The group had planned to watch C-SPAN together and cheer on those who were willing to fight for Trump.

But what they saw instead left them in a state of shock. Their fellow steal stoppers had not retired to opulent suites as they had. They were storming the Capitol. And it was violent. A few of the people went from the television to the window. They looked out and saw the sea of people that had surrounded them on the Mall marching toward the conflict.

"I don't remember talking a lot," she said.

As they nibbled on the room service, they heard reports about five people dead. They learned that Ashli Babbitt had been killed. They were all sick with worry. For the country. For the people involved. For whoever lost their lives and their families.

Caroline became more and more terrified as it all unfolded. She was racked with guilt hearing the reports. She couldn't believe that "their people" would do this. She had come to believe it was only the "other side" that was violent. The Antifas and the Black Lives Matter rioters and the Prius drivers with their coffee Coolattas.

Eventually, she couldn't take it any longer. She turned off the TV. Walked the ladies back to the Willard Hotel, where they were staying. Returned to her room, alone. She took nine Xanax and went to bed before the clock reached six.

Back in Santa Monica, I wanted to take this moment to finally break through to her. She was vulnerable and a little drunk. She had just walked through one of the most emotional days of her life and explained her own complicated and repressed feelings of guilt.

I wanted to be the Sean Maguire to her Will Hunting. To embrace her and tell her that it wasn't her fault. That Trump did it. That both she and the people storming the Capitol were sucked in by his lies. That in some ways they were victims of him.

He perpetuated this lie because he's a baby. He made up a fucking lie, fifty million people believe it, and our

Capitol was stormed. People that believed his lie died. That woman that got shot is dead because of him. He killed her.

No.

He killed her.

No, he didn't.

He did, he did. He killed her. If Mitt Romney, John McCain, John Kerry, Al Gore, Bob Dole, George H. W. Bush . . . that woman would've been alive if any of them lost, because none of them would've gone on and created this bullshit fucking lie. He. Killed. Her.

Ten seconds of silence.
For the first time, Caroline chokes up. Her voice catches.

I don't see it that way.

Whose fault is it then?

Its people make a series of decisions . . .

These people believed he had won. They loved him, he lied to them.

I don't think fifty million people are mindless idiots. They have legitimate reasons to believe . . .

I AGREE. Donald Trump lied to them. . . . He knows he lost. He's a child. He did this in 2015 in Iowa. He always said he'd never admit he's gonna lose. She's dead because he's a baby.

She's whispering now. "I don't think that."

We are interrupted. The bar is about to shut down. The waitress asks if we have time for one more drink. We do. But the moment has passed.

I can't break the spell.

She is in her feelings and yet undeterred. She attempts a joke. The tension breaks. My spirit deflates.

Caroline says that if Trump runs again, she will be back in the saddle, assuming they'll have her. (A few months following our meeting, it is reported that she was pushed out of her finance role by others as part of some indecipherable internal Trump war. But there are plenty of second acts in MAGA American life. Caroline has since begun appearing on Steve Bannon's Volksempfänger-esque podcast with other Trump influencers, so there is good reason to believe she'll be welcomed back when the time comes.)

It turns out my old friend has almost the full package of Trump rationalizations.

She has compartmentalized the bad, even when it comes to those she cares about. She has demonized the left and wants revenge against the cultural elite. She's caught up in this big imaginary game and enjoys the LOLs. She's wearing the orange crush team jersey. She loves being in the mix at Trump events. She has succumbed to inertia and doesn't know what she would do if not Republican politics, so she can't envision what a different, more fulfilling life for herself would look like.

But in her case, it is even more than all that.

Caroline has been sucked in by the cult. She is obsessed with Trump and adores him, as incommodious as that may seem. She's the masochistic follower who feels a compulsion to be tested, abused, and forced to prove they are deserving of the leader's love over and over and over again. And like many of our parents and grandparents and friends, she's become unreachable, thanks to consuming petty grievances and an impenetrable media bubble. She is so far gone that bumbling her way into being complicit in an insurrection that caused the death of some of her fellow travelers didn't shake her free. It should have been obvious that I couldn't, either, despite my private wishcasting.

As we leave the bar, we both light up a cigarette and walk together up Pico Boulevard, past the famous Shutters hotel, emotionally drained and unsure what comes next. As I go to veer off, she has a parting request:

"I hope your husband doesn't hate me anymore. I hope we can all be friends again."

I stutter in reply, finally spitting out, "I hope so, too," remaining vague on what exactly those hopes are.

The truth is, while I hope that the complexes that drove us apart might reverse or be mended, I have a hard time seeing how. All the reasons for why we both made the choices we did remain operable. The stories we are telling ourselves have a narrative arc that is unaltered despite the monumental plot twists.

The road that brought us to this place was long. It seems as if it might just go on forever.

Acknowledgments

Eternal thanks to Tyler, for being a better husband than anyone could have asked for when the writing took me to the bad place, for workshopping tweets, and for LTBT at least as long as it was appropriate. LYLW.

Thank you to Sarah Longwell, who actually got up off her ass and built *The Bulwark* and Republican Voters Against Trump while the rest of us were sitting around being sad. If you had not come back into my life, I'm not sure this book would exist.

To Jonathan V. Last, somehow both the best editor and newsletter writer in America. You turned me from a hack into an author (that's still kind of weird to write), and it changed my life.

To Bill Kristol, when basically everyone I admired let me down, you maintained a self-deprecating affability and moral identity worth aspiring to. And to Charlie Sykes for helping me work through this all in real time on Friday mornings.

To Mollie Glick, the no-bullshit book boss who was exactly the agent that my imposter syndrome required.

To Eric Nelson, for asking me the right questions, forcing me to look at what I thought to be true about my book in a fresh light, and providing precisely the type of edit this book required.

To my mom, for not just defeating inertia but blossoming and inspiring me in her seventh decade. This book's spark might just have been born on those late nights finishing up school projects like the Australia magazine or crafting that class treasurer campaign speech that you put all the flourishes into. And to my dad, for being the glue anytime things might've frayed, and for being behind me no matter what.

To Paul and Mark: The gift of siblings who are also close friends and confidants is so rare, and I'm unbelievably lucky to have you. You guys motivate me to be a better person and brother, and I hope this book bears that out.

To J. J. Conway, for being the one person I trusted to see the janky first drafts in all their non-glory. Geaux Browns.

To Dr. Jeff Sharp, for helping me sort through my shadow.

To Colonel Dr. Blake Williamson, because you would've rightly been mad if I hadn't acknowledged you. And to Nicole, because you wouldn't have been.

To Peter Hamby, Scott Conroy, and Jake Suski, for encouraging my pivot to content, brainstorming about steam tray hot dogs, and demonstrating men can in fact make close friends after thirty. And to Grant, for being the old friend who has offered the dankest support of the content pivot.

To Waylon and Teddy, I'm tryna be the shepherd for you, too. Don't do the bad stuff in this book and get me in trouble with your moms.

To Treina and Laurie, for becoming a part of our family, making it stronger, and giving me some clarity.

To Kochel, for your friendship, and Jeb, who I wish we could've done right by.

To Pompei and Lis, for listening to my random anxieties throughout the process.

To Brian McGuigan, who looked at me like I was insane one

night when I said I was thinking about giving up politics for corporate PR and set me back on the righteous path.

To Justin Wilson, appreciate you.

To Jane Lynch (!!), Nicolle Wallace, James Carville, Stuart Stevens, and David Frum, for the supportive blurbs that gave me a shot in the arm in the anxious moment I needed it most.

To Drew and Michael Bierut, for your creative energies, which are going to help make this writing pop off the shelf.

To Mark Leibovich, for telling me to write free.

To Mayor David Holt, for being the best Republican elected official in America, or at least the best who previously posted on GWhoops.com. And for letting me borrow the "comforting lie."

To Olivia Nuzzi, the only person whose work was quoted twice in the book and for Toulouse's baller motorcycle jacket.

To Alyssa and Caroline, for your unvarnished candor.

To Andrew Kaczynski, Jeremy Peters, and Maia Hibbett, whose reporting on Stefanik, Fleischer, and Spicer I leaned on to help animate those chapters.

To James "the Anvil" Neidhardt, for marshaling this to the finish line.

To every single person who emailed and DM'd about my writing. You buoyed me, and this would have never come together without all of you.

Peace.

Index

Heyer, Heather, 67
Hicks, Hope, 202
Holmes, Josh, 182–87, 212
"horse race" politics, 23
Howe, Ben, 111
Hubbell, Webster, 68
Hughes, Simon, 166
Huntsman, Jon, Jr.
  opposition research for,
    30–33, 36, 45
  Wren and 2012 campaign
    of, 215–17, 219
Hurd, Will, 162, 169

IJ Review, 57, 60, 71, 158
immigration reform
  McCain and, 1–6, 9–10
  RNC political "autopsy"
    after 2012 loss and, 84–85
  Romney and, 6–7
  self-deportation and, 7, 71,
    82, 83
Independent Journal Review
  (IJR), 54–61
Inert Team Players
  as enablers, 123–25
  see also Cartel Cashers
Ingraham, Laura, 196–97
IN Review, 60

Jaconi, Michelle, 57, 58
January 6, 2021, insurrection,
    72, 181
  Barbour and, 187–88
  consultants and, 183–87
  Alyssa Farah and, 194,
    211–12, 213
  Joe Farah and, 211–12
  Priebus and, 139

Shields and, 186–87
Trump's e-mails prior to,
    28–29
Wren and support for
    Trump, xii–xviii, 242–46
Johnson, Benny, 58–59, 60, 71
Johnson, Chuck, 67–70, 107,
    109–10, 112
Jones, Alex, xiii–xiv, 235, 240
Jones, Doug, 106–7
Jordan, Jim, 200
Joy of Hate, The (Gutfeld), 51
Junior Messiahs
  as enablers, 117
  Farah and, 189–213

Kagan, Robert, 156
Karl, Jonathan, 171
Kasich, John, 225
Katko, John, 161
Kelly, John, 107, 116
Kemp, Jack, 83
Kerry, John, 56, 78
Kimmel, Jimmy, 148, 150
Kinsey, Camryn, 122
Kraushaar, Josh, 183–84
Krebs, Chris, 71
Kremer, Amy, 240
Kremer, Kylie, 240
Kristol, Bill, 156
Kukowski, Kirsten, 80, 81
Kushner, Jared, 171

Lanza, Bryan, 103
Lauer, Matt, 15
Lewis, Michael, 42
Lieberman, Joe, 7–8
Lincoln Project, 8, 40, 118,
    179–80, 230

About the Author

Tim Miller is an MSNBC political analyst, writer at large at *The Bulwark*, and the host of *Not My Party* on Snapchat. He has written on politics and culture for *Rolling Stone*, *The Ringer*, *Playboy*, and *The Daily Beast*. Tim was communications director for Jeb Bush's 2016 presidential campaign and spokesman for the Republican National Committee during Mitt Romney's 2012 campaign. He has since left the GOP and become one of the leaders of the "Never Trump" movement. He lives in Oakland, California, with his husband, Tyler, and their daughter, Toulouse.